INSPIRE / PLAN / DISCOVER / EXPERIENCE

ALASKA

ALASKA

CONTENTS

DISCOVER 6

EXPERIENCE 62

NEED TO KNOW 250

Left: Former industrial buildings in Kennecot Mines
Previous page: The Alaska Range reflected in Wonder Lake
Front cover: Exit Glacier in Kenai Fjords National Park

DISCOVER

The verdant mountains of Hatcher Pass

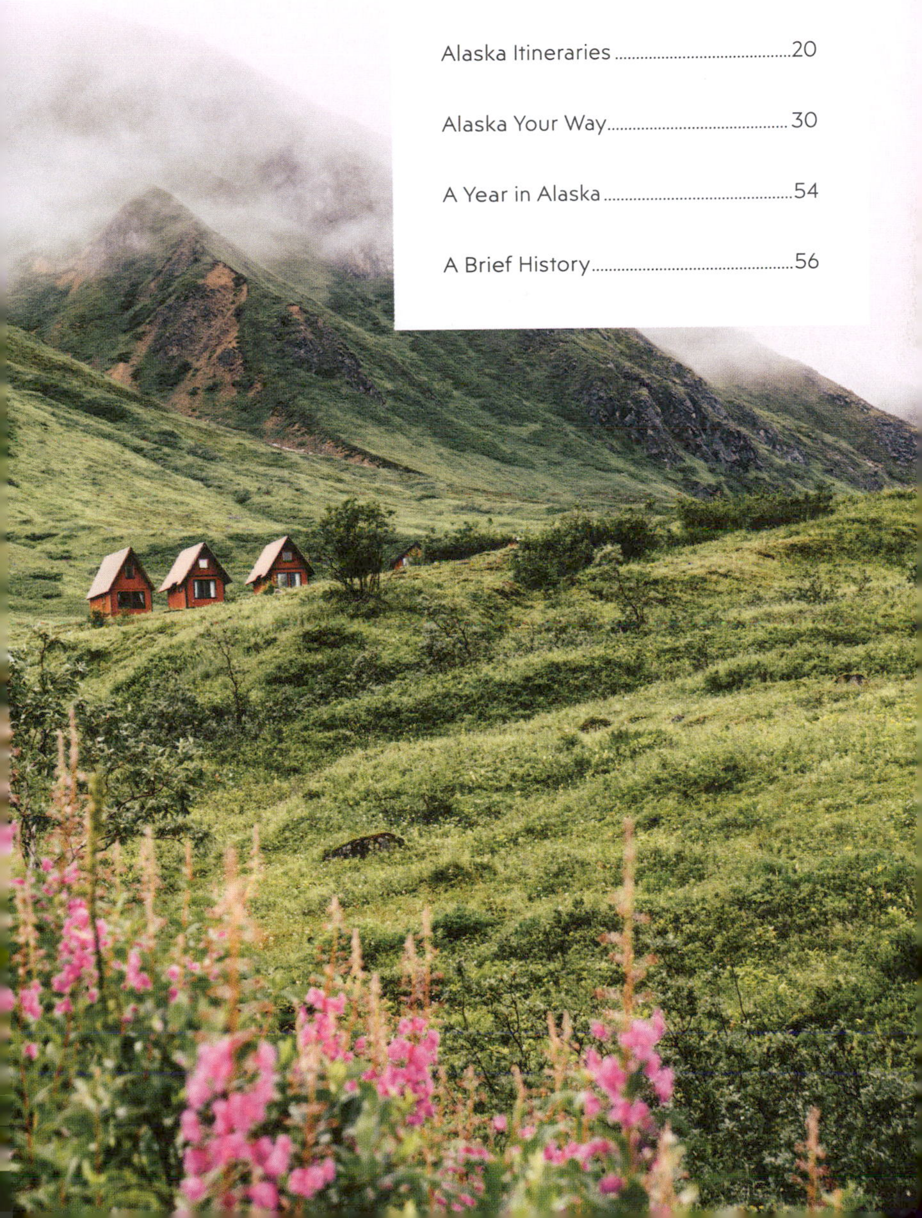

WELCOME TO
ALASKA

Roaming wildlife-rich wilderness by day and snuggling up in cosy cabins at night. Cruising through stunning, glacier-lined fjords and exploring friendly port towns packed with character. Whatever your dream trip to Alaska includes, this DK Eyewitness Travel Guide is the perfect companion.

1 Nagley's Store in the heart of Talkeetna.

2 A wild moose in Denali National Park.

3 A floatplane parked on the shore of Lake Clark.

4 Admiring the scenery on a cruise through Glacier Bay.

Home to the USA's highest peak and its largest national park, and more than double the size of the second-biggest state, Alaska is a land of epic proportions. Unforgettable adventures await all who journey here, with the range of outdoor activities as varied as the state's spectacular scenery. Go bear-spotting in Katmai National Park, canoe through the icy waters of Glacier Bay, or take a once-in-a-lifetime road trip along the rugged Denali Highway. From the misty rainforests of Southeast Alaska to the Arctic reaches of the far north, the lure of the landscape is impossible to resist.

Sprinkled across this wilderness is an appealing assortment of cities and towns, offering a warm welcome with hearty food and lip-smacking brews. Anchorage buzzes as the state's largest settlement, while Juneau and Fairbanks shine as monuments to the legendary Gold Rush. Small-town Alaska reveals the state's quirkier side, with a host of unusual festivals celebrating the individuality of communities such as Whittier and Cordova. Visible throughout is the presence of Alaska Native culture, infusing arts and activities, both ancient and modern, with a potent reminder of our intricate bond with nature.

With so many things to see and do, any visit to Alaska packs a punch. We've broken the state down into easily navigable chapters, with detailed itineraries and comprehensive maps to help plan the perfect adventure. Add insider tips, and a Need To Know section with all the practical essentials to be aware of, and you've got an indispensable guidebook. Enjoy the book, and enjoy Alaska.

REASONS TO LOVE
ALASKA

Diverse environments teeming with wildlife. Intriguing history and eclectic contemporary culture. Grand adventures in the great outdoors. There are so many reasons to love Alaska; here are our favorites.

1 EPIC LANDSCAPES
Every region has its own distinct terrain: roam barren tundra in the Arctic, lush rainforests in Southeast Alaska, or the craggy peaks of the Alaska Range in the Interior.

RECREATIONAL SPACES 2
This vast state is chock-full of national parks and other public lands, all ripe for adventure. Call in at the nearest Alaska Public Lands Information Center for some top tips.

3 SALMON, SALMON, AND MORE SALMON
Five salmon species spawn here, providing a major source of both sustenance and sport. You'll find the best fishing spots in Southeast Alaska and along the Kenai Peninsula.

SCENIC CRUISES 4

Alaska is home to some breathtaking boat journeys, and a cruise through the Inside Passage or Gulf of Alaska undoubtedly ranks among the best in the world *(p260)*.

WILDLIFE SPOTTING 5

Bears, moose, and bald eagles: Alaska's animals are as majestic as their domains. Glimpse them in the wild throughout the state, or get a close-up view at a conservation center *(p34)*.

GOLD RUSH LEGACY 6

Trace the colorful history of Alaska's Gold Rush in towns such as Juneau *(p136)*, Skagway *(p146)*, and Nome *(p238)*. You can even try panning for your own riches while you're there.

SEWARD HIGHWAY 7

With ample opportunities for whale-watching and hiking stops, a road trip along this 125-mile (200-km) National Scenic Byway is an experience you'll never forget *(p78)*.

GLACIER BAY NATIONAL PARK 8

A playground for visitors and a natural lab for climate scientists, Glacier Bay National Park *(p142)* is a wildlife-rich wonderland of dramatic ice formations and lush alpine meadows.

9 FUNKY FESTIVALS

Finding unusual ways to savor summer and endure winter has long been an Alaska tradition. Highlights include Cordova's Iceworm Festival and Golden Days in Fairbanks *(p54)*.

10 ADVENTURE ACTIVITIES

An abundance of outdoor activities - including ziplining over forests, scrambling up rocky trails, and rafting down rivers - make this the ideal place to get your adrenaline fix.

NATIVE CULTURE 11

Uncover the myriad arts and traditions of Alaska's 227 federally recognized Native groups, from the Inuit and Yup'ik in the Arctic to the Tlingit and Haida in the Southeast *(p38)*.

CRAFT BREWING 12

Alaska has more than 40 breweries, leaving no doubt that beer and cider are something of a local passion. Choose your favorite on a tasting tour of the finest local brews *(p42)*.

EXPLORE
ALASKA

This guide divides Alaska into seven colour-coded sightseeing areas, as shown on the map below. Find out more about each area on the following pages.

Utqiagvik

Wainwright

Point Lay

Colville

Point Hope

ARCTIC AND WESTERN ALASKA
p232

Noatak

Ambler

Kotzebue

RUSSIA

Shishmaref

Arctic Circle

Teller

Koyukuk

Nome

Koyukuk

Gambell

Unalakleet

Poorman

St. Lawrence Island

Stebbins

Yukon

Kotlik

McGrath

Bering Sea

Holy Cross

Iditarod

Kuskokwim

Newtok

SOUTHWEST ALASKA
p208

Bethel

Kipnuk

Iliamna

Platinum

Naknek

Dillingham

King Salmon

Egegik

Pribilof Islands St. George

Alaska Peninsula

Kodiak Island

Port Heiden

Akhiok

Chignik

Cold Bay

Sand Point

King Cove

Unalaska/ Dutch Harbor

Umnak Island

Amlia Island

Aleutian Islands

Arctic
Ocean

NORTH AMERICA

Arctic Ocean

RUSSIA
ALASKA

CANADA

Pacific
Ocean

USA

MEXICO

Prudhoe Bay
Kaktovik

Wiseman
Coldfoot
Fort Yukon

Yukon
Circle

Tanana
Livengood

Fairbanks
Eagle

Delta
Junction

Denali
Village
Tok

INTERIOR ALASKA
p164

Northway

Talkeetna
Glennallen

ANCHORAGE
p64
Valdez

McCarthy

Whittier

PRINCE
WILLIAM
SOUND
p112

Seward

THE KENAI
PENINSULA
p92

Kodiak

Gulf of
Alaska

CANADA

Norman Wells

Dawson City

Whitehorse

Watson
Lake

Haines
Junction

Skagway

Yakutat

Haines

Gustavus
Juneau

SOUTHEAST
ALASKA
p124

Sitka

Wrangell
Hyder

Ketchikan

Hydaburg

Prince
Rupert

Haida
Gwaii

Pacific
Ocean

0 kilometers   250

0 miles   250

N

GETTING TO KNOW
ALASKA

The state's vast territory encompasses a unique range of habitats, from the misty rainforests of Southeast Alaska to the treeless tundra of the Arctic. In between lie frosty glaciers, rugged mountains, remote island chains, and wide coastal plains, with most of the population settled around Anchorage.

PAGE 64

ANCHORAGE

Alaska's largest city, Anchorage is the cornerstone of transport, commerce, and government in the state. It is also a highly diverse place – more than 100 languages are spoken here – with an appealing blend of global cultures reflected in its inviting restaurants and intriguing festivals. To the west is the scenic Cook Inlet and to the east are the towering Chugach mountains, forming a spectacular outdoor playground within easy reach of downtown. Anchorage bustles all year, but it is at its liveliest in summer, when visitors and locals alike make the most of the city's myriad attractions.

Best for
International cuisine, state history, access to the rest of Alaska

Home to
Anchorage Museum, Alaska Native Heritage Center, Chugach State Park, Independence Mine State Park, Turnagain Arm

Experience
Learning about local culture at the Alaska Native Heritage Center and the Anchorage Museum

KENAI PENINSULA

PAGE 92

Known for its thriving fisheries, the Kenai Peninsula is a world-renowned paradise for anglers, laced with clear rivers and deep bays that teem with salmon, halibut, and cod. This region is also one of the most accessible places in the state to view glaciers and wildlife, and you'll find a wealth of recreational activities on offer in the communities here. Most of the options are centered around stunning Kenai Fjords National Park and Kachemak Bay State Park, where kayaks, fishing poles, and hiking boots are standard accessories for adventurers.

Best for
Fishing charters, day cruises to view glaciers and wildlife

Home to
Kenai Fjords National Park, Seward, Resurrection Pass Trail

Experience
Taking a guided walk to the magnificent Exit Glacier in Kenai Fjords National Park

PAGE 112

PRINCE WILLIAM SOUND

Gateway to the icy College Fjord, Prince William Sound provides a stunning reminder of just how rugged Alaska truly is. At its western end is the quirky town of Whittier, a short hop from Anchorage, while to the east is the deepwater port city of Valdez, the terminus of the Trans-Alaska Pipeline. The best way to delve into the heart of the sound is by boat, surrounded by whales, sea otters, seals, and an abundance of noisy shorebirds.

Best for
Remote wilderness, marine wildlife

Home to
Valdez

Experience
Hiring a charter boat for intimate kayaking or hiking adventures in quiet coves

→

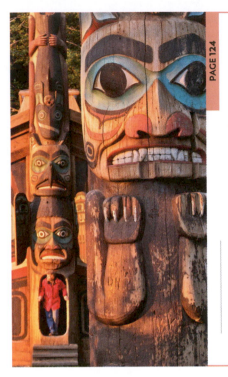

PAGE 124

SOUTHEAST ALASKA

A popular destination with visitors due to the high number of cruise lines sailing through the beautiful Inside Passage route, Southeast Alaska is defined by dense forest and archipelagos of islands both large and small. The fishing, tourism, and resource development industries reign supreme, but if you step away from the busy docks you'll find friendly communities with an easygoing charm. This is also a great place to learn about Alaska Native traditions and local seafaring culture, as well as the history of the Gold Rush era.

Best for
Alaska Native culture, Gold Rush history

Home to
Prince of Wales Island, Ketchikan, Sitka, Juneau, Glacier Bay National Park, Skagway, Haines

Experience
Immersing yourself in Tlingit, Tshimshian, and Haida culture at the Sealaska Heritage Institute

PAGE 164

INTERIOR ALASKA

Encompassing Denali National Park and the Denali, Richardson, and Parks highways, the Interior is a huge section of the state's north-central region. This is the Alaska you might recognize from magazines: grand landscapes, with jaw-dropping views of Mount Denali looming behind birch forests and muskeg. Rural roads, when they exist, are often dirt or gravel, and travel here takes a long time. It's worth it though, for the expanse of wilderness at your feet, and the soaring Alaska Range on the horizon. The Interior is home to the Athabascan people, and their culture is felt wherever you go.

Best for
Off-trail exploring, cross-border trips to Canada

Home to
Denali National Park, Denali Highway, Fairbanks, Talkeetna, Wrangell-St. Elias National Park, Kennecott, Dawson City

Experience
Journeying along the scenic Denali Park Road, with an overnight stay at the remote Kantishna Roadhouse

SOUTHWEST ALASKA

Situated on the Pacific Ring of Fire and the site of many a violent ocean-borne storm, Southwest Alaska is one of the state's most difficult areas to access, but also one of the most beautiful. Wild and wonderful in equal measure, it ranges from Dutch Harbor/Unalaska all the way north to Magrath and Hooper Bay. The rich wildlife here includes abundant Bristol Bay sockeye salmon and coastal brown bears, as well as the world's largest colony of northern fur seals and millions of migratory birds. Boating is the primary means of travel, making for adventure-filled excursions on the stormy seas.

Best for
Off-the-beaten-track adventures, wildlife-viewing, bird-watching

Home to
Katmai National Park, Dutch Harbor/Unalaska, Pribilof Islands, Kodiak

Experience
Watching hungry bears feed on salmon at Katmai National Park

ARCTIC AND WESTERN ALASKA

Challenging but not impossible to reach, the Arctic and Western region covers nearly two-thirds of the state and is the longstanding homeland of the Inuit, Yup'ik, and Aleut Native groups. Only a few thousand people live in this harsh landscape, along its barren coastal plains and in the valleys of its towering mountain passes, leaving vast swathes of starkly beautiful wilderness where great herds of caribou roam across the as yet untouched tundra.

Best for
Seeing the northern lights, polar bear viewing

Home to
Utqiagvik, Nome, Dalton Highway

Experience
Standing amid the pristine wilderness of Gates of the Arctic National Park

←

1 The Alaska Native Heritage Center.

2 Chugach State Park.

3 A moose at the Alaska Wildlife Conservation Center.

4 Mt. Aleyska in winter.

Vast and varied, Alaska brims with travel possibilities. These suggested itineraries pick out the highlights of each region, to help you plan your time in the 49th state.

3 DAYS

in Anchorage

Day 1

Start your day with a hearty breakfast at a downtown café, then make tracks to the Anchorage Museum (p68), a 40,000 sq ft (3,700 sq m) building packed with exhibits on Alaska's culture, history, and industry. Let your newfound knowledge sink in over lunch at the on-site restaurant, then catch a connecting shuttle to the Alaska Native Heritage Center (p70). Located a little way east of downtown, the center provides an in-depth insight into Native culture through an assortment of indoor and outdoor exhibits. These include a group of mock villages clustered around a small lake, as well as daily drumming and dancing presentations. Complete your introduction to Alaskan life with a dinner of locally caught seafood at one of downtown Anchorage's many restaurants.

Day 2

Get outdoors today with a helpful map from the Public Lands Information Center on 4th Avenue (p80). Stroll a section of the scenic Tony Knowles Coastal Trail (p82), an 11-mile (18-km) route that hugs the city's coastline and has numerous outlets for shorter excursions; or venture slightly further afield to Chugach State Park (p72), for a guided or self-guided hike with a chance of spotting moose and bears. In the afternoon, make your way over to the shores of Lake Hood (p84), the busiest seaplane base in the world. It's fun just to observe the planes in action, but if you've got the energy and time, then it's well worth paying a visit to the Alaska Aviation Museum (p82) to uncover the fascinating history of the state's intrepid bush pilots. For dinner, sit out on the patio of The Fancy Moose Lounge at The Lakefront Hotel (p85), accompanied by the sights and sounds of floatplanes roaring to life.

Day 3

Head south today for a road trip on the scenic Seward Highway, snaking along the shore of Turnagain Arm (p78) – you might catch a glimpse of a beluga whale in the waters if you're lucky. Just 35 miles (56 km) from Anchorage is the town of Girdwood (p88), known for its hanging glaciers. There are several helicopter tours offering the chance to see them up close, but if you're not a flyer then you can take the tram to the top of Mt. Alyeska for a panoramic view instead – there's also a restaurant at the summit, which makes a scenic spot for lunch. Spend the afternoon visiting the Alaska Wildlife Conservation Center (p79), an animal rescue and preservation facility located in a pristine area of Portage Valley, then enjoy a leisurely drive back to Anchorage with a hearty dinner at one of the restaurants along Turnagain Arm.

→

1 Enjoying a boat tour of Kenai
Fjords National Park.

2 Looking out over Exit Glacier
and the Harding Icefield.

3 Sled dogs ready for mushing.

4 Boats in Seward harbor.

3 DAYS
in Seward

Day 1

Wake up with a fragrant cup of coffee or tea at a local café before climbing aboard your day cruise vessel for a tour of Resurrection Bay and Kenai Fjords National Park *(p96)*. Humpback whales, harbor seals, sea otters, and orcas are all common visitors to these chilly northern waters – look out for them feeding within sight of the boat. Most tours also visit several towering glaciers within the national park; if you're lucky, you might experience the drama of a calving, when shards of ice fall noisily into the bay. Back on dry land, enjoy a seafood dinner at local favorite The Cookery *(p101)*.

Day 2

See a different side of Kenai Fjords National Park with a guided walk to Exit Glacier *(p101)*, and marvel at the dramatic retreat of ice here since the early 1900s. Hardy trekkers may want to continue on the 8-mile (13-km) circular trail to Harding Icefield, where most of the national park's glaciers originate; either way, be sure to stop by the visitor center to pick up a map and peruse the displays on glacial formation. In the afternoon, meet the dogs of one of Alaska's most famous mushing families, the Seaveys, on their Ididaride tour *(https://ididaride.com)*. The Iditarod National Historic Trail begins in Seward, and mushing was of vital importance to mail delivery and commerce here during the Gold Rush era. Round off the day with a peaceful pause at Caines Head State Recreation Area *(p101)*, listening to the waves lapping at its black sand beach.

Day 3

Head back to the water for a bit of salmon or halibut fishing. Numerous charter vessels depart from Seward's small boat harbor, offering either half- or full-day guided fishing experiences. Catches can be processed and packed for shipment home, so you don't have to worry about missing out on the rewards of your labor. If you have time later in the day, visit the Alaska SeaLife Center *(p101)*, the state's only rescue and rehabilitation facility for marine wildlife – it's an excellent place to gain a deeper insight into human connections with the sea. Toast your final night with a drink at Seward Brewing Company *(www.sewardbrewery.com)*, bidding farewell to this jolly seaside community.

7 DAYS
on the Kenai Peninsula

Day 1

Setting out from Anchorage, drive south along the Seward Highway to the scenic Turnagain Pass, pausing to hike a short section of the Iditarod National Historic Trail. Your end destination for the day is Cooper Landing *(p104)*; aim to arrive here in time for lunch at Gwin's Lodge and Roadhouse *(www.gwinslodge.com)* – be sure to try the pie. Spend the afternoon learning about the hardy homesteaders who settled this area, before overnighting by the Kenai River.

Day 2

Hit the Sterling Highway today to explore the towns of Soldotna *(p105)* and Kenai *(p106)*. The former has interesting exhibits on the peninsula's homesteading families in the Soldotna Historical Society Museum, while the latter's charming old town features historic buildings such as the Holy Assumption of the Virgin Mary Russian Orthodox Church. In the spring, snow geese make their way to the nearby Kenai Flats State Recreation Site, which makes

a good spot for a picnic. End the afternoon with a scenic drive to Homer *(p108)*, which will be your base for the next few days.

Day 3

Homer is known as the Halibut Capital of the World, and fishing is a major industry here. Learn about the science and history of the coast with visits to the Pratt Museum and the Islands and Ocean Visitor Center, then take a tour of Homer's docks with the Center for Alaskan Coastal Studies *(www. akcoastalstudies.org)* to view the local marine life in person. As evening falls, catch the Danny J ferry to The Saltry *(www.thesaltry.com)* in Halibut Cove *(p111)* for an intimate dinner in this small village.

Day 4

Hop aboard a private water taxi or an Alaska Marine Highway System ferry for a day trip to Seldovia *(p111)*. After picking up a map from the town visitor center, walk the short Otterbahn Trail to a secluded beach, where humpback whales can often

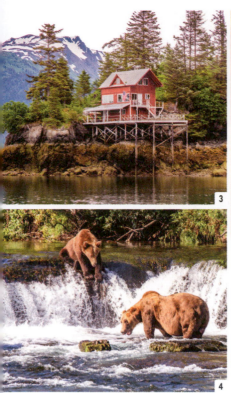

1 Fishing on the Kenai River.

2 The Holy Assumption of the Virgin Mary Russian Orthodox Church in the town of Kenai.

3 Halibut Cove, lying opposite Homer across Kachemak Bay.

4 Brown bears fishing for salmon in Katmai National Park.

5 Fruit-infused wines made by Bear Creek Winery.

be seen in the distance. Seldovia's gardens and parks are delightful places to stretch your legs, and there are several small cafés where you can get lunch. After the boat ride back to Homer, spend a relaxed evening sampling some fine local ales at the city's microbreweries (p109).

Day 5

Fuel up with fresh coffee and morning pastries at Two Sisters Bakery (http://twosistersbakery.net) for a day of bear viewing in remote Katmai National Park (p212). Fly-in tours last from a few hours to a full day, and are led by knowledgable guides who will bring you to the bears' feeding grounds to watch them fish for salmon. Dine tonight at Captain Pattie's Fish House (p109) on Homer Spit, in full view of the fishing boats returning from sea.

Day 6

Head upland to the Carl E. Wynn Nature Center for a guided hike amid the abundant flora and fauna. Back in Homer, have lunch at a central café and then set out to explore the town's east end. Travel past scenic homesteads and small farms, keeping an eye out for Kachemak Bay's glaciers, as well as roadside wildlife such as moose and sandhill cranes. On the way back to town, stop at Bear Creek Winery (p42) and sample wines featuring local berries and fruits. If there's time, call in at the Bunnell Street Arts Center to view their contemporary works, and perhaps even pick up a piece to take home.

Day 7

Drive north on the Sterling Highway to the small town of Anchor Point (p110). Only 11 miles (18 km) from Homer, it features delightful beaches for strolling upon, and offers stunning views of the Alaska Range to the west. Anglers will find plenty of fishing here, and there is a popular boat launch, campground, and restaurant. Anchor Point has plenty of appealing accomodation options, and makes a scenic spot to savor your final night on the Kenai Peninsula.

1

2

6 DAYS

in the Far North and Arctic

Day 1

Begin acquainting yourself with the far north by exploring Fairbanks (p174), the hub city for most Arctic regions. A good starting place is the Morris Thompson Cultural and Visitors Center, which provides interpretive displays, maps, and books about the region, and also screens some wonderful documentary films. After lunch at a local restaurant, swing uptown to the University of Alaska Fairbanks campus to visit the Museum of the North facility. With outstanding views of the Tanana Valley, the museum features geologic and archaeological exhibits related to Alaska's physical history, and there are also several worthwhile art galleries to explore. Finish the day with a meal at The Pump House (www.pumphouse.com).

Day 2

Embark on your Arctic adventure proper by climbing aboard a comfortable tour van for the journey into the far north. Explore the rural village of Joy and its Arctic Circle Trading Post, then sit back and enjoy scenic views of rugged mountain peaks and the mighty Yukon River as you cruise along the Dalton Highway (p242). After crossing the Arctic Circle, celebrate with dinner and an overnight stay in the rustic community of Coldfoot. Originally called "Slate Creek," it received its present name after miners got "cold feet" at the idea of spending an entire winter here in the frigid temperatures and ever-present darkness.

Day 3

Spend today floating the Middle Fork of the Koyukuk River, a scenic trip with plenty of opportunities to photograph the majestic mountain surrounds and abundant local wildlife. You may also pass an Athabascan fish camp, where Alaska Native families catch and preserve salmon. Alternatively, if water activities aren't your thing, you can go deeper into the Arctic wilderness with a day trip to Anaktuvuk Pass, a Nunamiut community of only about 200 people, surrounded by the stunning Gates of the Arctic National Park (p244).

1 Morris Thompson Cultural and Visitors Center in Fairbanks.

2 Musk oxen standing on the roadside of the Dalton Highway.

3 Gazing at the snowy scenery of Anaktuvuk Pass.

4 The Trans-Alaska Pipeline snaking through the Arctic countryside.

5 Pioneer Park in Fairbanks.

Day 4

Start the day with a stop at the Arctic Interagency Visitors Center in Coldfoot (*p242*) to learn about life in the far north, then travel to the historic village of Wiseman (*p243*) for a tour of its excellent open-air museum. Continue your journey north along the Dalton Highway, traversing the Brooks Range via the Atigun Pass – at 4,739 ft (1,444 m), this is the highest road pass in Alaska, and it also crosses the Continental Divide, which determines whether rivers drain into the Arctic or the Pacific. The final stop today is Deadhorse, gateway to the oil fields of Prudhoe Bay (*p244*) and home to a wide variety of wildlife, including bears, musk oxen, foxes, and flocks of shorebirds.

Day 5

Dedicate this morning to exploring the Prudhoe Bay oil fields, including a visit to the start of the Trans-Alaska Pipeline, as it embarks on its snaking 800-mile (1,300-km) route south to the terminus in Valdez. The pipeline is an engineering marvel and it is fascinating to see its simple origins, especially considering the manpower involved in its construction and the difficulties in protecting it against permafrost, earthquakes, and other hazards. Complete your trip to the Arctic by taking a few minutes to dip your toes in the frigid waters of the Beaufort Sea, before catching a flight back down to Fairbanks.

Day 6

Reconnect with Fairbanks history at the Fountainhead Antique Auto Museum (*p174*), housing an impressive collection of historic vehicles in pristine working condition. Get lunch afterward at the Tanana Valley Farmers Market, then make your way to Pioneer Park to view its vintage cabins, built in the style of the Gold Rush era. A trip to Gold Dredge 8 nicely rounds off the day, with an intimate look at Alaska's gold-mining industry and the chance to take a turn at panning for gold yourself. Relax in the evening with a quiet dinner, basking in the delights of the famous Alaska "midnight sun."

6 DAYS

in Gold Rush Country

Day 1

Start your Gold Rush explorations with a walking tour of Juneau, Alaska's capital city *(p136)*. With a map in hand from the Juneau Convention and Visitors Bureau, traverse the docks of downtown before climbing up into the hilly streets of the historic neighborhoods. The Juneau-Douglas City Museum makes a good stop for some background on local mining history, and there are plenty of cosy cafés around to choose from for lunch. In the afternoon, make your way to the Alaska State Museum, a beautiful facility that holds exquisite displays showcasing the state's rich culture and history. Stop the night at a historical hotel in the downtown district, with dinner at SALT *(p137)*.

Day 2

Today it's time for an immersive look at the laborious process of mining. Put on your hiking shoes and follow the short-but-steep forest trail to The Last Chance Mining Museum, housed in the remains of a former gold-mining camp; if the hike sounds too strenuous, a guided tour of the AJ/Gastineau Mine *(www.ajgastineau minetour.com)* makes a good alternative. Back in town, stop for a late lunch at one of the corner vendors selling freshly caught Alaska seafood. Spend the evening on the Juneau Food Tours Bites and Booze Tour *(www.juneaufoodtours.com)*, for an introduction to the city's thriving food scene with a side of local history.

Day 3

Hop aboard an Alaska Marine Highway System ferry for a five-hour cruise to the town of Skagway *(p146)*, once a bustling community of almost 100,000 during the heyday of the Klondike Gold Rush. Begin at the heart of it all, at the Klondike Gold Rush National Historical Park Visitor Center and Museum, where you can view exhibits on Skagway's notorious history and pick up a map for a self-guided walking tour. Dine tonight at Skagway Brewing Company *(https://skagwaybrewing.com)*, enjoying a tour of the facilities and a pint or two, along with a delicious meal.

1 Admiring the exhibits in the Alaska State Museum, Juneau.

2 Juneau's attractive waterfront.

3 Skagway's historic downtown.

4 The scenic White Pass and Yukon Route Railway.

5 Kayaking along the placid waters of Lynn Canal, near Haines.

Day 4

Follow in the footsteps of the many fortune-seekers who arrived during the Klondike Gold Rush of the 1890s, with a ride on Skagway's White Pass and Yukon Route Railway (p147). A variety of excursions are available, running up and over Chilkoot Pass. To make it a round trip, you can combine a rail journey with a visit to the village of Carcross, and then return to Skagway by motorcoach along the scenic Klondike Highway. Stretch your legs in the evening with a stroll about town, admiring the period architecture and beautiful summer flowers that line the sidewalks.

Day 5

Catch a shuttle from downtown Skagway to Dyea (p151), an historic site 10 miles (16 km) north of the city, where eager miners and businessmen took leave of steamships during the Gold Rush era. The natural splendor of this area is best experienced on a guided horseback tour through the rainforest and along the shoreline of Lynn Canal, or on foot with a hike through a forested section of the Chilkoot Trail (p151). Make your way back to Skagway for lunch, then board a fast ferry to the scenic town of Haines (p152), just 45 minutes away to the south.

Day 6

After fueling up with a hearty breakfast, hire a bicycle for a leisurely pedal around Haines. There are a number of charming businesses, parks, and museums to admire here, including Fort Seward, perched on a bluff overlooking town. If there's time afterward – or if cycling doesn't appeal – you can take a guided kayak or canoe tour in the beautiful surroundings of Chilkat Lake or Lynn Canal. Round off your afternoon with a visit to the Haines Sheldon Museum and Cultural Center for an insight into the town's culture – be sure to also call in at the kitsch Hammer Museum, opposite, which celebrates the ingenuity of the humble tool. Mark the end of your Gold Rush adventures with dinner at Pilot Light (766 2962), enjoying a view of Lynn Canal and the harbor.

ALASKA FOR
NATURAL
WONDERS

Alaska's dramatic scenery is one of the state's primary attractions, and for good reason. Shaped over thousands of years, the landscapes here are breathtaking reminders of nature's power and beauty.

Towering Glaciers

Alaska is home to 616 named glaciers – ever-moving "rivers of ice" that mark the march of time and climate. Witness the shift of ice on a cruise through Glacier Bay National Park *(p142),* a biosphere reserve where you can observe thunderous calving episodes. An even closer view can be had at Kenai Fjords National Park *(p96),* with a whole icefield of glaciers accessible by foot.

←

Kayaking through Glacier Bay National Park

Dramatic Geology

Mount Denali is North America's highest peak, rising 20,210 ft (6,160 m) above sea level. Forming the 400-mile- (650-km-) long Alaska Range, Denali and its neighbors are undeniable evidence of the state's precarious position on the Pacific "Ring of Fire." A visit to Denali National Park *(p168)* offers an informative look at this tumultuous geology, while a trip to the Valley of 10,000 Smokes in Katmai National Park *(p212)* shows the fallout of Alaska's explosive volcanic nature.

←

Volcanic landscapes in Katmai National Park and *(inset)* Denali National Park

A SHAKY HISTORY

At 5:36pm on March 27, 1964, a magnitude 9.2 earthquake shook Alaska for nearly five minutes. It was one of the most destructive earthquakes in recorded history, and its epicenter was near Valdez. The sights, sounds, and emotions of that day are shared in exhibits at both the Anchorage Museum *(p68)* and the Valdez Museum *(p116)*.

Abundant Flora

Despite its seemingly harsh environment, Alaska is rich in plant life, ranging from tiny wildflowers to giant trees. Learn more about this hardy flora at the Alaska Botanical Garden in Anchorage *(p85)*, the Georgeson Botanical Garden in Fairbanks *(p175)*, and in the lush rainforest surrounds of Glacier Gardens in Juneau *(p141)*.

→

Arctic lupine in the foothills of Sheep Mountain, on the Kenai Peninsula

CLIMATE CHANGE IN ALASKA

Alaska's remote locations and wild spaces inspire awe among the thousands of people who visit each year, as well as those who live here. But the state is changing, rapidly and dramatically, as a result of climate shifts that have affected every aspect of life in the far north of the United States. Alaska has warmed twice as fast as global averages, its annual snowpacks have decreased, and record temperatures in summer 2019 measured 30 degrees higher than normal. These changes are extreme, and in some cases tragic, as plants, animals, and humans struggle to maintain their symbiosis.

CULTURE

The hunting and gathering practices of Alaska Natives have revolved for centuries around the habits of mammals and events such as salmon runs and the migration of birds. Dramatic changes to shorelines, habitats, and temperatures affect the availability of foods and materials, thereby impacting the ability of Alaska Natives to carry out certain cultural traditions.

WILDLIFE

A shifting climate means changes to habitats and food chains. Polar bears no longer have adequate sea ice upon which to hunt, requiring them to swim longer distances in search of prey. Warmer waters also affect salmon, which need cold water to return to their birthplace to spawn, and seabirds, which are struggling to find enough small fish to eat.

↑ Salmon on their way to spawn in Katmai National Park

→ Matanuska Glacier, one of many ice formations in Alaska being affected by rising temperatures, which are also *(inset)* impacting polar bears

ECONOMICS

At 1 million metric tons, the Alaska seafood industry is a major income generator for the US. A loss of product means a loss of dollars, and the consequences of this could be severe. Elsewhere, tourists who come to Alaska expecting to ski, ice skate, or mush behind a sled dog team are instead arriving to rain, sleet, and warm winds. The projected cost of adapting to a warmer climate is estimated between $3.3 and $7.9 billion.

ENVIRONMENTS

In the summer of 2019, more than 2 million acres (800,000 ha) of Alaskan land burned in one of the most devastating wildfire seasons in recorded history. A warmer-than-normal winter followed by a hot, dry, and windy summer was part of the reason, but it was also due to an infestation of spruce bark beetles: insects that destroy the inner bark layer of spruce trees, leaving them as standing, dead tinder. The resulting fires burned homes, halted rail and air services, and choked most of Southcentral Alaska in thick smoke for several weeks.

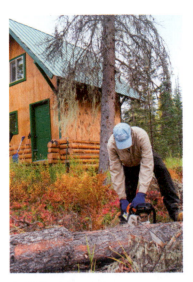

↑ Cutting up the remains of a tree infected by spruce bark beetles

Marvellous Moose

Urban moose are prevalent in most city neighborhoods, munching on shrubbery and even giving birth in backyards. The Anchorage Park Foundation has paid tribute to these gangly creatures by designing a city bike ride that traces the outline of a moose's head *(www.bikeanchorage. org/bike_the_moose)*. See how many you can spot along the 32-mile (51-km) route.

→

A moose and her two calves grazing in Anchorage

ALASKA FOR
WILDLIFE

Alaska's wild creatures have the benefit of thousands of square miles in which to roam, soar, or swim. Many are readily visible, providing ample opportunities for a whole host of unforgettable encounters.

MODERN CONSERVATION EFFORTS

You can help support efforts to preserve and protect Alaska's iconic species by visiting sanctuaries and wildlife conservation centers throughout the state. The Alaska Wildlife Conservation Center near Anchorage *(p79)* offers behind-the-scenes tours to learn more about the animals living on the property; the Alaska Raptor Center in Sitka *(p134)* provides rehabilitation to injured or sick birds of prey; and the Alaska SeaLife Center in Seward *(p101)* is the only rescue and rehabilitation organization in the state for marine mammals.

Big Bears

By far the most popular of Alaska's animals, bears can be spotted in every region of the state. Brown (grizzly) and black bears are often seen on fly-in adventures to places such as Lake Clark *(p228)* or Katmai National Park *(p212)*, while polar bears can only be viewed in the Arctic on a specialist guided excursion *(www.northernalaska.com)*.

A majestic brown bear surveying its domain in Denali National Park ↑

Thar She Blows!
Whales of all sizes can be found swimming in Alaska's cold Pacific waters. Look for belugas at Turnagain Arm *(p78)*, or follow humpbacks and orcas through the Gulf of Alaska, from the Southeast region to Prince William Sound or Resurrection Bay at Seward. The months between April and October are prime time for spotting these mammoths of the sea, gliding through the water to feed on krill, herring, and other fish.

→

Two orcas surfacing in Lynn Canal, Southeast Alaska

Birding Bonanza
Shorebirds from all over the world flock to Alaska's coastal areas in spring and summer to feed and raise their chicks. Their arrival is celebrated with an array of local festivals featuring lectures, walks, and plenty of opportunities to hear the noisy chatter of these seasonal residents. Highlights include Ketchikan's Hummingbird Festival *(p55)* and Homer's Kachemak Bay Shorebird Festival *(p54)*.

←

A dunlin, one of the many migratory birds that breed in Alaska

Hardy Reindeer
Herds of fleet-footed reindeer (or caribou) are present throughout Alaska, but the easiest way to meet Santa's helpers in person is at the Reindeer Farm *(p86)* in Palmer or at the Large Animal Research Station in Fairbanks *(www.uaf.edu/lars)*. Also in Fairbanks is the Running Reindeer Ranch *(https://runningreindeer.com)*, where you can take an enchanting walk through the boreal forest in the company of a friendly herd.

→

A winter walk led by the Running Reindeer Ranch in Fairbanks

Drumming and Dancing

Gatherings to mark key events and seasons are a regular feature of Alaska Native life, with the celebrations often featuring performances by multi-generational dancing and drumming groups. Catch a scheduled show by Sitka Tribal Tours *(www.sitka tours.com)* or head to a festival such as Cama-i Dance in Bethel *(http://camai.org)* for an introduction to the delights of these powerful musical artforms.

→

A dance demonstration at Anchorage's Alaska Native Heritage Center

ALASKA FOR
NATIVE CULTURES

Native groups have lived in Alaska for almost 10,000 years, successfully subsisting on the bounties of land and sea. Each community has developed its own distinct culture, with arts and activities woven around a deep relationship to nature and storytelling.

Storytelling Through Art

From masks to totem poles, Alaska Native artworks tell the rich stories of Native communities. Shops and galleries display a wealth of stunning items made by skilled local artisans, who use themes and materials that draw on their cultural heritage. Artistic hotspots include Sitka National Historic Park *(p134)*, the Sealaska Heritage Institute in Juneau *(p139)*, and the Arctic Studies Center in Anchorage Museum *(p68)*, all of which host artists in residence.

💬 INSIDER TIP
Reading a Totem Pole

Totem poles are built in three sections, and are read from bottom to top. The bottom section is the most important, with displays and images in prominent positions.

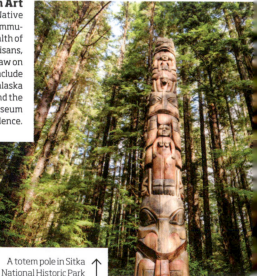

A totem pole in Sitka National Historic Park ↑

Games People Play

For Native culture with a twist, don't miss the annual NYO Games, or Native Youth Olympics. Held in Anchorage every April, this event sees more than 2,000 young athletes compete in skills tests mimicking the actions of traditional hunting activities. If your visit doesn't coincide with the competition, you can still view a demonstration at the Alaska Native Heritage Center (p70).

←

An athlete attempting to kick a seal skin ball in the Two-Foot High Kick competition

Living History

Opportunities to learn about the traditions of Alaska Native groups are readily available in every region of the state. Good places to start include the Alaska Native Heritage Center in Anchorage (p70), the Morris Thompson Cultural and Visitors Center in Fairbanks (p175), and the Sealaska Heritage Institute in Juneau (p139), all packed with illuminating exhibits. Make sure to check their schedules for demonstrations, classes, and events.

→

The Morris Thompson Cultural and Visitors Center in Fairbanks

NATIVE PEOPLES OF ALASKA

Many anthropologists believe that the first Native peoples migrated to Alaska 30,000 to 12,000 years ago, during an Ice Age that lowered sea levels and created a land bridge across the Bering Strait. Today, about 15 percent of Alaska's population claims Native descent, and the largest Native groups include the Tsimshian, Athabascan, Eyak, Tlingit, Haida, Inupiat, Alutiiq, Aleut, and Yup'ik. Alaska Natives usually refer to themselves as members of a particular group, or collectively as Natives.

ATHABASCAN

Historically, the Athabascans occupied the vast taiga forests of the Interior. Largely a hunting and gathering society, they spent summers in riverside tent camps and in winter lived in houses made of sod and wood. Their decorative clothing was made primarily of caribou or moose hide. Many modern Athabascans live in Fairbanks.

TLINGIT

Alaska's Tlingit (pronounced klink-it) have long inhabited Southeast Alaska. Historically, the Tlingit were a seafaring people, and their traders traveled as far as present-day Washington State. Traditional Tlingit society had no central government, but each village had a stratified society. Like other Northwest Coast cultures, the Tlingit carved totem poles *(p131)*; these and other Tlingit arts are widely popular.

↑ Creating Athabascan beadwork and embroidery

Tlingit, Haida, and Tsimshian peoples at a totem pole raising, and *(inset)* Aleut women weaving grass baskets ↑

HAIDA

The Haida share many cultural traditions with the Tlingit. Expert sailors, they traditionally depended on salmon and sea mammals for their subsistence lifestyle. As many as 10,000 Haida once lived in Alaska, but by the 1890s, their numbers had been decimated by diseases brought in by Western explorers. While they are now centered on Hydaburg on Prince of Wales Island, people of Haida descent live across southern Alaska.

TSIMSHIAN

Alaska's Tsimshian are descendants of 823 people who left Canada with an Anglican missionary. Settling on Annette Island, in a village they named Metlakatla, they set up a model Protestant Christian community. The Tsimshian are the only Native group to retain sovereignty over their land, after rejecting the Alaska Native Claims Settlement Act of 1971 *(p60)*.

INUPIAT

The Inupiat (singular Inupiaq) mainly occupy areas along the Arctic Ocean coast and on the northern slope of the Brooks Range. Historically, some groups were settled, but others traveled great distances to hunt seals, whales, caribou, and other animals. The Inupiat had no chiefs, but each family

↑ An Inupiaq hunter in a traditional parka, next to a skin boat

was headed by an *umialik*, who managed food and other needs. Today, many rural Inupiat still make a livelihood from subsistence hunting, fishing, and gathering.

YUP'IK

The Yup'ik traditionally lived on the Yukon-Kuskokwim Delta, as well as on the Bering Sea coast and parts of the Seward Peninsula, in both summer hunting camps and permanent villages. Due to the milder and more vegetated environment, they made more use of wood, vegetables, and land animals than the Inupiat. Some Yup'ik still practice subsistence hunting or spend the summers working in family fish camps.

ALEUT (UNANGAX) AND ALUTIIQ (SUGPIAQ)

Both the Aleut and Alutiiq live in Southwest Alaska, but the difference in their languages suggests that they have entirely separate origins. Both groups had a maritime hunting culture, using skin boats to chase seals, otters, and whales. Many individuals were killed or enslaved by early Russian otter hunters, but Russian Orthodox clergy later converted large numbers to the church, which remains a strong spiritual force. Aleut people often prefer the name Unangax and Alutiiq call themselves Sugpiaq.

Catch of the Day

Five species of salmon inhabit Alaska waters, and the fish is a common item on local menus. Feel the thrill of catching your own on a guided salmon charter in Homer *(p108)*, Seward *(p100)*, or Kenai *(p106)*, or purchase a license and give it a go along the Kenai River *(p104)*; any leftovers can be shipped home through a processor. Gourmets should look out for Copper River salmon *(p121)* – a luxurious local delicacy.

←

Fresh salmon cooking on an open grill

ALASKA FOR
FOODIES

When it comes to food, Alaska is a bountiful basket of flavors, colors, and textures. Take your time to savor each region's specialities – whether it's just-picked vegetables or succulent salmon, you'll enjoy delicious local produce bursting with freshness.

Farm Fresh

The beautiful Matanuska-Susitna Valley near Anchorage is a rich, fertile region famed for its sweet, homegrown fruits and vegetables. Treat your taste buds with a visit to Pyrah's Pioneer Peak Farm *(http://pppfarm.net)*, located in the shadow of its craggy, snow-capped namesake, or pick up some produce at one of Anchorage's weekly summer farmers markets.

ALASKA'S RECORD GOURDS

Alaska's long summer days are perfect for growing giant vegetables. In 2019, Anchorage resident Dale Marshall shattered his previous state record by almost 600 lbs (270 kg) when the pumpkin he entered at the Alaska State Fair tipped the scales at an astonishing 2,051 lbs (930 kg) in the annual weigh-off.

The South Anchorage Farmers Market ↑

Tasty Tours

Fill your belly in Alaska's capital on an outing with Juneau Food Tours *(www. juneaufoodtours.com)*. Explore a unique spectrum of tastes that ranges from trendy specials such as Asian-fusion nachos to classic Alaska favorites such as foraged greens and succulent fresh seafood. Anchorage Culinary Tours *(www.anchorage-culinarytours.com)* offers a similar experience in the state's largest city.

$\rightarrow$

Fueling up on local seafood at a food shack in Juneau

Keeping it Green

For centuries, Alaskans have taken advantage of the readily available edible plants that grow naturally on their doorstep. Take a class on foraging at the Alaska Botanical Garden in Anchorage *(p85)* or the Alaska Folk School in Fairbanks *(https://folk.school)*, then put your new skills into practice by harvesting wild blueberries and cranberries from the state's forests, or picking beach greens along its shore.

$\leftarrow$

Golden and red salmonberries, foraged on the Aleutian Islands

Subsistence Rules

Alaska Native foods are an important part of the subsistence lifestyles that connect people here to the land. Centers such as the Alutiiq Museum in Kodiak *(p224)* and the Museum of the Aleutians in Unalaska *(p218)* offer an interesting insight into the hunting and gathering activities of each region. And at Icy Strait Point in the Tlingit village of Hoonah *(p162)* you can sample the delicate flavor of freshly caught halibut or salmon that has been prepared traditionally.

$\rightarrow$

Browsing the exhibits at the Alutiiq Museum in Kodiak

A Harvest of Flavor

Always looking for ways to utilize the bounty of Alaska's rich environments, local drinks producers are proud of their ability to harvest from the land - make sure to ask about the seasonal special when you visit any bar or brewery. How about an Alaska Brewing Company Winter Ale made with spruce tips, or an Alaska Distillery vodka flavored with - wait for it - smoked salmon?

→

A tasting flight of craft beers made by Girdwood Brewing

ALASKA
RAISE A GLASS

While Alaska's natural attractions tend to hog the headlines, the state's craft beer and spirits industry also demands a look. Using local ingredients and crystal-clear glacier water, innovative producers are putting a unique Alaska twist on some standard classics.

Wilderness Wines

Much to the surprise of many visitors, Alaska is home to several successful wineries. Alaska Denali Winery in Anchorage (*www.alaska denaliwinery.com*) creates small-batch wines tailored to individual customers, while Bear Creek Winery in Homer (*www.bearcreekwinery.com*) specializes in combining imported grapes with local flavors such as blueberry, gooseberry, or rhubarb for an exquisite sipping experience.

Did You Know?

Alaska is ranked sixth in the US for the number of breweries per capita.

Sampling a glass of fruit-infused wine at Bear Creek Winery ↑

Get Festive

Due to Alaska's varied terrain and limited number of roadways, it takes a long time to visit all of the state's breweries or distilleries. To help make life easier for consumers, a growing number of annual beer and spirits festivals have been established, offering lots of samples in one place. The largest of these is the Alaska Craft Brew & Barley Wine Festival, held each January in Anchorage, but Haines' Great Alaska Craft Beer and Homebrew Festival in May and the Talkeetna Beer Festival in September are also good options.

← The Alaska Craft Brew & Barley Wine Festival

Looking behind the scenes at a brewery with Big Swig Tours ↑

Sip while Sightseeing

Exploring Alaska's stunning countryside can be thirsty work, so why not refresh with some handcrafted beer along the way. Big Swig Tours in Anchorage *(www.bigswigtours.com)* provides a designated driver for curated trips to Southcentral Alaska's most popular breweries, combining sightseeing and history with a host of lip-smacking beverages. You can even throw in an Alaska Railroad adventure for good measure, or take to the saddle for a pedal-powered tour.

Hit the Trails

Whether you're after a quiet stroll or a challenging mountain hike, Alaska has thousands of trails to choose from. Anchorage's Chugach State Park *(p72)* is perfect for an easy excursion into the backcountry, with numerous options within striking distance of town. The ranger-led hikes in Denali National Park *(p168)* are a great opportunity to learn more about the local flora and fauna, while the Flume Trail in Juneau offers an insight into Alaska's Gold Rush history. You'll find a wealth of helpful advice at the Alaska Public Lands Information Centers in Anchorage *(p80)*, Tok *(p202)*, Fairbanks *(p174)*, and Ketchikan *(p130)*, which provide listings of all public lands trails and associated campgrounds statewide.

→
Hiking through the scenic surrounds of Chugach State Park

ALASKA FOR
OUTDOOR
ADVENTURE

From high alpine hiking to an ATV tour of the backcountry, Alaska is packed with opportunities for adventure seekers. Immerse yourself in the state's wild spaces for an experience you'll never forget.

Start Your Engine

With so few roads, locals often take to firing up All-Terrain Vehicles (ATVs) or snowmobiles to reach the backcountry. If you've never driven one and fancy giving it a go, join a guided tour with 49th State Motor Tours near Anchorage *(https://49smt.com)* or embark on an excursion with Skagway Shore Tours *(https://skagwayshoretours.com)*. Keep an eye out for moose, bears, and caribou along the way.

←
Watching polar bears on an ATV tour

Mush On

Dog sleds were long a key mode of transportation among Interior and Arctic communities – used for hauling people, freight, and mail – and mushing is still the state sport. You can meet the canine athletes on a tour of a working sled dog kennel; be sure to choose one that ascribes to the highest standards of care by referencing the Alaska State visitors bureau website *(www.travelalaska.com)*.

← A hard-working sled dog pausing for a rest in Utqiagvik

Sporting For Fish

Sportfishing is one of Alaska's most popular activities. Charters are the best way to ensure a productive trip, but casting a line on your own is great fun, too. Try Cooper Landing *(p104)* on the world-renowned Kenai River for salmon, or visit Homer *(p108)* to try your luck at catching a giant "barn door" halibut.

→ Fishing for salmon in the bountiful waters of Kenai River

Stroll the Streets

Alaska's cities are full of history and culture, and a free walking tour is a great way to get to know each area's character. The Alaska Public Lands Information Center in Anchorage *(p80)* offers daily city tours in summer, and in Southeast Alaska you can pick up helpful walking tour maps from each of the port towns' visitor centers.

←

Learning about Skagway's history on a guided tour of the town

ALASKA ON A
SHOESTRING

Visiting Alaska isn't cheap, but it doesn't have to be expensive, either. Using a little insider know-how, you can live like a local and enjoy a wealth of activities that are accessible on even the tightest of budgets.

Pick a Different Season

The bulk of visitors arrive between May and September, but there's plenty of fun to be had outside the peak summer months, when hotel rates can be up to half those of the high season. As the weather cools, Alaska's fall colors shine in Denali National Park *(p168)* and along the Seward Highway, while winter's snowfall brings the prospect of skiing at the Alyeska Resort in Girdwood *(p88)* or cosying up before a roaring fire. In April or early May, try a deeply discounted cruise up the Inside Passage *(p260)* to watch for whales, bear cubs, and migratory shorebirds.

Hit the Road

A self-drive tour makes an affordable option for exploring the state, with Alaska's network of highways providing a natural route planner. Start by renting a Recreational Vehicle (RV) in Anchorage, then head either north toward the Interior or south along the Kenai Peninsula, camping along the way. Be sure to grab a copy of *The Milepost (www.themilepost.com)* before you set off – this long-standing guide to traveling the roadways of Alaska is packed with valuable tips and advice.

→

Driving along Exit Glacier Road in the Kenai Peninsula

Get Rustic

For those wanting to experience the great outdoors, Alaska's campgrounds and public-use cabins are a bargain. Whether it's pitching a tent next to a wilderness lake or dining al fresco on the porch of a simple log cabin, this is how Alaskans themselves unwind. For full listings of all the different options that are available, check online at www.alaskacenters.gov.

←

A cosy wooden cabin in the wilds of Interior Alaska

Go Back to School

Meet Alaskans and learn new skills by taking a free class. The Alaska Folk School in Fairbanks *(https://folk.school)* runs courses on everything from wooden spoon-making to felting, while the Eagle River Nature Center near Anchorage *(p72)* offers various classes on wilderness recreation, including wildlife safety and edible plants.

→

A guided walk at the Eagle River Nature Centre

↑ Golden fall foliage in Denali National Park's Polychrome Pass

Learn Together

Got a budding ranger in the family? Sign up for one of the Junior Ranger programs run by the National Park Service or US Forest Service – they give kids the opportunity to meet rangers and learn about nature while participating in a variety of fun activities. Ranger-led walks are available at many of Alaska's public lands sites, and Alaska State Parks offers quarterly "Family Adventure Days" designed to include kids of any age in outdoor activities such as crafts and wayfinding. You'll find a host of interpretive displays at park visitor centers, as well as classes for the whole family and presentations on everything from bear safety to plant identification.

→

Learning to light a
fire at Kachemak Bay
near Homer

ALASKA FOR
FAMILIES

Alaska is the perfect venue for a family vacation, no matter your budget or timeline. Children thrive in the Last Frontier, with so many ways to explore the outdoors: whether you're fishing, hiking or looking for wildlife, Alaska's magical landscapes will provide family memories to last a lifetime.

All Aboard!

It's hard to beat an adventure on the Alaska Railroad *(www. alaskarailroad.com),* which offers cars with domed windows and plentiful wildlife-spotting opportunities. Catch the train to Spencer Glacier for a short rafting trip or hike, or travel to Talkeetna *(p180),* then on to Denali National Park *(p168).* The Hurricane Turn train is the nation's only flag stop route *(p255),* and kids will love helping the conductor assist passengers with their gear at each stop.

←

Alaska Railroad's Glacier
Discovery Train in Chugach
National Forest

Where the Wild Things Are

For a chance to meet Alaska's wildlife without the challenges of the wilderness, head to the Alaska Zoo in Anchorage *(p85)*, or the beautiful Alaska Wildlife Conservation Center in Portage *(p79)*. Young birders will delight in the Bald Eagle Foundation in Haines *(p152)* and Sitka's Raptor Center *(p134)*, with their close-up viewings of rehabilitated birds of prey.

→

Wolves at the Alaska Wildlife Conservation Center

Sail Away

Most of Alaska's ever-popular cruises are a good fit for younger guests. The larger ships often have onboard children's clubs, as well as affordable shore excursions. Smaller ships, like UnCruise Adventures *(www.uncruise adventures.com)*, provide scheduled departures for families, with an onboard youth leader. These boutique-style experiences are usually more expensive but include activities and meals, often resulting in overall savings.

←

Cruising past glaciers in Prince William Sound

Location, Location

With so much wilderness, it can be hard to know where to begin. Your best bet for bear photos is Lake Clark (p228) or Katmai National Park (p212); Anchorage (p64) and Denali National Park (p168) are top spots for moose; and Haines (p152) is the place to go for bald eagles. Especially scenic landscapes include the misty forests of the Inside Passage, and the towering mountains of the Seward Highway.

←

A brown bear and its reflection in the waters of Lake Clark

ALASKA FOR
PHOTOGRAPHERS

With opportunities to capture images of feeding bears and the swirling aurora borealis, Alaska is a photographer's dream location. Whether you're a seasoned pro or just starting out, here are some top tips for getting the best shots.

TOP 3 ICONIC ALASKA SHOTS

Arctic Brotherhood Hall
This unusual building in Skagway (p144), made of driftwood, is said to be Alaska's most-photographed structure.

Mount Denali
The best angle of this supremely photogenic mountain is from Wonder Lake at the end of the Denali National Park Road (p170).

Bears at Brooks Falls
Brown bears feeding on salmon at Brooks Falls in Katmai National Park (p212) is one of the most iconic images of the state.

Hone Your Technique

Taking pictures of moving wildlife and awkwardly lit landscapes isn't always easy, so get some expert advice on a photography tour with Alaska Photo Treks *(https://alaska phototreks.com)* or Jeff Schultz Photography *(www.schultz photo.com)* in Anchorage. Rainbow Glacier Adventures *(https://tourhaines.com)* in Haines is helpful for pointers on snapping bald eagles, which are notoriously difficult to capture due to their active movements and fine features.

→

Taking photos on a tour in Chugach State Park

💬 INSIDER TIP
Safe Shooting

Never openly approach a wild animal, no matter how small, for the sake of capturing a photo. Alaska's animals are unpredictable and should be left alone for their safety and yours.

←

Photographing the changing colors of the aurora borealis, or northern lights

Capture the Northern Lights

The aurora borealis, or northern lights, illuminate Alaska's winter skies with swirls of green, red, and purple, making for some incredibly evocative night shots. They appear from late August to April and are usually at their best around 1am; the farther north you are, the more likely it is that you'll see them. To get the best pictures of the phenomenon, it's worth joining an aurora-viewing tour with an expert guide. Fairbanks has a number of good options: The Aurora Chasers *(www. theaurorachasers.com)* visit several viewing locations, including remote areas outside of town, while Alaska Tours *(https://alaskatours.com)* provides an introduction to aurora photography from the comfort of an enclosed yurt.

Traverse the Passes

The drive from Anchorage (p64) to Valdez (p116) is a popular road trip among Alaska residents, twisting along the Matanuska River on the Glenn Highway, before joining the Richardson Highway and crossing the rugged Thompson Pass. There are various stops where you can learn about the Gold Rush, plus peaks and glaciers to ogle en route.

↑ Driving through the Matanuska Valley on the Glenn Highway

ALASKA FOR
SCENIC JOURNEYS

Explore Alaska for any length of time at all and you're likely to run out of ways to describe its beauty. With spectacular scenery wherever you travel, journeying through the state by road, rail, or sea is as much of a delight as arriving at your destination.

Sail Away

The ferries of the Alaska Marine Highway System (p255) carry scores of passengers each year, especially around the Inside Passage, where roads are few and air travel is expensive. The "Blue Canoes" are known for their steadiness, and their simple-yet-spotless accommodations are wonderfully offset by the grandeur of the surrounding scenery. Hop aboard at Juneau (p136) and travel to the surrounding port towns for a taste of small-town Alaska life.

←

Looking toward Skagway from the deck of an Alaska Marine Highway ferry

Ride the Hurricane

Go back to a bygone era with a ride on the last flag-stop train route in the US: Alaska Railroad's Hurricane Turn Train *(p255)*. Traveling from Talkeetna to Hurricane via the wilds of the backcountry, the train serves as a lifeline for rural homesteaders and is particularly scenic during the golden months of fall.

→

Taking pictures of the view from the Hurricane Turn Train

Take the Alaska Highway

Known fondly by its nickname, the "AlCan," the Alaska Highway is a 1,390-mile (2,237-km) stretch of road between British Columbia's Dawson Creek and Alaska's Delta Junction *(p191)*. Built to connect Alaska to Canada and the Lower 48 states during World War II, it offers a breathtaking drive through stunning scenery, and will leave you overwhelmed with respect for the US Army Corps of Engineers who laid it.

←

The start of the Alaska Highway in Dawson Creek, Canada

Do the Denali

Soak up sweeping views of the Alaska Range and miles and miles of open tundra on the 135-mile (217-km) Denali Highway *(p172)*. Its largely gravel surface means that most rental companies prohibit driving here, so instead relax as a passenger on an excursion with Denali Highway Cabins and Tours *(www.denalihwy.com)*.

↑ Evening light illuminating the Denali Highway as it winds its way east

A YEAR IN
ALASKA

JANUARY

Polar Bear Jump *(third weekend in Jan)*. People in costumes jump into the icy waters of Seward's Resurrection Bay for charity.

△ **Cordova Iceworm Festival** *(last week of Jan)*. A festival designed to beat the winter blues, by honoring a tiny worm that lives in glacial ice.

FEBRUARY

Fur Rendezvous *(last week of Feb)*. Held in Anchorage, this large festival celebrates the end of winter and the history of Alaska pioneer life.

△ **World Ice Art Championships** *(Feb–Mar)*. Amazing ice sculptures are created by champion ice carvers, who travel from all over the world to compete in Fairbanks.

MAY

△ **Kachemak Bay Shorebird Festival** *(mid-May)*. A weeklong festival in Homer to observe and learn about the shorebirds of Southcentral Alaska.

Little Norway Festival *(mid-May)*. A vibrant celebration of Petersburg's Norwegian heritage, packed with plenty of food, dancing, and other events.

JUNE

Sitka Summer Music Festival *(Jun)*. A popular classical music series, held at various venues around Sitka since 1972.

△ **Colony Days** *(first week in Jun)*. A festival of farming, homesteading, and agriculture in the Matanuska-Susitna Valley, held in Palmer.

SEPTEMBER

△ **Labor Day** *(first Mon in Sep)*. This national holiday is celebrated statewide, but the quirkiest events – including a Rubber Duck Race and a Bathtub Race – are hosted by Nome.

Seward Music and Arts Festival *(last weekend in Sep)*. A musical revue for all ages, featuring local bands and artisans of food and crafts.

OCTOBER

△ **Alaska Day Festival** *(Oct 18)*. Sitka marks the day when Russia relinquished ownership of Alaska to the United States with a grand parade and traditional ball, as well as various activities for kids.

MARCH

△ **Iditarod Trail Sled Dog Race** *(starts first weekend in Mar)*. Mushing teams race along a historic 1,000-mile (1,600-km) trail from Anchorage to Nome *(p238)*.

Festival of Native Arts *(late Mar)*. A collaboration between the University of Alaska Fairbanks and Alaska Native groups since 1973, this festival in Fairbanks is a celebration of dances, stories, and songs from cultures around the world.

APRIL

Hummingbird Festival *(Apr)*. Ketchikan welcomes the Rufous hummingbird's return to Southeast Alaska after its winter migrations.

△ **Native Youth Olympics** *(late Apr)*. Young athletes from across Alaska meet in Anchorage to compete in traditional games of skill and strength.

JULY

△ **Seward's Mount Marathon Race and July 4th Celebration** *(Jul 4)*. Brave runners race up and down Mount Marathon as part of Seward's signature celebrations for Independence Day.

Golden Days *(mid-Jul)*. Alaska's midnight sun is celebrated in Fairbanks with games, artisan crafts, and a parade.

AUGUST

Blueberry Arts Festival *(first weekend in Aug)*. A happy celebration of blueberries, arts, and crafts in downtown Ketchikan.

△ **Alaska State Fair** *(late Aug–early Sep)*. Held in Palmer, this showcase for giant vegetables, food, crafts, and livestock has been running since 1936.

NOVEMBER

Sitka Whalefest *(early Nov)*. A multiday symposium on Alaska's whale species, with opportunities to go whale-watching in Sitka Sound and beyond.

△ **Alaska Bald Eagle Festival** *(mid-Nov)*. Haines honors the hundreds of bald eagles that reside in the town over winter.

DECEMBER

Anchorage International Film Festival *(early Dec)*. Billed as "Films worth freezing for," this celebration of independent filmmaking features more than 100 screenings, plus discussions with artists.

△ **Colony Christmas, Palmer** *(mid-Dec)*. A laidback country Christmas parade in Palmer, resurrecting the pioneer spirit with fireworks and a community festival.

MAP OF THE
TERRITORY of ALASKA

1

A BRIEF
HISTORY

Alaxsxaq (Aleut for "The Great Land") has provided much for the humans who have eked out an existence from its land and seas. The discovery of natural resources here has brought great wealth – but also great strife – and the environment continues to play an important role in Alaska's fortunes today.

Land Bridges to European Explorers

The first Native groups are thought to have arrived in Alaska at least 12,000 years ago, via a land bridge from Siberia. They were later followed by the Inuit and Aleut, who likely arrived by umiak (hide-covered canoe). These communities expanded, adapting their hunter-gatherer lifestyles to the local climate and terrain.

Spaniard Bartolomew de Fonte is said to have been the first European to view Alaska, when he sailed up the Inside Passage in around 1640 on an exploratory mission. Danish captain Vitus Bering followed in 1728 on behalf of Russia, and British captain James Cook arrived at the site of present-day Anchorage in 1778.

1 A map of Alaska dating from 1878.

2 An Aleut visor, worn while hunting in kayaks.

3 A 1776 portrait of Captain James Cook by Nathaniel Dance.

4 A painting commemorating the Alaska Purchase in 1867.

Timeline of events

9,000 years ago
The first Inuit begin arriving in western Alaska, reaching land via skin boats.

15,000 years ago
Paleolithic people begin moving into the northern reaches of North America.

1640
Spaniard Bartolomew de Fonte becomes the first European to view Alaska.

1728
Vitus Bering arrives in the to-be-named Bering Strait, claiming the new territory for Russia.

1778
James Cook visits the site of present-day Anchorage while searching for the Northwest Passage.

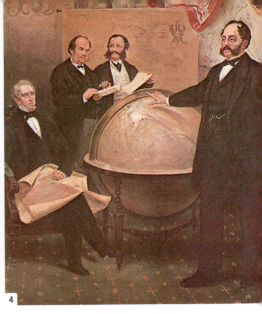

The Russian Era

By the late 18th century, a booming trade in sea otter pelts had brought many Russians to Alaska, keen to seek their fortune. These hunters and traders frequently exploited local Native groups, often tricking them into abject slavery. To discourage British interest in the region, Russian merchants began settling coastal communities, and in 1799 the Russian-American Company, headed by salesman Alexander Baranov, was granted a trade monoloply by Czar Paul I. Local Tlingit groups protested this incursion, violently destroying a fort built in Sitka in 1802, but were ultimately unable to halt the Russian encroachment.

By the 1830s, however, the Russian fur trade had all but ceased due to overhunting and Russia began to lose interest. In 1859, Czar Alexander II offered to sell Alaska to the United States. The US Congress was initially hesistant, but in 1867, Secretary of State William H. Seward pushed for the purchase, and President Andrew Johnson – and Congress – agreed. Alaska was bought for about 2 cents per acre; a total sum of $7.2 million. Official ownership was transfered in a ceremony in Sitka on October 18, 1867.

↑ *Unknown First Family,* a statue in Fairbanks by Malcolm Alexander

---

1799
Russia assigns the town of Sitka as the seat of its colonial government, even as local Native groups push back.

1859
Czar Alexander II authorizes his agent to negotiate the sale of Alaska to the US.

1867
The US formally purchases Alaska from Russia for $7.2 million.

1790
The sea otter population is decimated by overhunting for pelts, known for their softness.

1824
Russia, Britain, and the US sign a treaty forming the boundary of Russian America.

1

2

3

The Gold Rush and its Aftermath

The American public generally thought that Alaska was a waste of money, and the early years after the state's purchase were rather unremarkable – until the discovery of gold in 1880, at the site of present-day Juneau. By the 1890s, "gold fever" had also spread to the Canadian Klondike and farther west near Nome. Thousands flocked to Alaska to make their fortunes, and the territory appeared in newspaper headlines worldwide. By the time the Gold Rushes ended around 1905, Alaska's capital had moved from Sitka to Juneau, and by 1906, Alaska had a non-voting member in Congress.

In the years that followed, an increasing population and interest in timber resources and seafood transformed the new territory's economy. In the 1920s, Alaska Natives, along with other American Indians, were granted voting rights and then US citizenship. The Alaska Railroad between Seward and Fairbanks was completed in 1923, rejuvenating the city of Anchorage, and President Franklin D. Roosevelt's New Deal established the Matanuska Valley Colony at Palmer in the mid-1930s, during the Great Depression.

CHILKOOT TRAIL

During the Klondike Gold Rush, more than 33,000 people set out in search of riches on the Chilkoot Trail (p150). Beginning in Dyea and ending at Lake Bennett, British Columbia, miners would make the journey, often at their peril. By 1898, Canada's North-West Mounted Police, frustrated by the ill-prepared hikers, required all to bring a year's worth of supplies.

Timeline of events

1872

Gold is found on the Kenai Peninsula, not far from Sitka.

1880

The area around Juneau is found to be rich in gold.

1886

Alaska's Gold Rush begins in earnest when a major gold strike occurs near Fortymile River.

1890

Christian missionaries arrive with the aim of converting all Alaska Natives.

1898

More than 30,000 miners reach the Klondike and Nome District.

The War Years

When Japan attacked Pearl Harbor on December 7, 1941, the vulnerability of Alaska's location was brought into sharp focus. Fears of a Japanese invasion were validated by an air attack on the Aleutians and the capture of Attu Island in 1942. The US regained control of the Aleutians by August 1943, after the establishment of bases on Akutan, Amchitka, and Adak. Many Alaska Native families were abruptly relocated during this period – ostensibly for their safety, but ultimately most of them never returned home.

Many of Alaska's highways were constructed during the early part of World War II to aid in the delivery of goods to support the war effort. The greatest of these was the Alaska Highway, a 1,440-mile (2,304-km) gravel road that connected Alaska to the rest of the United States via Canada. This phenomenal feat involved punching through trackless territory, felling trees, and bridging wild rivers. Similarly, the expansion of the port of Whittier required the construction of what is known today as the Anton Anderson Memorial Tunnel, the longest highway tunnel in North America.

1 A stream of miners on the Chilkoot Trail.

2 Transporting supplies for gold mining.

3 The Aleutian Islands during World War II.

4 The Anton Anderson Memorial Tunnel.

Did You Know?

The Alaska Highway was built in just eight months and 12 days.

1906

Juneau becomes the official territorial capital of Alaska.

1910

Petersburg in Southeast - part of a thriving fish cannery industry - is incorporated as a town.

1923

Construction of the Alaska Railroad between Anchorage and Fairbanks is completed.

1935

Farming families from the Midwest arrive in Matanuska-Susitna Valley under the New Deal.

1942

Japanese forces attack bases on the Aleutian Islands, and hundreds of Alaska Native families are relocated.

Statehood and the Oil Boom

The population growth during World War II made Alaska a clear candidate for statehood. In 1955, Alaska elected delegates to draft a constitution, which was adopted the following year. After President Dwight D. Eisenhower signed the Statehood Bill in 1958, Alaska became the 49th state in the Union on January 3, 1959.

In 1968, the Atlantic-Richfield Company (ARCO) drilled an exploratory well near Prudhoe Bay. The resulting 9.6 billion barrels of oil found on state land sent Alaska into a frenzy. The state sold oil leases worth $900 billion, and in 1974 the Alyeska Corporation began construction of the Trans-Alaska Pipeline. Thousands of workers flooded into the state for lucrative jobs along the pipeline route, and after just 39 months, oil began to flow.

Landmark Acts

During this rush for "black gold," Alaska's Native population questioned their rights to land that had been integral to centuries of tradition. In 1971, Congress passed the Alaska Native Claims Settlement Act (ANCSA) to compensate Native

1 President Eisenhower signs the bill making Alaska a state.

2 Trans-Alaska Pipeline.

3 President Carter with Alaska Natives in 1979.

4 Caribou in Wrangell-St. Elias National Park.

Did You Know?

The Trans-Alaska Pipeline can move up to 88,000 barrels of oil per hour.

Timeline of events

1957
Oil is discovered in Cook Inlet, and small platforms begin to appear along the shoreline.

1964
A 9.2 earthquake causes tsunamis and coastal devastation.

1968
Rich oil reserves are discovered in the Arctic on state land.

1959
Alaska becomes the 49th state in the Union.

1971
The Alaska Native Claims Settlement Act is enacted, creating 12 Native corporations.

groups for the loss of their ancestral property. Instead of establishing reservations, as was general practice elsewhere in the US, the Act transferred 68,750 square miles (178,000 sq km) of land to Native Corporations within a rough set of tribal boundaries. As shareholders in their respective corporations, Alaska Natives had control over most assets, but any claims to Native sovereignty were nullified.

In 1980, President Jimmy Carter signed the Alaska National Interest Lands Conservation Act (ANILCA), setting aside 162,000 sq miles (420,870 sq km) as protected wilderness. A slew of new national parks were created, including Katmai, Gates of the Arctic, Kenai Fjords, and Wrangell-St. Elias.

Alaska Today

Two million visitors flock to Alaska each year, and numbers continue to grow, especially among the lucrative cruise line industry. But the ripple effects of climate change pose a threat to the economy, and leaders will need to overcome a range of environmental challenges to ensure a profitable future for the state.

↑ Tourists from a cruise ship booking shore excursions in Juneau

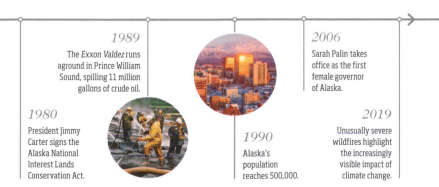

1989
The *Exxon Valdez* runs aground in Prince William Sound, spilling 11 million gallons of crude oil.

1980
President Jimmy Carter signs the Alaska National Interest Lands Conservation Act.

1990
Alaska's population reaches 500,000.

2006
Sarah Palin takes office as the first female governor of Alaska.

2019
Unusually severe wildfires highlight the increasingly visible impact of climate change.

EXPERIENCE

Kayakers in the pretty town of Ketchikan

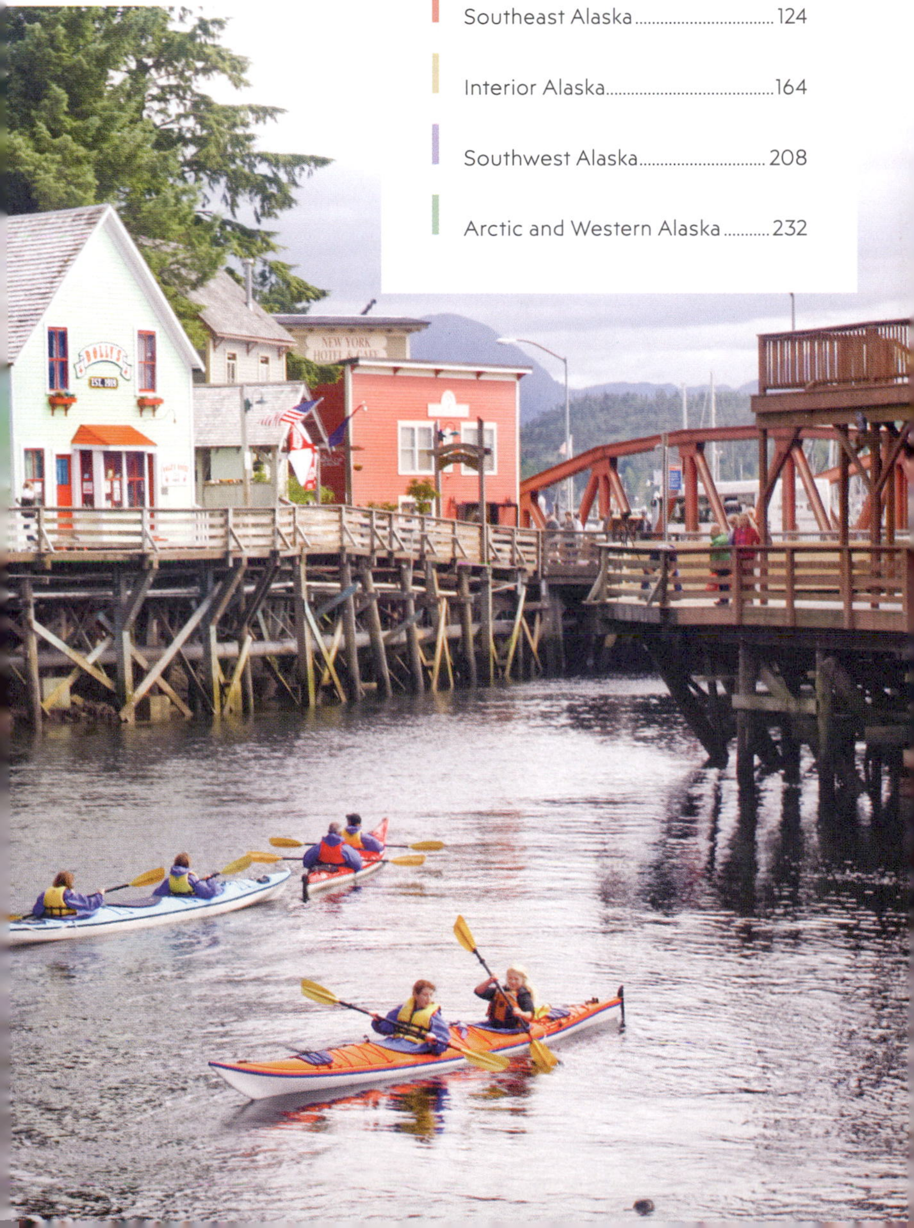

Downtown Anchorage reflected in Cook Inlet

ANCHORAGE

The "bowl" of land occupied by present-day Anchorage has been inhabited by humans for at least 10,000 years, when the Dena'ina people settled in the area. Dena'ina groups like the Eklutna and Knik peacefully coexisted here until 1778, when British explorer Captain James Cook landed near the entrance of Turnagain Arm. Word soon spread about Cook Inlet's abundant resources and accessible harbors, and fur traders and merchants, many from Russia, quickly began settling here, to the ever-increasing cost of the Dena'ina's cultural traditions and subsistence lifestyle.

A decade after Alaska was purchased from Russia by the United States in 1867, massive Gold Rushes drew attention to the area's easy access to northern and southern trade and supply routes. In 1914, President Wilson commissioned a survey of the entire basin in an attempt to lay out plans for a railroad connecting the tiny community of Seward on the Kenai Peninsula to Fairbanks in the Interior. The original townsite of Anchorage was established by Alaska Railroad crews in 1915 as Ship Creek, which started off as a ramshackle tent city but quickly grew to a large town.

During World War II, Anchorage was considered vital to the US war effort due to its proximity to the Pacific Rim, and the military base established here became an integral part of the city's growth. Today, Anchorage is Alaska's largest city, with a diverse population of 350,000 and a major role as a commercial and transportation hub.

ANCHORAGE

Must Sees
1. Anchorage Museum
2. Alaska Native Heritage Center
3. Chugach State Park
4. Independence Mine State Historical Park
5. Turnagain Arm

Experience More
6. Log Cabin Visitor Information Center
7. Alaska Law Enforcement Museum
8. Alaska Public Lands Information Center
9. Oscar Anderson House
10. Resolution Park
11. Alaska Aviation Museum
12. Tony Knowles Coastal Trail
13. St. Innocent Russian Orthodox Cathedral
14. Ship Creek Salmon Viewing Platform
15. Spenard
16. Lake Hood and Lake Spenard

17. Hilltop Ski Area
18. Alaska Zoo
19. Alaska Botanical Garden
20. Palmer
21. Reindeer Farm
22. Bodenburg Butte
23. Eklutna Historical Park
24. Wasilla
25. Musk Ox Farm
26. Hatcher Pass
27. Girdwood

Eat
1. Bear Tooth Grill
2. Crow's Nest
3. Glacier Brewhouse
4. The Marx Bros Café
5. Turkey Red
6. Palmer Alehouse
7. Raven's Perch Restaurant

Stay
8. Copper Whale Inn B&B
9. The Lakefront Anchorage
10. Hotel Captain Cook

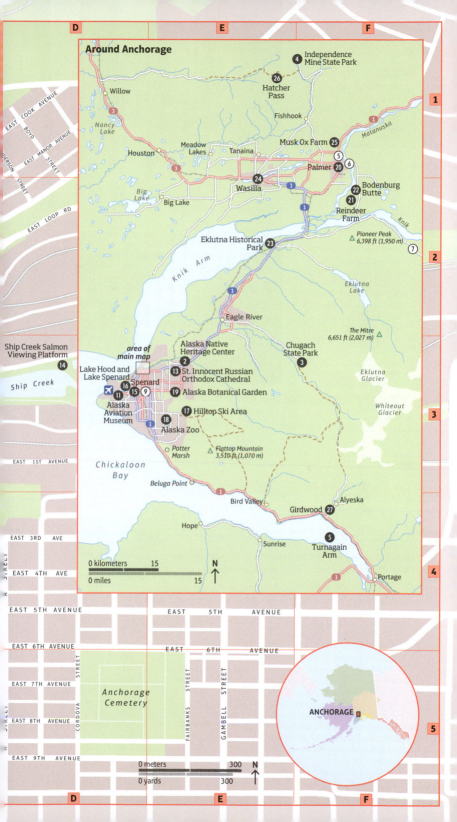

Around Anchorage

D **E** **F**

1

Willow

3

Nancy Lake

Houston

Meadow Lakes

Tanaina

4 Independence Mine State Park

26 Hatcher Pass

Fishhook

Musk Ox Farm **25**

Palmer **5** **6**
20

Matanuska **1**

22 Bodenburg Butte

21 Reindeer Farm

Wasilla **24**

Big Lake

Big Lake

3

3

1

1

Knik

Pioneer Peak 6,398 ft (1,950 m) **7**

2

Eklutna Historical Park **23**

Knik Arm

Eklutna Lake

1

Ship Creek Salmon Viewing Platform

14

Ship Creek

Eagle River

Alaska Native Heritage Center **2**

St. Innocent Russian Orthodox Cathedral **13**

Alaska Botanical Garden **19**

Chugach State Park **3**

The Mitre 6,651 ft (2,027 m)

Eklutna Glacier

Whiteout Glacier

3

area of main map

Lake Hood and Lake Spenard

16 **11**

15 **9**

Alaska Aviation Museum

18

Alaska Zoo

Spenard

1

Hilltop Ski Area **17**

Potter Marsh

Flattop Mountain 3,510 ft (1,070 m)

Chickaloon Bay

Beluga Point **1**

Bird Valley

Alyeska

Girdwood **27**

Hope

Sunrise

5 Turnagain Arm

Portage **1**

0 kilometers   15
0 miles   15

N

EAST COOK AVENUE

EAST MANOR AVENUE

EAST LOOP RD

EAST 1ST AVENUE

EAST 3RD AVE

EAST 4TH AVE

EAST 5TH AVENUE

EAST 6TH AVENUE

EAST 7TH AVENUE

EAST 8TH AVENUE

EAST 9TH AVENUE

EAST 5TH AVENUE

EAST 6TH AVENUE

CORDOVA STREET

FAIRBANKS STREET

GAMBELL STREET

Anchorage Cemetery

0 meters   300
0 yards   300

N

ANCHORAGE

D **E** **F**

1

2

3

4

5

GALLERY GUIDE

The Discovery Center covers much of the first floor, which also houses the Alaska Resource Center (open for public research). The second-level galleries are home to the permanent exhibitions exploring 10,000 years of Alaska history. The Art of the North galleries, which feature a broad swathe of Alaska art through the ages, occupy level three; temporary exhibits are displayed here, too. The fourth-floor gallery affords expansive views of the Chugach Mountains.

The Smithsonian Arctic Studies Center, housed within Anchorage Museum ↑

ANCHORAGE MUSEUM

📍 C5 🏠 625 C Street 🚌 2, 14 🕐 May-Sep: 9am-6pm daily; Oct-Apr: 10am-6pm Tue-Sat, noon-6pm Sun 🌐 anchoragemuseum.org

Covering 170,000 sq ft (16,000 sq km), including 2 acres (1 ha) of landscaped public space, Alaska's largest museum provides a fascinating introduction to life in the state.

Anchorage Museum houses exhibits on the history, land, and culture of Alaska and its Indigenous peoples. There are many fascinating artifacts, including beautiful ivory carvings and ceremonial masks from Native peoples such as the Yup'ik and Inupiaq. The Rasmuson Wing, part of an extension built in 2017, houses the Art of the North galleries, containing some of the state's finest art, including 19th- and 20th-century Romantic landscapes. Other highlights are the Planetarium and the Discovery Center, a child-friendly science space exploring Alaska's constantly changing landscape through plenty of hands-on attractions. The museum also hosts approximately 20 visiting exhibits annually from around the world.

> 💬 INSIDER TIP
> **Culture Pass**
>
> Buy a Culture Pass (*www.alaskaculture pass.org*), which grants admission to both the Anchorage Museum and Alaska Native Heritage Center, with a free shuttle between the two.

1

2

3

1 The major extension to the Anchorage Museum, designed by David Chipperfield in 2009, is a graceful four-storey building faced with shimmering glass.

2 The museum holds an extensive collection of Alaska Native art and artifacts, including exquisite carvings of animals, and masks such as this one, carved in wood.

3 This atmospheric depiction of Denali (formerly known as Mount McKinley) was painted by Sydney Laurence (1865-1940), one of Alaska's most popular artists. Several of Laurence's landscapes are on display here.

②

ALASKA NATIVE HERITAGE CENTER

⊙ E3 🏠 Muldoon Rd North, exit from Glenn Hwy 🚌 Free shuttle from Anchorage Museum and from some hotels 🕐 Mid-May–mid-Sep: 9am–5pm daily; mid-Sep–mid-May: for special events only ⓦ alaskanative.net

Situated in a lovely wooded corner of Anchorage, the Alaska Native Heritage Center uses exhibits, workshops, and outdoor displays to preserve and perpetuate Alaska Native culture.

One of Anchorage's most popular attractions, this educational and cultural institution gives visitors the opportunity to experience a range of diverse Native traditions at a single site. Among the center's highlights are five Native "villages," which are based on broad tribal groupings that draw upon cultural similarities or geographic proximity. In each of these "villages," Alaska Natives, dressed in traditional clothing, interpret aspects of their cultures and give demonstrations of arts and activities such as totem pole carving. The center also presents workshops, films, and numerous other cultural programs.

↑ A Tlingit clan house and totem pole at the Southeast Alaska Natives Village Site

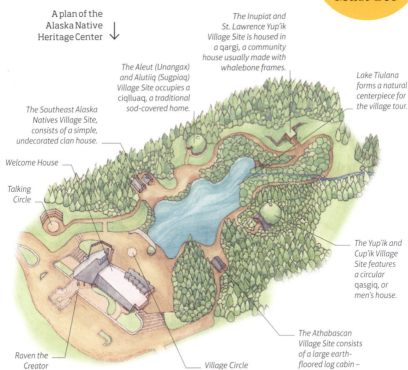

A plan of the Alaska Native Heritage Center ↓

The Inupiat and St. Lawrence Yup'ik Village Site is housed in a qargi, a community house usually made with whalebone frames.

The Aleut (Unangax) and Alutiiq (Sugpiaq) Village Site occupies a ciqlluaq, a traditional sod-covered home.

Lake Tiulana forms a natural centerpiece for the village tour.

The Southeast Alaska Natives Village Site, consists of a simple, undecorated clan house.

Welcome House

Talking Circle

The Yup'ik and Cup'ik Village Site features a circular qasgiq, or men's house.

Raven the Creator

Village Circle

The Athabascan Village Site consists of a large earth-floored log cabin – a traditional Athabascan home.

←
A traditional Alaska Native dance performance at the Heritage Center and *(inset)* traditional handicrafts on display

③

CHUGACH STATE PARK

🅿 F3 🏠 Eastern part of the Municipality of Anchorage 🕐 May–Sep: 10am–5pm Wed–Sun; Oct–Apr: 10am–5pm Fri–Sun 🅵 Park: Potter Section House, Mile 115, Seward Hwy; www.dnr.alaska.gov/parks

Encompassing almost 770 sq miles (2,000 sq km), Chugach State Park is America's third-largest state park. Surrounded by the Alaska range and the Wrangell and Chugach mountains, it makes a fabulously scenic setting for hiking and wildlife-spotting.

This glaciated region is one of Alaska's most easily accessible outdoor recreation areas, since it is only 7 miles (11 km) from downtown Anchorage. The park includes ice fields, massive glaciers, high peaks, forests, and mountain lakes, all within hiking distance of the city. While no roads cross the park, there are several hiking trails winding through spectacular scenery, as well as plenty of opportunities to view wildlife, including moose, black and brown bears, Dall sheep, mountain goats, marmots, and a host of smaller animals. Birdlife is profuse, especially along the park's many rivers, and close-up views of salmon are available from a platform near the Eagle River Nature Center. Entry to the park is free, though there is a fee for parking at the trailhead parking lot.

EAGLE RIVER NATURE CENTER

Located about an hour from Anchorage along the scenic Eagle River Valley, the Eagle River Nature Center *(www.ernc. org)* provides visitors with excellent interpretive programs and a network of trails leading further into Chugach State Park. Founded as a non-profit organization in 1996 to support a busy park staff, the center now offers a host of classes for all ages, including plant ID, guided hikes, foraging, and bear safety. There are also two yurts and one cabin available for rent via the public-use cabin system. The center has a small gift shop and natural science exhibits.

Did You Know?

The highest mountain in the park is Bashful Peak, at an impressive 8,005 ft (2,440 m).

→
Kayaks available for rent on Eklutna Lake, the park's largest lake

←
Hiking up to Flattop Mountain, Alaska's most climbed peak

↑ The scenic Eagle River Valley backed by the Chugach Mountains

A moose drinking from a pond as the sun sets over Polar Bear peak

EXPLORING CHUGACH STATE PARK

The Glen Alps area above Anchorage is by far the most popular place in the park to hike, ski, or mountain bike. Its parking lot is often full during the summer months, thanks to the sweeping views of the Anchorage Bowl and Cook Inlet. But smaller, quieter trails crossing a variety of terrain are also plentiful, ranging from Thunderbird Falls to the north and the Turnagain Arm Trail to the south. A good location for a bike ride or level walking trail is the Eklutna Lakeside Trail, running alongside scenic Eklutna Lake, the site of Anchorage's main watershed. At higher elevations, Williwaw and Rabbit lakes offer quieter alternatives to the Glen Alps, as well as providing stunning panoramic views. Watch for bears and moose, and the occasional wolverine, while hiking along the alpine trails.

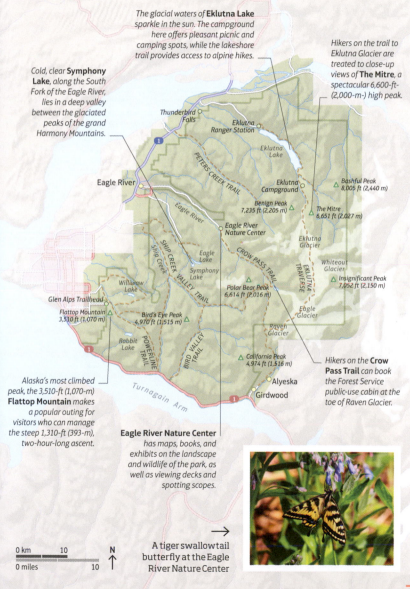

*The glacial waters of **Eklutna Lake** sparkle in the sun. The campground here offers pleasant picnic and camping spots, while the lakeshore trail provides access to alpine hikes.*

*Hikers on the trail to Eklutna Glacier are treated to close-up views of **The Mitre**, a spectacular 6,600-ft- (2,000-m-) high peak.*

*Cold, clear **Symphony Lake**, along the South Fork of the Eagle River, lies in a deep valley between the glaciated peaks of the grand Harmony Mountains.*

Thunderbird Falls

Eklutna Ranger Station

Eklutna Lake

Bashful Peak
8,005 ft (2,440 m)

Eagle River

Eklutna Campground

Benign Peak
7,235 ft (2,205 m)

The Mitre
6,651 ft (2,027 m)

PETERS CREEK TRAIL

Eagle River

Eagle River Nature Center

Eklutna Glacier

Eagle Lake

CROW PASS TRAIL

Whiteout Glacier

SHIP CREEK VALLEY TRAIL

Symphony Lake

Ship Creek

Williwaw Lake

Polar Bear Peak
6,614 ft (2,016 m)

Insignificant Peak
7,052 ft (2,150 m)

EKLUTNA TRAVERSE

Eagle Glacier

Glen Alps Trailhead

Flattop Mountain
3,510 ft (1,070 m)

Bird's Eye Peak
4,970 ft (1,515 m)

POWERLINE TRAIL

Rabbit Lake

BIRD VALLEY TRAIL

Raven Glacier

California Peak
4,974 ft (1,516 m)

Alyeska

Girdwood

Turnagain Arm

*Hikers on the **Crow Pass Trail** can book the Forest Service public-use cabin at the toe of Raven Glacier.*

*Alaska's most climbed peak, the 3,510-ft (1,070-m) **Flattop Mountain** makes a popular outing for visitors who can manage the steep 1,310-ft (393-m), two-hour-long ascent.*

***Eagle River Nature Center** has maps, books, and exhibits on the landscape and wildlife of the park, as well as viewing decks and spotting scopes.*

0 km   10
0 miles   10

N ↑

→ A tiger swallowtail butterfly at the Eagle River Nature Center

EXPERIENCE Anchorage

INDEPENDENCE MINE STATE HISTORICAL PARK

◆E1 ⌂19 miles (31 km) N of Palmer at Mile 17.3, Hatcher Pass Road
◔Mid-Jun–Labor Day ⓘdnr.alaska.gov/parks/units/indmine.htm

Independence Mine was once one of Alaska's largest gold-mining camps. Today, its well-preserved workshops and bunkhouses give a fascinating glimpse of what it was like to live and work here.

Most people associate gold mining in Alaska with the stream bed diggings in the Klondike. However, starting in 1906, a gold-bearing quartz lode was being tapped in the Talkeetna Mountains. Two mines were established in the scenic mountain valley of the Little Susitna River: the Alaska Free Gold Mine on Skyscraper Mountain and the Independence Mine on Granite Mountain. In 1938, the two were merged into the Alaska-Pacific Consolidated Mining Company.

Although the mines were producing large amounts of gold, the activity was deemed non-essential during World War II, and after the war, government restrictions on private ownership of gold spelled the end of the mine. The site was designated a State Historical Park in the late 1970s. A self-guided interpretive tour leads through the camp; guided tours are also available.

EXPLORING THE MINE

A full exploration of the park's historic buildings and ruins will take two to three hours. The Main Trail is an easy, level route that begins at the Mine Manager's House and loops past the Mess Hall, Administrative Building, and Bunk Houses, with a short detour to the Museum (Assay Office). The more challenging 20-minute Hard Rock Trail climbs the tundra-covered hillside to an overlook near the Water Tunnel Portal and Mine Shops.

The New Mess Hall, constructed in 1941, had a well-equipped kitchen, bakery, butchery, scullery, and a dining hall that seated 160 people.

The Administrative Building was used as an office, storeroom, and bunkhouse during an attempt to reopen the mine in 1946.

Three of the larger buildings at Independence Mine served as bunk-houses. One functioned as a warehouse and school.

The Mine Manager's House was constructed in 1939 for the mine manager's family and guests. Today, it is the park's Visitor Center.

↑ Bunkhouses built for the mine workers

→ The remains of tracks that were once used to transport the ore

Mechanical, plumbing, carpentry, and electrical repair shops

The 1937 mill complex, uphill from the mine offices, includes a welding shed, ore sorting plant, machine shop, and blacksmith.

An ore conveyor brought ore into the mill where it was sorted and crushed to extract the gold.

The Hard Rock Trail leads to a park overlook near the Water Tunnel Portal.

The Assay Office now houses the site museum.

The New Bunkhouse was built in 1940 to accommodate 50 people. It also contained rooms used for classes.

↑ A plan of Independence Mine State Park

 INSIDER TIP
Parking

Parking at the site is tricky due to the area's popularity, so be sure to arrive early in the day. Purchase a day parking pass for $5 on site, or get an annual pass for $60 if you plan to visit several state park sites.

Trail runners in the Chugach
Mountains, with fabulous
views of Turnagain Arm below ↑

5

TURNAGAIN ARM

⬛ F4　⌂ Highway starts 12 miles (19 km) S of downtown Anchorage

Easily reached from Anchorage, Turnagain Arm is a dramatic 50-mile-
(80-km-) long fjord off the Cook Inlet. The drive along its north shore
is one of America's most spectacular, affording dramatic vistas of
majestic mountains plunging down to the water.

The curious name of the fjord was bestowed
by explorer Captain James Cook in 1778. He
was forced to "turn again" after discovering
that it was impossible to navigate a sea route
between Cook Inlet and the fabled Northwest
Passage. Today, a drive along the fjord's shore
makes a rewarding day trip from Anchorage. A
lovely stretch of the 120-mile (200-km) Seward
Highway connects Anchorage and Seward, following the fjord's north shore through Chugach
State Park (p72) and Chugach National Forest,
and offering magnificent views of the Kenai
Mountains across the water. Along the way,
there are numerous stop-off points where
you can drink in the scenery.

↑ The scenic Seward Highway, which hugs
the Turnagain Arm fjord

Anchorage Coastal Wildlife Refuge

Just south of Anchorage at Mile 117, a series of boardwalks provide views across Potter Marsh, frequented in the summer by nesting ducks, geese, swans, and other waterfowl.

Beluga Point

▷ At Beluga Point (Mile 110) visitors can observe Turnagain Arm empty and refill twice daily in a wall of water known as the Bore Tide.

"Bird-to-Gird Trail"

▽ The Indian to Girdwood pathway, (known as the "Bird-to-Gird Trail," as it also passes through Bird) is a 13-mile (21-km) paved bike and pedestrian path alongside the Seward Highway. The trail buzzes with bikers and walkers during the summer.

Crow Creek Trail

From Crow Creek Road, a 4-mile (6-km) trail climbs past Gold Rush relics to Crow Pass, with views of Raven Glacier, then continues through Chugach State Park to the Eagle River Nature Center.

BELUGA WHALES

The distinctive whale known as the beluga (*Delphinapterus leucas*) is one of several beaked whales that inhabit the Arctic, North Atlantic, and North Pacific oceans. The name beluga, meaning "the white one," was given by Russian explorers, who probably first observed the creatures in the Bering Sea. These mammals are usually 13 to 15 ft (4 to 4.5 m) in length and weigh about 2,500 to 3,500 lbs (1,100 to 1,600 kg). They use echolocation to communicate and are sometimes called "sea canaries" because of their wide variety of calls. In the summer, from around mid-July to the end of August, pods migrate into Turnagain Arm to feed and may be observed from the shore, although the Cook Inlet population has been declining dramatically in recent years, to the alarm of scientists.

The "Ghost Forest"

At the head of the fjord, the highway passes through a "ghost forest" of bleached dead trees. It was created when the 1964 earthquake (*p31*) caused the land to slump 4 ft (1.2 m), allowing salt seawater to rush in.

Alaska Wildlife Conservation Center

▷ This center (*www.alaskawildlife.org*) houses and cares for displaced animals, including bears, moose, and wood bison.

Begich-Boggs Visitors' Center

Built on a terminal moraine left by the receding Portage Glacier, the center has exhibits on Alaskan glaciers.

Portage Glacier

Portage Glacier extends into Portage Lake and is best viewed on cruises from the visitor center.

← The flower-bedecked Log Cabin Visitor Center, found in downtown Anchorage

EXPERIENCE MORE

6

Log Cabin Visitor Information Center

⦿ B4 ⬛ 546 W 4th Ave
🚌 To Downtown Transit Center 🕐 Mid-May-mid-Sep: 8am-7pm daily; mid-Sep-mid-May: 9am-4pm daily 🚫 Federal hols
🌐 anchorage.net

Operated by the Anchorage Convention and Visitors Bureau, this helpful center is in the heart of downtown Anchorage. The sod-roofed log cabin is a favorite spot for photos, and outside there are equally picturesque signposts showing the distance in miles to many international cities. The main visitor center fills a second building directly

> 💬 INSIDER TIP
> **Made in Alaska**
>
> Alaska artisans work hard at their respective crafts. Look for the distinctive "Made In Alaska" logo that marks authentic merchandise before purchasing.

behind the log cabin. It has visitor brochures, free guides to nearby parks, and other publications, plus helpful staff to answer travel questions.

7

Alaska Law Enforcement Museum

⦿ C4 ⬛ 245 W 5th Ave
🚌 To Downtown Transit Center 🕐 10am-4pm Mon-Fri, noon-4pm Sat
🌐 foast.org

Founded with a handful of officers in 1941 as the Alaska State Highway Patrol, Alaska's law enforcement agency also served as the Territorial Police and the State Police before being named the Alaska State Troopers in 1967. The Fraternal Order of the Alaska State Troopers established the museum in 1991.

In the early days, the Troopers protected half a million sq miles (1,295,000 sq km) of territory using the fairly basic technology of the time. One display exhibits a typical 1940s law enforcement office, where sealskin boots,

snowshoes, a clunky period radio, and a telephone illustrate the range of duties a trooper was expected to fulfill.

The most popular exhibit is the shiny 1952 Hudson Hornet patrol car, one of the fastest vehicles of its era, now lovingly restored. Other displays here showcase memorabilia from the days of the US Marshals, including a poster offering a $1,000 reward for Alaska's first serial killer, Edward Krause, who killed ten people between 1912 and 1915. Another interesting device is the Harger Drunkometer, a forerunner of the modern breathalyzer.

8

Alaska Public Lands Information Center

⦿ B4 ⬛ 605 W 4th Ave
🚌 To Downtown Transit Center 🕐 Late-May-mid-Sep: 9am-5pm daily; mid-Sep-late-May: 9am-5pm Mon-Fri 🚫 Federal hols
🌐 alaskacenters.gov

The Federal government manages more than 60 percent of Alaska lands, including

ANCHORAGE MARKET AND FESTIVAL

A favorite of both locals and tourists, this weekend market attracts hundreds of people during summer to a large downtown parking lot. Come rain or shine, you'll find over 300 vendors selling Alaskan-made items - from pottery to nesting dolls - as well as a range of fast food stalls.

15 national parks, the nation's two largest national forests, and 16 national wildlife refuges. This information center, housed within the old Federal Building, has displays on Alaska's wildlife and natural areas, a wealth of books and other publications, and an auditorium for nature videos and talks.

It is also a great place to ask experienced staff for their advice on anything from buses into Denali National Park or bush flights into the Arctic National Wildlife Refuge. Daily historical walks are also offered, and there are information branches in Fairbanks, Tok, and Ketchikan. The center was recently renovated to include interactive exhibits and a user-friendly database of the state's campgrounds, cabins, and trails.

---

9 ♿ Ⓜ

Oscar Anderson House

📍 A4 🏠 420 M St 📞 274-2336 🚌 To Downtown Transit Center 🕐 Jun-Aug: noon-4pm Wed-Sat

This historic home was built in 1915 by Oscar Anderson, a Swede who is said to have been the 18th resident of the original tent city of Anchorage. While still residing on the beach after his arrival in town, Anderson established the Ship Creek Meat Company and the Evan Jones Fuel Company. Due to a shortage of building materials, his house, the town's first permanent wood-frame structure, had only one-and-a-half stories and measured just 800 sq ft (72 sq m). Anderson lived here until his death in 1974, and two years later, it was deeded to the City of Anchorage by his widow.

The building has since been meticulously restored to reflect the period in which it was built, and is listed on the National Register of Historic Places. Various exhibits reveal the history of the city, and many of Anderson's original belongings are on display, including a working 1909 piano. A Swedish Christmas open house is held here in traditional style each December.

10

Resolution Park

📍 A4 🏠 320 L St 🚌 To Downtown Transit Center 🕐 24 hrs daily

Named after Captain Cook's flagship, Resolution Park offers visitors one of the best views in Anchorage, taking

→

The commanding bronze statue of Captain Cook, which stands in Resolution Park

in Cook Inlet and both Mount Susitna (a magnificent low mountain to the northwest, also known as The Sleeping Lady) and spectacular Denali on a clear day. The active volcanoes to the south of Denali – Mount Spurr and Redoubt – are also visible.

The centerpiece of this small park is the Captain Cook Monument, commemorating the 200th anniversary of British naval officer James Cook's exploration of Alaska. In 1776, on his third voyage in HMS *Resolution*, Cook sailed north along the continent's west coast in search of the Northwest Passage (a navigable link between the Atlantic and Pacific oceans), and passed the present-day site of Anchorage, giving his name to Cook Inlet. Derek Freeborn's life-sized bronze statue, based on the one in Whitby, UK, from where Cook first set sail, was donated to Anchorage during the US Bicentennial celebrations in 1976.

Just one block east, in front of the Carr-Gottstein Building, is Josef Princiotta's fabulous 1973 bronze sculpture, *The Last Blue Whale*. Adding a wonderful sense of perspective is a small beleaguered boat sitting on the ripples of water near the tail of the gigantic whale.

EAT

Bear Tooth Grill

Hugely popular with Anchorage residents, this spot specializes in Southwest flavors. It's attached to Bear Tooth Theaterpub, which has movie screenings and good craft brews.

📍 **A5** 🏠 **1230 W 27th**
🌐 **beartoothgrill.net**

💲💲💲

Crow's Nest

Offering stellar views and impeccable service, but still managing to retain Alaska's casual charm, this restaurant in the Hotel Captain Cook is a great pick for special occasions. Reservations are advised.

📍 **A4** 🏠 **939 W 5th Ave**
🕐 **Dinner only**
🌐 **captaincook.com**

💲💲💲

Glacier Brewhouse

A popular local spot that's busy most evenings, with a rowdy, rustic dining room. The menu is varied, and there's a huge selection of craft beers on tap.

📍 **B4** 🏠 **737 W 5th Ave**
Ste 110 🌐 **glacier brewhouse.com**

💲💲💲

The Marx Bros Café

Fine dining in a simple, quiet dining room. Desserts are elegant and there's a great wine selection – but limited seating, so book ahead. Dinner only.

📍 **B4** 🏠 **627 W 3rd Ave**
🕐 **Sun & Mon**
🌐 **marxcafe.com**

💲💲💲

11 🔶 🏛

Alaska Aviation Museum

📍 **D3** 🏠 **4721 Aircraft Dr**
🚌 **40** 🕐 **Mid-May–mid-Sep: 10am–6pm daily; mid-Sep–mid-May: 10am–5pm Tue–Sun** 🌐 **alaskaairmuseum.org**

Located on the shores of Lake Hood, the Alaska Aviation Museum is a must-see for anyone interested in traditional bush pilots and their planes. There is detailed coverage of the state's World War II history, along with collections of artifacts, photographs, and newspaper clippings.

The museum also preserves an extensive collection of historic aircraft, including a 1928 Stearman bush plane that was among the first to land on Denali in 1932, and one of only two remaining 1928 Hamilton Metalplanes. A theater shows film footage about Alaska's early pilots.

Renovated in 2018 to better reflect its multigenerational visitors, the museum now has a children's area, flight simulators, and a thriving educational program. The museum also hosts a number of events throughout the year designed to encourage youngsters to consider a career in aviation.

12

Tony Knowles Coastal Trail

📍 **A4** 🏠 **Western end of 2nd Ave** 🚌 **25**

The most popular biking and jogging trail in Anchorage, the Tony Knowles Coastal Trail passes attractive Elderberry Park on the downtown waterfront and follows the coastline south to Kincaid Park. A

↑ Colorful exhibits on display inside the Alaska Aviation Museum

↑ Cyclists making their way around part of the popular Tony Knowles Coastal Trail

highlight along the 11-mile (17-km) trail is Westchester Lagoon, where walkers can observe waterfowl. On clear days, there are great views across Cook Inlet to the volcano, Mount Spurr. Midway along the route, Earthquake Park has exhibits on the devastating 1964 earthquake (p31), which created the dramatic bluff visible here.

At the southern end of the trail, the 2-sq-mile (5-sq-km) Kincaid Park offers excellent summer hiking and a network of Nordic ski trails in winter.

⑬
St. Innocent Russian Orthodox Cathedral

📍 E3 🏠 401 Turpin St
🚌 31 🕐 Only for services
🌐 sicanc.org

The heart of Russian Orthodox activity in the Anchorage area, this beautiful cathedral is instantly recognizable for its striking blue onion domes. Strangely, the church is not named after St. Innocent of Alaska – a 19th-century missionary priest and bishop

known for translating parts of the Bible into the Aleut language – but rather for St. Innocent, Bishop of Irkutsk, who was born in 1680 and educated in Kiev.

As with most Orthodox places of worship, the cathedral's interiors are incredibly opulent. Although the cathedral is usually closed to the public, these can be glimpsed during services, on feast days, or during other key events of the Russian Orthodox calendar.

⑭
Ship Creek Salmon Viewing Platform

📍 D3 🏠 North side of Ship Creek footbridge, off Whitney Ave 🕐 24 hrs daily

Ship Creek is a mecca for urban fishermen. Each year, the nearby salmon hatchery releases up to 250,000 king salmon smolt, which swim downstream into Cook Inlet, spending seven years at sea before returning to spawn. To the north of the bridge across Ship Creek, a viewing platform gives visitors the opportunity

to observe the salmon as they crowd their way upstream and jump at the weir.

In the summer, anglers descend to the riverbanks in the hope of reeling in one of the 5,000 fish that are caught here each year. An Alaska fishing license is required, available in local shops. Fishing derbies may yield up to $10,000 for lucky anglers who catch specially tagged fish.

ALASKA'S SPORT FISH HATCHERY

Fishing is one of Alaska's most popular outdoor activities, generating millions of dollars in revenue each year. The William Jack Hernandez Sport Fish Hatchery (www.adfg.alaska.gov) offers a fascinating look at the industry; it's open daily in summer for tank viewings. There are also interpretive displays, an outdoor walking path, and a viewing deck to watch salmon make the jump upstream to spawn.

15

Spenard

📍 D3 🚌 7

Anchorage's funky Spenard district was once a separate town, connected to downtown by the winding Spenard Road. Visitors to the neighborhood may come across a scattering of less-than-reputable businesses, which are throwbacks to Spenard's grittier days.

Despite its past and its somewhat unsavory reputation, Spenard is rapidly becoming a fashionable neighborhood. The derelict buildings and trailer parks are steadily giving way to houses, health-food eateries, second-hand shops, motels, and atmospheric bars and clubs. The corner of Spenard and Northern Lights is home to one of Alaska's finest bookstores, Title Wave Books, along with the busy Middle Way Café and the exceptionally popular Bear Tooth Theaterpub (*p82*).

BUSH FLYING IN ALASKA

Visitors who wish to fly into a remote lodge or enjoy a wilderness fishing trip are likely to employ an Alaskan bush pilot. These legendary aviators fly across untracked country, land on lakes and gravel bars, and defy natural conditions that most conventional pilots prefer to avoid. About 1 in 50 Alaskans has a pilot's license, and the state supports over 290 charter companies. Careful preparations are essential as drop-offs and pickups are prescheduled and can be disrupted by bad weather or unforeseen circumstances.

16

Lake Hood and Lake Spenard

📍 D3 🏠 Lakeshore Drive
🚌 40 🕐 24 hrs daily

Keeping Anchorage in touch with Alaska wilderness, this is the largest and busiest float-plane base in the US. It handles up to 800 flights per day and anyone chartering a bush flight into a remote area will likely depart from here. The best viewpoint to watch the flights is behind the Department of Transportation building.

17

Hilltop Ski Area

📍 E3 🏠 Upper Abbot Rd
🕐 Winter: 3–8pm Mon–Fri,
9am–8pm Sat, 9am–5pm
Sun 🌐 hilltopskiarea.org

New skiers and those without the time or money to head for the larger Alyeska Resort in Girdwood (*p88*) will appreciate the 30-acre (12-ha) Hilltop Ski Area, Anchorage proper's only ski resort. Here, the longest run (2,090 ft/637 m) offers a gradient that drops a gentle 295 ft (90 m), and there are

many other runs of varying difficulty. In the adjacent Hillside Park, Nordic skiers will find 22 miles (32 km) of groomed cross-country trails.

18

Alaska Zoo

📍 E3 🏠 4731 O'Malley Rd
🚌 Shuttle from downtown
🕐 Mar, Apr & Oct: 10am–5pm daily; May & Sep: 9am–6pm daily; Jun–Aug: 9am–9pm daily; Nov–Feb: 10am–4pm daily 🌐 alaskazoo.org

In 1966, an Anchorage grocer won a baby Asian elephant in a contest. Eventually, Annabelle the elephant was donated to horse rancher Mrs. Seawell, who decided that the local community needed a public zoo. The Alaska Children's Zoo opened in 1969, developing slowly into what is today the sprawling Alaska Zoo.

Although Annabelle is no longer alive, visitors can see a host of Alaskan and exotic animals, including moose, reindeer, snow leopards, and Siberian tigers, as well as a brown bear and polar bears. There's also an excellent behind-the-scenes tour that focuses on a specific animal species, and kids can attend themed summer day camps.

19

Alaska Botanical Garden

📍 E3 🏠 4601 Campbell Airstrip Rd 🚌 25 🕐 Year-round: daylight hours daily 🌐 alaskabg.org

Amid the beautiful birch and spruce forests of Far North Bicentennial Park nestles the 110-acre (44-ha) Alaska Botanical Garden. Opened in 1993, the area features a formal herb garden, two perennial gardens, and a wildflower path dotted with boulders left behind by glaciers. Boreal flora is showcased with more than 1,100 perennials and 150 native species of hardy flowering plants, shrubs, and other northern vegetation. The 1-mile- (2-km-) long interpretive Lowenfels Family Nature Trail follows the north fork of Campbell Creek, which is home to a summer run of king salmon, and offers views of the Chugach Range. The area is ideal for photography and bird-watching in summer, while in winter, the trails serve as Nordic ski routes. As the plants in the area are fragile, dogs are not allowed.

STAY

Copper Whale Inn B&B

Housed in a historic building just a block from the Coastal Trail, this hotel offers views across Cook Inlet.

📍 A4 🏠 440 L St
🌐 copperwhale.com

💲💲💲

The Lakefront Anchorage

Set along the east shore of Lake Hood, guests can watch floatplanes as they take off and land at the busy seaplane base.

📍 D3 🏠 4800 Spenard Rd 📞 907-243-2300

💲💲💲

Hotel Captain Cook

A premier business hotel with excellent amenities and gorgeous views of Cook Inlet.

📍 A4 🏠 939 W 5th Ave
🌐 captaincook.com

💲💲💲

← Brightly painted floatplanes at Lake Hood, the world's largest seaplane base

GREEN GIANTS

Alaskans are rightfully proud of the produce grown in the Matanuska Valley. The growing season may be short, but thanks to the long summer days, vegetables continue to grow around the clock, resulting in huge produce. At the annual Alaska State Fair, awards are given for the largest vegetable of each variety. The most popular category is for the cabbage - the world-record holder, grown in Palmer in 2012, tipped the scales at 138 lb (63 kg), winning the $2,000 grand prize.

20
Palmer

F1 **42 miles (70 km) NE of Anchorage** **From Anchorage** **723 S Valley Way; www.palmer chamber.org**

Historically best known as a farming community, the town of Palmer nestles beneath Matanuska Peak and the Talkeetna Range along the glacial Matanuska River. Set up as a social experiment in 1935 as part of President Franklin D. Roosevelt's New Deal, it was settled by 200 Midwestern families (p58). Each family in the newly founded Matanuska Colony was given 40 acres (16 ha) of land for vegetable farming, growing hay, and raising dairy cattle.

Today, while farming is still important, Palmer's outskirts are rapidly turning into bedroom suburbs for Anchorage, due mainly to the city's dwindling land and high costs. The surrounding Matanuska and Susitna valleys, popularly abbreviated to Mat-Su, are now among the fastest-growing regions of Alaska.

Well worth visiting is the **Colony House Museum**, which reflects one of the five basic farmhouse styles available to the colony's farmers. Inside, their story is told with old newspaper articles, period furnishings, and intriguing artifacts.

For 12 days in August and September, Palmer hosts the Alaska State Fair (p55), the state's biggest annual event, drawing nearly half of Alaska's population. The fair features the valley's famous giant vegetables, as well as other agricultural displays, crafts, live music, a rodeo, Native dancing and blanket tossing (p247), a funfair, and a range of competitions.

Colony House Museum

316 E Elmwood Ave **May-Aug: 10am-4pm Tue-Sat** **palmerhistorical society.org**

→

The welcoming town of Palmer, host of the (inset) hugely popular Alaska State Fair

21
Reindeer Farm

F2 **5561 S Bodenburg Loop Rd, Palmer** **May-mid-Sep: 10am-6pm daily** **reindeerfarm.com**

Located in one of the original Colony farmhouses on the flat farmlands off the Old Glenn Highway, the Reindeer Farm, in operation since 1987, lets visitors see reindeer close-up. The herd here once comprised as many as 300 reindeer, but there are currently around 100 animals. Children are invited to hand-feed the reindeer, as well as to meet an elk, a moose, and a black-tailed deer. Those inclined to outdoor activities can join a horseback trail ride.

22
Bodenburg Butte

F2 **Mile 11.5, Old Glenn Hwy**

Rising out of the farmlands on the Knik River flats south of Palmer, Bodenburg Butte is one of the Matanuska Valley's

1,500

moose live within the city limits of Anchorage Bowl.

most prominent landmarks, at 900 ft (270m) high. It was created when Knik Glacier rode over a small knob of resistant bedrock, leaving a glacier-scraped dome known as a *roche moutonnée*. Once used for military training, it is now a popular picnic and hiking spot with a windy summit from where para-sailers can launch out over the flats. The steep trail leading to the summit starts opposite the Reindeer Farm and soon passes from the stands of birch at the base into open grassy ridges and rocky bluffs near the top. The two-hour-long round trek is worth it for the lovely views from the summit, which take in the Palmer area and the impressive Knik Glacier.

23

Eklutna Historical Park

E2 **Mile 26, Glenn Hwy** **Anchorage-Mat-Su** **Mid-May–mid-Sep: 10am–5pm Mon-Sat** **eklutna historicalpark.org**

Forming the centerpiece of the tiny village of Eklutna, this site was established to pre-serve and portray the heritage of the Athabascan people. Founded in 1650, it is the oldest continually inhabited village in the Anchorage area. With the coming of Russian missionaries in the early 19th century, most locals converted to Russian Orthodoxy, as evidenced by the onion-domed St. Nicholas church. Graves in the adjacent cemetery are covered with colorful "spirit houses," decorated according to individual family traditions. Athabascan beadwork and snowshoes can be seen at the Heritage House museum.

A 3-mile (5-km) return walk, over the Glenn Highway, leads to scenic Thunderbird Falls, which turns spectacularly to ice in winter.

EAT

Turkey Red
Baked goods and daily specials, made with local organic ingredients.

F1 **550 S Alaska St, Palmer** **turkey redak.com**

$ $ $

Palmer Alehouse
Perfect for casual dining and sampling local beers.

F1 **320 E Dahlia, Palmer** **palmer alehouse.com**

$ $ $

Raven's Perch Restaurant
Dine while gazing upon stunning Knik Glacier.

F2 **29979 E Knik River Rd, Palmer** **knikriverlodge.com**

$ $ $

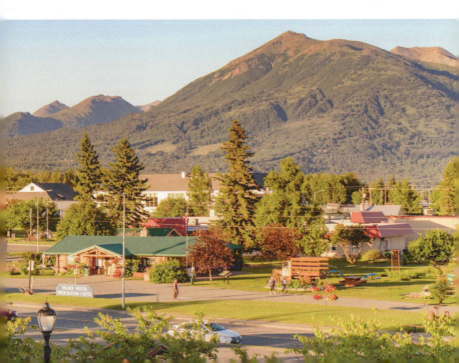

24

Wasilla

E2 45 miles (72 km) N of Anchorage From Anchorage Mat-Su Convention and Visitors Bureau; www.cityof wasilla.com

Wasilla is a long strip of unfocused development along the Parks Highway. The town was founded in 1917 and eventually grew to become the commercial center of the Mat-Su Borough. Although not the prettiest of Alaskan towns, Wasilla does have several worthwhile attractions – mostly clustered at the Old Wasilla Townsite Park. The park includes the original Wasilla School, an old barn and blacksmith shop, a reconstructed bathhouse, and the Dorothy Page Museum, named for the woman who founded the famous Iditarod Trail Sled Dog Race (p238) with musher Joe Redington.

The **Museum of Alaska Transportation and Industry** moved to its present home west of Wasilla in 1992, having outgrown its previous site in Palmer. In addition to a large gallery and exhibit hall, the museum has an outdoor collection that includes umiaks (hide-covered canoes), railroad memorabilia, and vintage steam engines, aircraft, and motor vehicles.

↑ A pair of sturdy musk ox bulls grazing at the Musk Ox Farm in springtime

Situated near the former Iditarod restart site is the **Knik Museum and Musher's Hall of Fame**. Visitors can see objects from the now-defunct town of Knik, as well as Iditarod exhibits such as race trophies and a presentation on famous Alaskan mushers.

Museum of Alaska Transportation and Industry

3800 W Museum Drive May-Sep: 10am-5pm daily museumofalaska.org

Knik Museum and Musher's Hall of Fame

Mile 13.9, Knik Rd May-Oct: 1pm-6pm Wed-Sun wkhsociety.org

25

Musk Ox Farm

F1 12850 E Archie Rd, Mile 50, Glenn Hwy Mid-May-Sep: 10am-6pm daily; Oct-Apr: 11am-4pm Wed-Sat muskoxfarm.org

The Musk Ox Farm is home to the only domestic herd of musk oxen in the world. Hunted to extinction in Alaska

← Wasilla's memorial to musher Joe Redington

in the 19th century, they were reintroduced from Greenland in the 1930s. Musk oxen now inhabit Nunivak Island, the Seward Peninsula, and the North Slope of Alaska.

Anthropologist John Teal started the farm in Fairbanks in 1964. Now located in Palmer, the farm gathers qiviut, the fine underwool of the musk ox, and distributes it to Native women. They spin and knit the qiviut into soft, warm garments using patterns and motifs unique to their villages. The farm is open to the public and runs short tours.

26

Hatcher Pass

E1 21 miles (34 km) N of Palmer at Mile 19 of the Hatcher Pass Rd

Beyond Independence Mine (p76), the Hatcher Pass Road climbs up onto the "tail" of the Talkeetna Range that reaches westward toward the small town of Willow (p192) and makes a wonderful driving or biking route. The road is paved only as far as the turn-off for Independence Mine and Hatcher Pass Lodge at Mile 17. At Mile 19 it crosses Hatcher Pass, one of Alaska's highest road passes at 3,886 ft (1,166 m), before twisting on 31 miles (50 km) to Willow. Just beyond the pass, the road passes through the Summit

Lake State Recreation Site. The lake itself is a small alpine tarn in a glacial cirque, or steep-walled basin, and is accessed by a trail around its perimeter and along the bluff overlooking it. The inspiring views take in the Susitna Valley, Willow Creek, and the Alaska Range in the distance.

In the summer, Hatcher Pass is an excellent place to watch paragliders, and explore a number of hiking trails, including the popular Gold Mint Trail, that take off into the peaks and valleys. In the winter, the attraction is the network of Nordic skiing and snowmoviling trails that lead into the wilds of the Talkeetna Mountains. The pass is often closed between September and May, so do check ahead.

27

Girdwood

📍 F4 🚗 36 miles (61 km) S of Anchorage ♿
ℹ Girdwood Chamber of Commerce; www. girdwoodchamber.com

Located just 40 minutes south of downtown Anchorage, the mountain hamlet of Girdwood is scenically situated in a valley of boreal forest. Originally known as Glacier City for the multitude of hanging glaciers visible from nearly every angle, Girdwood was a mining town founded in the late 1800s. Its name was later changed in honor of James Girdwood, an enterprising Irish linen merchant and miner, who saw the necessity of an adequate supply of provisions and tools to the Gold Rush town. Spurred on by the development of transport links, Girdwood grew rapidly, and soon gained a reputation for outdoor recreation.

Alyeska Resort, a world-class ski resort and huge draw to the town, was opened in 1960. Although the 1964 earthquake (p31) caused the original townsite to be moved inland to the current location, Girdwood has flourished ever since. The present-day community is a mix of outdoor enthusiasts, commuters to Anchorage, seasonal workers, and a healthy population of miners still seeking gold. It makes a lovely side trip for visitors, with hiking, biking, good restaurants, and, of course, skiing.

> In the summer, Hatcher Pass is an excellent place to watch paragliders and explore a number of hiking trails that take off into the peaks and valleys.

Hiking the popular Gold Mint Trail of the scenic Hatcher Pass ↑

A SHORT WALK

DOWNTOWN ANCHORAGE

Distance 1 mile (2 km) **Nearest bus stop**
Downtown Transit Center **Time** 30 minutes

Although Anchorage began life as a tented construction camp on the shores of Ship Creek, the 1915 sale of lots shifted its center to the site of the city's present-day downtown. After more than a century of growth and development, along with restoration work after the massive 1964 earthquake (p31), downtown Anchorage today features a mix of historic buildings and modern high-rises interspersed with small private homes. The compact area is a joy to explore on foot – you'll find an open-air weekend market, a variety of shops, and most of the city's main sights. There is also a lovely town square with pleasant ornamentation, including public artwork and flower baskets hanging from lampposts.

Relaxing outside the iconic Log Cabin Vistor Information Center

The **Anchorage Market and Festival** is held on summer weekends, with Alaskan arts and crafts and fresh produce for sale.

The **Alaska Public Lands Information Center** has details on Alaska's millions of acres of wild places, including Denali and 14 other national parks.

The picturesque **Log Cabin Visitor Information Center** has an oft-photographed sign showing the distance to other cities around the globe.

2ND AVENUE

3RD AVENUE

F STREET

4TH AVENUE

G STREET

0 meters 100
0 yards 100

N

EXPERIENCE Anchorage

Traditional exhibits on display at the city's celebrated Anchorage Museum

Locator Map
For more detail see p66

A **statue of champion sled dog Balto** *stands outside the turreted Wendler Building.*

One of the most prominent exhibits in the **Alaska Law Enforcement Museum** *is a fully restored 1952 Hudson Hornet patrol car.*

Anchorage Museum *houses excellent collections of historical artifacts, as well as traditional Native and modern Alaskan art.*

A STREET

C STREET

FINISH

STREET

5TH AVENUE

6TH AVENUE

7TH AVENUE

START

The **Wyland Whale Mural** *was created freehand by Robert Wyland in 1994 and depicts a family of bowhead whales.*

With over 9,000 plants, **Town Square** *is a popular lunch and concert spot that hosts an ice rink in winter.*

→

A bronze statue of Balto, the legendary husky sled dog

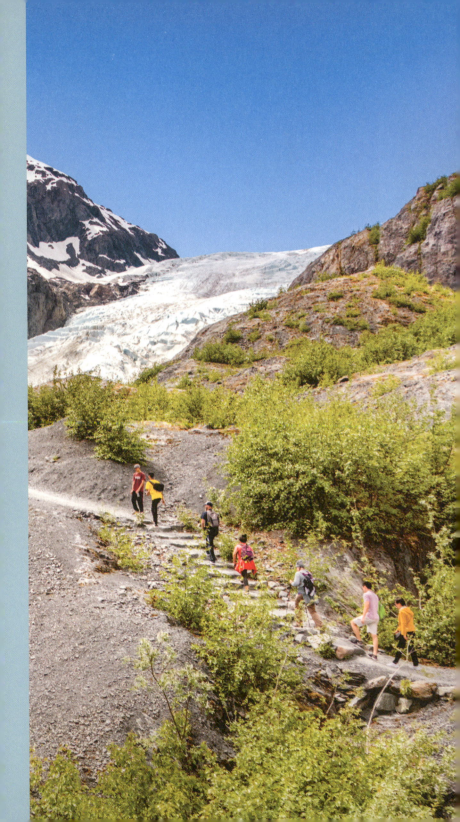

THE KENAI PENINSULA

Sitting between Cook Inlet to the west and Prince William Sound to the east, the Kenai Peninsula has long been a key transportation route. The earliest archeological evidence of human occupation dates back 10,000 years, with the Riverine Kachemak people arriving about 2,000 years ago. They were later followed by the Dena'ina Athabascan people, and until Russian fur traders landed in 1741, the town of Kenai was a small Dena'ina village called Shk'ituk't.

By 1791, the Russians had built a trading post – Fort St. Nicholas – and had established a somewhat tenuous working relationship with the Dena'ina, whom they called "Kenaitze," meaning "people of the flats," or "Kenai People." In 1869, shortly after the purchase of Alaska from the Russians, the US Army established a post on the peninsula called "Fort Kenay," but it only lasted a year before being abandoned.

The peninsula's proximity to shipping lanes saw many salteries and canneries spring up in the early 1900s, and commercial fishing for salmon, halibut, and other offshore fish became a booming industry that continued through the 1920s. Other settlers began clearing the fertile lands for homesteads, and a road to Anchorage was constructed in 1951. By 1965, offshore oil discoveries and platforms began to dot the horizon, and the town of Kenai has been a stalwart fixture in the state's oil production and exploration ever since.

THE KENAI PENINSULA

Must Sees

1. Kenai Fjords National Park
2. Seward
3. Resurrection Pass Trail

Experience More

4. Kenai River
5. Moose Pass
6. Cooper Landing
7. Hope
8. Soldotna
9. Kenai
10. Sterling
11. Kenai National Wildlife Refuge
12. Captain Cook State Recreation Area
13. Homer
14. Ninilchik
15. Nikolaevsk
16. Anchor Point
17. Seldovia
18. Kachemak Bay State Park
19. Halibut Cove

The dramatic mountain and glacial landscape at Kenai Fjords National Park ↑

❶

KENAI FJORDS NATIONAL PARK

🅰 D7   🏠 Seward   🚌 🚐 To Seward, then shuttle van to Exit Glacier
🚢 Day cruises to the fjords   🚹 1212 4th Ave, Seward; www.nps.gov/kefj

Covering around 950 sq miles (2,460 sq km), the Kenai Fjords National Park takes in some of Alaska's finest and most accessible coastal scenery and glacial landscapes, and is a haven for a rich diversity of marine wildlife.

TOP 5   LAND ANIMALS TO SPOT

Black Bear
Black bears exist in large numbers around the park's forests and along its shorelines.

Brown Bear
These bears eat salmon, berries, grasses, and clams foraged from coastal areas and rivers.

Beaver
This rodent uses wood to pare down its fast-growing teeth and to fell trees to build canals and dams.

River Otter
River otters are fun to watch as they snack on aquatic clams and snails, and fish near estuaries and riverbanks.

Mountain Goat
Look for these surefooted, shaggy, horned animals along narrow rock ledges.

The crown of the park is the Harding Icefield, 70 miles (113 km) long and 30 km (48 km) long. This vast expanse of ice, interrupted only by an occasional *nunatak* (exposed rocky ridge) stretches across the Kenai Mountains and is the source of at least 38 glaciers. These massive rivers of ice flow down from the heights to form the park's deep valleys and fjords. The seas, rich in fish, crustaceans, shellfish, and plankton, also provide a habitat for a wide range of readily observed birds and marine mammals, including sea otters, Dall porpoises, Steller sea lions, and several whale species.

↑ A *nunatak* in one of the glaciers

→ Kayaking, a popular activity on the waters of Kenai Fjords

→ Steller sea lions, also known as northern sea lions, in Kenai Fjords National Park

EXPLORING KENAI FJORDS NATIONAL PARK

Most visitors to Kenai Fjords National Park spend time viewing the sights from aboard a day cruise vessel, watching for tidewater glaciers in the process of calving – shedding their outer layers with a thunderous crash. On land, you can take a guided ranger walk from the Exit Glacier Nature Center, or venture further up the trail to the glacier's toe. Hardy trekkers can also hike the 8 miles (13 km) to Harding Icefield, where glacial ice seems to continue into infinity. Those who want to try kayaking or stand-up paddleboarding will enjoy Bear Glacier Lagoon, a pool of beautiful blue-hued water 12 miles (19 km) from Seward. The park also manages two coastal public-use cabins near Aialik Bay.

Did You Know?

Glaciers look blue because they absorb long (red) wavelengths of light and reflect short (blue) ones.

*The 70-mile- (113-km-) long and 30-mile- (48-km-) wide **Harding Icefield** stretches across the Kenai Mountains and creates all of Kenai Fjord's glaciers. Hikers can access it via a trail from Exit Glacier. The icefield also draws experienced backcountry skiers.*

*Tidewater glaciers such as **Holgate Glacier** regularly calve icebergs into the fjords in the park. Kayakers must watch out for large waves generated by falling house-sized chunks.*

*Summer visitors often spot sounding or breaching **whales** in these waters, which serve as summer feeding grounds for humpbacks and migratory routes each spring and fall for gray whales. Minke whales and pods of porpoises are also seen in the summer.*

Harding

Holgate Glacier

Northwestern Glacier

McCarty Glacier

Northwestern Fjord

Harris Bay

McCarty Fjord

Pedersen Arm

Surok Point

0 kilometers 10

0 miles 10

N ↑

← Looking out over the vast expanse of the impressive Harding Icefield

The rugged scenery of Aialik Bay, a popular location for day cruises →

Resurrection River

Exit Glacier
Nature Center

Exit
Glacier

Phoenix Peak
5,155 ft (1,571 m)

Seward

Marathon Mt.
4,603 ft (1,403 m)

Information
Center

Icefield

Resurrection Bay

Bear
Glacier

Skee
Glacier

State Park Cabins

Callisto Peak
3,223 ft (983 m)

State Park
Cabins

Aialik
Glacier

Bear Glacier
Lagoon

Resurrection
Peninsula

Addison
Glacier

Slate
Island

Fox
Island

Kenai Fjords
Wilderness Lodge

Pedersen
Glacier

Aialik Bay Cabin

Hive
Island

Cape
Resurrection

Aialik Bay
Ranger Station

Rugged
Island

Aialik
Peninsula

Aialik Bay

Harris
Peninsula

Chiswell
Islands

Granite
Island

The **Kenai Fjords National Park Information Center** in Seward (p100) issues backcountry permits and provides information.

The 20-mile- (32-km-) long **Aialik Bay** is the most popular destination for day cruises. Visitors are usually guaranteed a dynamic show as huge chunks of ice calve off the towering face of Aialik Glacier.

FOX ISLAND RETREAT

In 1918, looking for a place to paint and write, frustrated artist Rockwell Kent settled in an old cabin on remote Fox Island with his son, Rockie. The pair's experience is described in Kent's book *Wilderness: A Journal of Quiet Adventure in Alaska,* which relaunched his career back in New York. Today, visitors can retrace Kent's steps with a stay at Kenai Fjords Wilderness Lodge on Fox Island *(www.alaskacollection.com/ lodging/kenai-fjords-wilderness-lodge).*

On the lonely, rocky outcrops of the **Chiswell Islands**, passengers on day cruises can approach one of Alaska's most prominent Steller sea lion rookeries.

SEWARD

⚠ E7 🚗 127 miles (204 km) S of Anchorage
✈🚌🚃⛴ ℹ Mile 2, Seward Hwy; www.seward.com

Enjoying one of Alaska's most scenic locations, Seward is also known for its saltwater salmon fishing, its rollicking Independence Day celebrations, and its access to Kenai Fjords National Park). The town was founded in 1903 by John Ballaine, who decided that its deepwater port would be an ideal location for a railhead. The railroad came to fruition in 1923 and Seward has since thrived, despite suffering major damage in the 1964 earthquake.

① Benny Benson Memorial

🏠 Dairy Hill Lane

Standing next to the lagoon is a memorial honoring former Seward resident Benny Benson. In 1926, schoolchildren were asked to submit ideas for a state flag, and Benson – a 13-year-old Alutiiq boy who lived in Seward's orphanage – was the winner. Benson explained that the flag's blue field represented the Alaska sky and the forget-me-not, the state flower. The North Star stood for the future State of Alaska, while the Great Bear constellation symbolized strength. Alaska's flag is now generally regarded as the most beautiful of the US state flags.

The memorial – carved on Alaska stone by artist Damon Capurro – depicts the flag and is engraved with the words of the Alaska flag song.

② Seward Waterfront

In the summer, Seward's waterfront bustles with thousands of visitors and cruise ship passengers. Here it is possible to organize tours and fishing trips, join Kenai Fjords cruises, plan outdoor activities, and shop for gifts in a growing number of souvenir shops. At the southern end of the waterfront, the shops give way to an often packed tent and RV campground that stretches along the shore for almost 2 miles (3 km).

③ 🛍 Kenai Fjords National Park Information Center

🚗 1212 4th Ave ⏰ Late May–mid-Sep: 9am–5pm daily; mid-Sep–late May: 8am–5pm Mon–Fri 🌐 nps.gov/kefj

The handsome building that houses the Kenai Fjords National Park Information Center sits on the Seward waterfront. It features several exhibits detailing aspects of the glaciation that created the park's spectacular landscapes, as well as the wildlife and prolific birdlife that inhabit it (p96). Further advice can be obtained from the park's other visitor center, the Exit Glacier Nature Center at the Exit Glacier trailhead, which has exhibits and information.

Benny Benson Memorial ①
The Lagoon
Exit Glacier 8 miles (13 km) ⑥
Seward Boat Harbor
② Seward Waterfront
③ Kenai Fjords National Park Information Center

SECOND AVENUE
THIRD AVENUE
FOURTH AVENUE

Two Lakes Park

Resurrection Bay

B STREET
A STREET
MONROE ST
FIRST AVENUE
SECOND AVENUE
THIRD AVENUE
MADISON ST
FOURTH AVE
FIFTH AVE
SIXTH AVE
BALLAINE BOULEVARD
Waterfront Park
JEFFERSON ST
LOWELL CANYON RD
ADAMS ST
④ Seward Community Library and Museum
Thorn's Showcase Lounge
The Cookery
Caines Head SRA 5 miles (8 km)
⑤
⑦ Alaska SeaLife Center

0 meters 500
0 yards 500
N

EAT

Exit Glacier Salmon Bake
Salmon, halibut, and red snapper in a casual cabin-style dining room.

🏠 31832 Herman Leirer Rd 📞 907-224-2204

💲💲💲

The Cookery
Locally sourced ingredients prepared in traditional and not-so-traditional ways.

🏠 205 5th Ave
🌐 cookeryseward.com

💲💲💲

Thorn's Showcase Lounge
Outstanding burgers and freshly caught fish.

🏠 208 4th Ave
📞 907-224-3700

💲💲💲

④

Seward Community Library and Museum

🏠 6th & Adams ⏰ Hours vary, check website
🌐 cityofseward.us

The Seward Museum offers a glimpse of the history of the Resurrection Bay area, from pre-Russian contact to the 1964 Good Friday earthquake.

---

⑤

Caines Head State Recreation Area

🚢 Water taxi from Seward
ℹ️ alaskastateparks.org

During World War II, the US Army built Fort McGilvray on the rocky headland known as

←

An aerial view of Seward, arguably the most scenically located of all Alaska's towns

Caines Head, as well as a dock at North Beach, and a garrison (the remains of which are unstable) at South Beach. The 3-mile (5-km) walk from Tonsina Point is possible only at low tide, so hikers on the return trip will probably need to camp overnight – there are public-use cabins and camping sites available.

---

⑥

Exit Glacier

🏠 8 miles (13 km) W of Seward on Exit Glacier/Herman Leirer Rd
ℹ️ nps.gov/kefj

The impressive Exit Glacier, 2,500 ft (762 m) high and 3 miles (5 km) long, is the most readily accessible walk-up glacier in Alaska. From the seasonal visitor center at the end of the road, a short wheel-chair-accessible trail leads to a hiking route across the rocky terminal moraines to

the glacier face. The energetic can hike the steep 4-mile (6-km) Harding Icefield Trail up the western flank of Exit Glacier to the vast Harding Icefield. Camping is not permitted on the trail, but there is a campground nearby.

---

⑦

Alaska SeaLife Center

🏠 301 Railway Ave
⏰ Hours vary, check website
🌐 alaskasealife.org

The popular SeaLife Center introduces the maritime world of Alaska's southern coasts. Highlights include a series of spectacular tanks with underwater viewing windows that allow visitors to see octopus, Steller sea lions and many species of fish up close.

3

RESURRECTION PASS TRAIL

△ D6 ⌂ South trailhead: Mile 53.2, Sterling Hwy; north trailhead: 4 miles (6.5 km) up Resurrection Creek Rd from Mile 15, Hope Hwy ℹ fs.usda.gov/activity/chugach/recreation/hiking

The 39-mile (63-km) Resurrection Pass Trail is Alaska's most popular multiday hiking route. Hikers take anything from two to six days to walk the trail, overnighting in scenic campgrounds or rustic cabins.

Beginning at the Kenai River along the Sterling Highway, the trail climbs through spruce forest and past the dramatic Juneau Creek Falls into the subalpine zone. Crossing the 2,600-ft- (780-m-) high Resurrection Pass, it descends along Resurrection Creek to the trailhead near the village of Hope (p105). An alternative is to hike the 10-mile (16-km) Devil's Pass Trail from Mile 39.5 on the Seward Highway, then take the Resurrection Pass Trail to either Hope or the Sterling Highway. Campers will find lovely wild campgrounds near the northern end of the trail, and there are also plenty of forest and lakeside cabins with bunks.

←

A hoary marmot, known for its whistle, which is often heard on the trail

💬 INSIDER TIP
**Hiking
Practicalities**

It is best to hike the trail from south to north due to the net altitude loss. Book to stay in one of the Chugach National Forest cabins *(www. recreation.gov).*

↑ Juneau Creek Falls, one of the highlights of the Resurrection Pass Trail

Resurrection Pass Summit

▽ For 5 miles (8 km) the trail passes through a treeless alpine zone. Its highest point is the 2,500-ft (780-m) Resurrection Pass, with views of Denali and the Harding Icefield.

Trail Highlights

Juneau Lake

△ Juneau Lake makes a great place for an overnight stop, with three campgrounds and two cabins. Its beautiful natural setting makes it a popular spot with trail users in summer, and the lake also attracts anglers with its excellent fishing opportunities.

Abandoned Gold Diggings

△ The northern end of the trail passes through a gold-mining area, where prospectors have been mining and leaving behind detritus since the Gold Rush days of the late 19th century.

EXPERIENCE MORE

4 (M)

Kenai River

D6 **Anchorage-Homer**

Originating between high peaks above the glacier-blue Kenai Lake, the Kenai River rushes westward from Cooper Landing, where whitewater rafting, kayaking, and canoeing are on offer. The Kenai then passes the mouth of the Russian River before flowing out of the mountains and onto the flats around Skilak Lake.

Among the world's most productive salmon streams, the lower Kenai is the original combat fishing river, with fierce competition among anglers for fishing space. People flock to the river on summer weekends, temporarily making the Sterling Highway one of Alaska's busiest roads. Continuing west from its Skilak Lake outlet, the

river flows past many public campgrounds and private cabins to its mouth at Kenai.

Beyond fishing, this area is also rich in other forms of recreation, including river rafting, photography, abundant hiking trails, and bird-watching, especially in the early summer months.

5

Moose Pass

E6 **98 miles (158 km) S of Anchorage** **Anchorage-Seward** **moosepassalaska.com**

Moose Pass village began life in 1912 as a construction camp on the Alaska Railroad. The area was named in 1903, after a moose reputedly blocked the passage of a mail-carrying dog team. The town sits on the south side of Trail Lake, and a local air taxi provides flightseeing trips. To the west of the Seward Highway stands a landmark

waterwheel, constructed in 1976 by the Estes Brothers, who still run a grocery located in the adjacent 1928 building.

North of Moose Pass, a salmon hatchery by North Trail Lake is the starting point of the 21-mile (35-km) Johnson Pass Trail. Following the lakeshore, the trail climbs over its namesake before descending to Granite Creek at Mile 62.9 of the Seward Highway.

6

Cooper Landing

D6 **98 miles (158 km) S of Anchorage** **Anchorage-Homer** **Mile 48, Sterling Hwy; www.cooper landingchamber.com**

Named after Joseph Cooper, who was the first to discover gold here in 1894, Cooper Landing was one of the few places in Alaska that continued producing gold into the 20th century. The town sprawls along the Sterling Highway in a string of eateries, lodges, fishing guides, and rafting companies. At the K'Beq Kenaitze Footprints Heritage Site, Dena'ina Natives share their traditions through

The gorgeous turquoise waters of the Kenai River, which is renowned *(inset)* for its salmon fishing

↑ A quiet street in downtown Hope, which was once a booming Gold Rush town

interpretive walks featuring archaeological sites. Local artists make and sell Dena'ina arts and crafts.

Hope

🅰E6 🏠88 miles (141 km) S of Anchorage ☑ ℹ www.hope alaska.us

The historic gold-mining town of Hope nestles at the mouth of Resurrection Creek on the southern shore of Turnagain Arm *(p78)*. Named after Percy Hope, a 17-year-old prospector, Hope had its heyday in the late 1890s, when it was a rollicking Gold Rush town. By the end of the decade, however, many inhabitants had pulled up stakes and set off for the Klondike goldfields.

Today, despite its proximity to Anchorage and the Seward Highway, Hope remains a quiet place. Most visitors take in the 1902 log social hall and the old 1896 general store, now home to a café-bar. Recreational opportunities here include camping at Porcupine Campground, rafting on Six-Mile Creek, and hiking the Gull Rock Trail. More energetic hikers can try the Resurrection Pass Trail *(p102)*, which passes both

historical and modern-day gold diggings. Hope Point Trail is also excellent; it's a 2.5-mile (4-km) climb through spruce and birch forests to a ridge straddling the mountains and Turnagain Arm. Hikers should look out for fallen trees on windy days, and be bear aware.

Soldotna

🅰D6 🏠148 miles (238 km) SW of Anchorage ☑ 🚌 Anchorage–Homer ℹ 44790 Sterling Highway; www.soldotna chamber.com

As the primary commercial and service center of the Kenai Peninsula, Soldotna features fast-food franchises, stores, and visitor accommodation options. Founded in the 1940s as a retail hub, it was incorporated only in 1967. While the area experienced steady growth, unbridled sprawl, and congestion in the late 20th century, much of the surrounding land remains protected under federal management.

Five sites around town – the Soldotna Visitor Center, Rotary Park, Soldotna Creek Park, and the Centennial and Swiftwater Campgrounds – have set up "Fishwalks" along

EAT

Kenai Brewing Company
This local microbrewery offers full meals during the day, in addition to a great beer selection.

🅰D6 🏠308 Homestead Lane, Soldotna 🔲 kenai riverbrewing.com

$$(§)

Addie Camp
This environmentally friendly eatery is housed in an old rail car. The menus feature unique takes on Alaska cuisine, and there's also a beer and wine bar on site.

🅰D6 🏠43550 Whistle Hill Loop, Soldotna 🔲 whistle hillsoldotna.com

$$(§)

The Flats Bistro
Dine in full view of Kenai River Flats, where eagles and caribou regularly wander. The house-smoked meats are spectacular.

🅰D6 🏠39846 Kalifornsky Rd, Kenai 🔲 theflatsbistro.com

$$(§)

the Kenai River. These boardwalks, designed to protect the fragile riverbank, allow public access to the river for fishing and salmon-viewing.

The Soldotna Historical Society Museum features a collection of homesteaders' cabins from the 1940s. It also has a Territorial log school and Native artifacts.

Soldotna Creek Park is a lovely, family-friendly space with many walking paths. It is also the site of many local music, art, and food festivals.

⑨ Kenai

**🅐D6 🚗11 miles (18 km)
NW of Soldotna
🚍 Anchorage–Homer
ℹ️11471 Kenai Spur Hwy;
www.kenaichamber.com**

The peninsula's largest city, Kenai also ranks as one of Alaska's best-preserved historic communities. In 1791, Russian fur traders came into contact with the region's Dena'ina Athabascan people and established St. Nicholas Redoubt, the second permanent Russian settlement in Alaska. In 1869, two years after the purchase of Alaska, the US Army built Fort Kenay to provide a military presence in the Cook Inlet region. Major oil exploration began in the 1950s, and the Tesoro Alaska refinery at Nikiski is now an important economic player.

Visitors can stroll around the historic Old Town near the beach, which has the 1881 Parish Rectory House, the 1906 St. Nicholas Chapel, a replica of Fort Kenay, and the Holy Assumption of the Virgin Mary Russian Orthodox Church. Founded in 1846, the church's present building was constructed between 1894 and 1895. The interior is decorated with antique Russian artifacts.

In spring, the salt marsh at Kenai Flats State Recreation Site, across the Warren Ames Bridge over the Kenai River, attracts large flocks of Siberian snow geese. With interpretive panels, picnic tables, a boardwalk, and viewing scope, it will delight keen birders.

⑩ Sterling

**🅐D6 🚗134 miles (215 km)
SW of Anchorage
🚍Anchorage–Homer**

The name of the game in this 5-mile- (8-km-) long strip is fish. Nearly all the businesses along the Sterling Highway cater to the anglers who flock to the town when the salmon are running. Anyone who has ever wanted to try their hand at landing a monster salmon will find plenty of equipment and advice in Sterling, as well as along the highway between here, Soldotna, Kenai, and Homer.

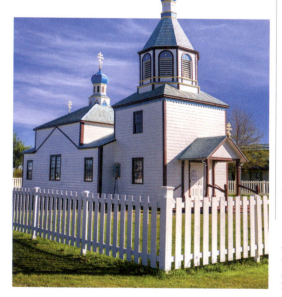

This community is also home to numerous private recreational cabins on the banks of the Kenai River.

The area's most worthwhile site is Skilak Lake, which features lovely wild lakeside campgrounds and hiking trails. In the winter, Sterling's numerous frozen lakes – including Seven Lakes and Hidden Lake – make a pretty sight, but in the summer, the congestion in this area can be frustrating.

⑪ Kenai National Wildlife Refuge

**🅐D7 🚗30 miles (50 km)
SE of Kenai 🚍Anchorage–Homer ℹ️2139 Ski Hill Rd, Soldotna; www.kenai.fws.gov**

The Alaska National Interest Lands Conservation Act of 1980 *(p61)* changed the name

←

The distinctive blue-domed roof of Kenai's Russian Orthodox church

Paddling through lily pads in Canoe Lake, within the Kenai National Wildlife Refuge

of the Kenai National Moose Range to the Kenai National Wildlife Refuge, and increased it to its current area of almost 3,125 sq miles (8,094 sq km). The refuge covers high peaks, glaciers, muskeg, and lake-studded bog. This landscape provides habitat for a range of wildlife, from mountain goats, Dall sheep, and bears to moose, caribou, and wolves. The refuge is also home to lynx, coyotes, and waterfowl such as trumpeter swans and migratory birds.

Access to the refuge's wild southern part can be challenging, but the northern areas feature a number of public campgrounds, 200 miles (322 km) of hiking trails, and two world-class canoe routes. The 80-mile (128-km) Swanson River Canoe Route links over 40 lakes with the Swanson River, ending in the Captain Cook State Recreation Area. The 60-mile (96-km) Swan Lakes Loop is a system of 32 lakes, accessible from the Swanson River and Swan Lake roads. Equipment can be hired and tours organized in nearby towns.

Stop by the Kenai National Wildlife Refuge Visitor Center for interpretive displays, guided hikes and walks, and programs specially designed for kids of any age. Preschool programs for under-sixes, held throughout the year, are a highlight. Most activities are free and open to all.

12
Captain Cook State Recreation Area

D6 **25 miles (40 km) N of Kenai at Mile 36, Kenai Spur Hwy** dnr. alaska.gov/parks/aspunits/kenai/captcook.htm

Located on the shores of Cook Inlet, the Captain Cook State Recreation Area is named after British explorer Captain James Cook, who explored the region in 1778 (p56). One of Alaska's quieter parks, it has forests, lakes, streams, and beaches offering picnic sites, hiking routes, and camping at the peaceful Discovery Campground, as well as swimming, canoeing, and fishing in Stormy Lake. A variety of wildlife, including moose, bears, loons, and sandhill cranes, can be spotted in the park. The beach is popular with agate hunters, but visitors should avoid the dangerous mudflats just offshore.

Along the dead-end road to the recreation area, visitors can pick up supplies and look around the oil town of Nikiski, 9 miles (14 km) to the south. Formerly known as North Kenai, this town began as a homesteading area in the 1940s and grew with the discovery of oil in Cook Inlet. At the end of Nikiski Beach Road, expansive views open up across Nikishka Bay and the Cook Inlet oil drilling platforms, and beyond to the active volcano Mount Spurr. The large domed Nikiski pool, which is funded by the oil companies, features a hot tub and a winding 136-ft (41-m) waterslide that is extremely popular with residents and visitors.

> **INSIDER TIP**
> **Salmon Run**
>
> Alaskans flock to the Kenai River each July for the run of red, or sockeye, salmon. Alaska residents are allowed a designated number of fish per family member through a dip net license. Walk along the beach near Cook Inlet to take in this spectacular sight.

13

Homer

D7 84 miles (135 km) S of Soldotna 201 Sterling Highway; www.homeralaska.org

Founded in 1895 and named for Homer Pennock, a New York con man who spent a few months in the area, Homer sells itself as the "end of the road." In 1886, Homer got its first post office, and in the late 1890s, a coal-shipping settlement occupied the tip of Homer Spit, which runs into Kachemak Bay. However, the village was abandoned in 1902 when the coal seams became unviable. The handful of residents who remained in town turned to farming and fishing. From 1910 onward, Homer expanded from a fishing village into a pleasant small city. Today, Homer is a refuge for visitors, artists, and anglers from all over the world, which has resulted in the rapid development of the city's bluffs and foothills. For most visitors, a stay here means bird-watching, halibut fishing, shopping for local arts, and visits to explore the nearby Kachemak Bay State Park (p111).

Homer is also home to several interesting museums, foremost among which is the world-class **Alaska Islands and Ocean Visitor Center**. This highly worthwhile stop is probably the finest center of its kind in Alaska. A wealth of original exhibits – including a replica of a Bering Sea seabird rookery and a recording of conservationist and researcher Olaus Murie dictating his journal – detail the natural history of the Alaska Maritime National Wildlife Refuge and the Kachemak Bay Research Reserve. Visitors can also hike along a boardwalk to Beluga Slough's tidal marshes or watch an award-winning film about the Aleutian Islands.

Natural history is also the subject of the **Pratt Museum**, which features exhibits on the geology, flora, fauna, and oceanography of the peninsula, as well as homesteader and Native cultures. There is a Kachemak Bay exhibit, and detailed coverage of the 1964 earthquake (p31) and the 1989 *Exxon Valdez* oil spill displayed downstairs. Trails through the botanical gardens outside the main building lead past 150 identified species of local plants. Also in the grounds is the Harrington

↑ Homer's small harbor, overlooked by mountains and heaving with boats

Cabin, which displays artifacts from Homer's homesteading era of the 1940s.

Homer's scenic location has made it a popular place with artists, and the city is home to an array of street fairs, workshops, and galleries. One of the most renowned is the **Bunnell Street Arts Center**, which was founded by an artists' group in 1989. Housed in the 1937 Old Inlet Trading Post building, which was once a commercial hub for homesteaders, the gallery now showcases an impressive collection of contemporary fine art.

To the north of the city is the **Carl E. Wynn Nature Center**, set amid spruce forests and meadows on the bluffs overlooking Homer. Formerly the homestead of naturalist Carl E. Wynn, it was donated to the Center for Alaskan Coastal Studies in 1990. Visitors can enjoy bird-watching, strolling amid wildflowers, and exploring the vegetation. The center also offers guided walks highlighting local wildlife and shrubs.

Homer's scenic location has made it a popular place with artists, and the city is home to an array of street fairs, workshops, and galleries.

Jutting out from the south of the city is Homer Spit. Thought to be a remnant of an ancient glacial moraine, it has been spared the ravages of the sea by reclamation and rock walls. This is Homer's main tourist district, taking in the small boat harbor, the ferry terminal, a hotel, myriad eateries, and a host of fishing charter companies. The Salty Dawg Saloon, with its light-house tower, is listed as a maritime landmark. Around 1900, it served as the head-quarters for the Cook Inlet Coal Fields Company.

The Spit is also a popular camping venue, and com-munities of RVs and tents can be found strung along the northern shore.

The Salty Dawg Saloon, a must-visit bar in the city's lively neighborhood of Homer Spit

Alaska Islands and Ocean Visitor Center
📷 🏠95 Sterling Hwy
🕐Late May–mid-Sep: 9am–5pm daily; mid-Sep–late May: noon–5pm Tue–Sat
🌐islandsandocean.org

Pratt Museum
🎦📷 🏠3779 Bartlett St 🕐Mid-May–mid-Sep: 10am–6pm daily; mid-Sep–Dec & Feb–mid-May: noon–5pm Tue–Sat 🌐pratt museum.org

Bunnell Street Arts Center
📷 🏠106 W Bunnell Ave
🕐11am–6pm Mon–Sat, noon–4pm Sun 🌐bunnellarts.org

Carl E. Wynn Nature Center
🎦📷 🏠E Skyline Dr
🕐Mid-Jun–early Sep: 10am–6pm daily 🌐akcoastal studies.org

EAT

Fat Olives
Head here to enjoy hand-tossed pizza, fresh oysters and seafood, and a gourmet wine selection. An excellent option for takeout meals.

🗺D7 🏠276 Ohlson Lane, Homer 📞907-235-8408
💲💲💲

Captain Pattie's Fish House
The city's best spot for fish 'n' chips – plus you can have your own catch served right to your table. Open seasonally for lunch and dinner.

🗺D7 🏠4241 Homer Spit Road, Homer 🌐captainpatties.com
💲💲💲

DRINK

Homer Brewing Company
Homer's first brewery is small but thriving. Growlers (glass jugs) are available, as are samples and smaller bottles.

🗺D7 🏠1411 Lake Shore Drive, Homer 🌐homerbrew.com

Grace Ridge Brewing
This is a small and cosy spot serving up unique beers featuring an assortment of local flavors.

🗺D7 🏠3388 B Street, Homer 🌐grace ridgebrewing.com

⑭ Ninilchik

🅰D7 📍40 miles (65 km) S of Soldotna 🚌Anchorage-Homer ℹ️ www.ninilchik chamber.com

This traditional Russian-era Native village, whose name means "peaceful riverside place," is centered around the 1901 Transfiguration of Our Lord Church. The photogenic onion-domed church sits beside a rambling Russian Orthodox cemetery and offers fine views across the inlet. While the church is open for Sunday services, it is closed to the public on other days.

The Ninilchik River, a short walk to the north of the Visitor Center, and Deep Creek, to the south, are world-class salmon fishing streams. Deep-sea charters provide access to offshore halibut and salmon. When the king salmon are running upstream (usually the first two weeks of June), the Deep Creek State Recreation Area Campground and the nearby Ninilchik River Campground fill up and spill over into surrounding private sites and RV parks. Anglers will probably enjoy the scene, while others may prefer quieter areas. The village's links to salmon fishing are so strong that the Salmonfest Music Festival is held in this area on the first weekend of August. The festival began life as a conservation-oriented fundraising concert, and has been running since 2010.

---

⑮ Nikolaevsk

🅰D7 📍64 miles (103 km) S of Soldotna

Settled in 1960, Nikolaevsk village is home to the Old Believers, a sect of Russian Orthodoxy that broke away from the mother church and settled in Siberia after 17th-century religious reforms. Those who later wound up in Alaska established Nikolaevsk and several of the surrounding villages.

Visitors arriving along the 9-mile (14-km) drive from Anchor Point might feel as if they have passed through a time warp. The village's distinctive architecture and demeanor has remained largely unchanged, and the way of life here has only been lightly touched by the 21st century. One exception is an enterprising local woman who runs the Samovar Café and a gallery of costumes and art.

The village is also home to a photogenic Russian Orthodox Church, although its interior is closed to the public.

---

⑯ Anchor Point

🅰D7 📍61 miles (98 km) S of Soldotna 🚌Anchorage-Homer ℹ️Sterling Hwy, opposite Anchor River Inn; www.anchorpoint chamber.org

Named after an anchor that the British explorer Captain James Cook lost on his voyage up Cook Inlet, the Anchor Point community was established by homesteaders in 1949. The major attraction at this westernmost point on the contiguous US Highway system is the Anchor River, with its abundant supply of king and silver salmon, and rainbow, Dolly Varden, and steelhead trout. The seas around the area are rich in saltwater salmon and halibut.

Anglers usually stay at the Anchor River State Recreation Area at Anchor Point. Those who prefer a quieter campsite

← The Transfiguration of Our Lord Russian Orthodox church in Ninilchik and (inset) its gilded artifacts

Hiking a trail with glorious sea views in Kachemak Bay State Park

Center, and visit the 1891 St. Nicholas Russian Orthodox Church, which crowns a hill overlooking the harbor.

can opt for the beautiful (and angler-free) Stariski State Recreation Area to the north of Anchor Point. The park is perched on a bluff with views across Cook Inlet toward the volcanoes beyond.

17 Seldovia

ⒶD7 Ⓓ20 nautical miles (32 km) S of Homer ✈ Charter floatplane from Homer 🚢 From Homer 🌐 youotterbehere.com

One of the most gorgeously sited seaside towns in Alaska, Seldovia was inhabited by Dena'ina people as early as the 16th century. Russian settlers arrived here around 1800, naming the place Zaliv Seldevoe (Herring Bay). In the early 20th century, the area's flourishing herring trade increased Seldovia's population to about 2,000, but the boom was shortlived.

Today, Seldovia is a small fishing town with an active Native association. Visitors can stroll along the waterfront boardwalk, explore the Village Tribe Museum and Visitor

18 Kachemak Bay State Park

ⒶD7 Ⓓ8 nautical miles (12 km) across the bay from Homer 🚢 From Homer 🌐 alaskastateparks.org

Alaska's first state park and one of the largest coastal state parks in the US, the Kachemak Bay State Park and the adjoining Kachemak Bay State Wilderness Park take in 625 sq miles (1,619 sq km) of islands, forests, glaciers, beaches, and rocky coastlines. This critical habitat area supports several species of marine life, including whales and sea otters, land mammals such as coyotes and black bears, and birds that include eagles and puffins. There are also excellent hiking opportunities in the park; about 80 miles (130 km) of hiking trails lace the waterfront area that lies across the bay from Homer. Trails from the primitive beach campgrounds track across beautiful and varied landscapes, leading to dramatic ridges and remote coastlines.

Did You Know?

"Barn door" halibut caught in Kachemak Bay can weigh up to 300 lbs (140 kg).

19 Halibut Cove

ⒶD7 Ⓓ12 miles (19 km) SE of Homer 🚢 From Homer 🌐 halibutcove.com

Halibut Cove happily receives short-term visitors, but has just a handful of permanent residents who are keen to avoid the unbridled growth of nearby Homer. This scenic little cove makes an excellent launch point for hikes into the adjacent Kachemak Bay State Park. There is also a restaurant and several lodges, as well as a number of artists' galleries. The most renowned of these is the Cove Gallery of the late Diana Tillion (1928–2010), who used octopus ink for her works. Quiet Place Lodge is also of interest; it's a unique music venue whose stage floats out into the cove.

Access to the community is by local water taxi, but day tours are also available.

PRINCE WILLIAM SOUND

A massive swathe of salt water roughly the size of Massachusetts, Prince William Sound is characterized by a series of irregular coastlines. The region was first explored by Europeans in 1741, when Danish ship captain Vitus Bering, sailing for the czar of Russia, landed on Kayak Island near the Copper River and present-day Cordova. The region was also visited in 1778 by British captain James Cook and in 1779 by Spanish explorer Don Salvador Fidalgo, both of whom were searching for the elusive Northwest Passage.

Valdez was settled during the 1897 Gold Rush, when an "All-American Route" to the goldfields of the Klondike was proposed. It was a hazardous journey for the unprepared miners, however, and thousands perished along the as yet uncharted mountainsides and canyons. Mining was also key to the growth of Cordova, which became the rail terminus for copper ore from Kennecott Mines near McCarthy. A boomtown between 1916 and 1938, the community suffered greatly when the mines closed and the railroad ceased operations.

The northwest end of Prince William Sound had long served as a trade and transit route for Alaska Native groups, and at the beginning of World War II the US military constructed a facility at the ice-free deepwater port of Whittier. The 1964 earthquake took a tremendous toll on Prince William Sound, with many seaside towns forced to rebuild after being devastated by the tsunami that followed the 9.2 temblor. The area has steadily recovered, however, thanks to a thriving commercial fishing industry and the selection of Valdez as the terminus for the Trans-Alaska Pipeline.

Sheep

Talkeetna

Kashwitna

Talkeetna Mountains

Chickaloon

Matanuska

GLENN HIGHWAY

Tazlina Lake

INTERIOR ALASKA
p164

Wasilla

Palmer

Knik Arm

Knik Glacier

Mount Marcus Baker
13,178 ft (4,016 m)

Chugach Mountains

ANCHORAGE
p64

Chugach State Park

Mount Goode
10,611 ft (3,234 m)

Harvard Glacier

Yale Glacier

Meares Glacier

Shoup Glacier

COLUMBIA GLACIER

❻

VALDEZ

Valdez Airport

❶

COLLEGE FJORD

❷

Harriman Fjord

Esther Island

Eagle Bay

Valdez Arm

Tatitlek

Bligh Island

Port Fidalgo

Port Gravina

Portage

WHITTIER ❹

Whittier Glacier

BLACKSTONE BAY ❸

Blackstone Glacier

Perry Island

Naked Island

Prince William Sound

Hinchinbrook Island

THE KENAI
PENINSULA
p92

Sargent Icefield

Knight Island

Montague Peak
2,162 ft (658 m)

Seward Airport

Seward

Bainbridge Island

Chenega Bay

Montague Island

Jeanie Peak
571 ft (174 m)

Resurrection Bay

ALASKA MARINE HIGHWAY

Kodiak

0 kilometers   30

0 miles   30

N

PRINCE WILLIAM SOUND

Must See
❶ Valdez

Experience More
❷ College Fjord
❸ Blackstone Bay
❹ Whittier
❺ Copper River Highway
❻ Columbia Glacier
❼ Cordova

❶
VALDEZ

🅰 E4 🏠 304 miles (487 km) E of Anchorage ✈🚢 From Whittier, Cordova
ℹ 309 Fairbanks Dr; www.valdezalaska.org

The most important town of the Prince William Sound region, Valdez enjoys a lovely setting between the mountains and the sea. It makes an excellent base for day trips and organized cruises to northeastern Prince William Sound, which provide good opportunities for sightings of whales, seals, sea otters, and birds around Columbia Glacier.

↑ Transportation exhibits on display at the Valdez Museum

Valdez, which is named after 18th-century Spanish naval officer Antonio Valdes y Basan, was founded in 1897 about 4 miles (6 km) east of its current location as a jumping-off point for hopeful prospectors heading to the Klondike goldfields. After the 1964 earthquake (p31) destroyed Old Valdez, the town was rebuilt at its present location. As the northernmost ice-free port in North America, it was chosen to be the terminus of the Trans-Alaska Pipeline (p201). The best place to find out about the history of the Alaska oil industry and Valdez itself is the excellent Valdez Museum. Its best-known display is probably the 1886 hand-pumped Ahrens steam fire engine, lovingly polished and tended. A replica of the Pipeline Workers' Monument, dedicated to

A small boat harbor on Prince William Sound in Valdez and *(inset)* the Worthington Glacier ↑

the men who built the pipeline, is among the displays. There are photographs documenting the 1964 earthquake and Valdez's rebirth as an oil town, as well as mockups of an old miner's cabin, a historic 1880s bar, and Native artifacts.

More Native artifacts are on display at the Whitney Museum, which is thought to hold the world's largest private collection of Alaska Native art, artifacts, and stuffed wildlife. It houses some of the finest examples of Inuit scrimshaw, as well as a ship and an aircraft carved entirely from ivory. There is also an extensive collection of Native dolls, garments, weapons, and masks, as well as an old Inuit kayak with whale baleen stays.

Around Valdez

East of Valdez, Keystone Canyon contains both buried stretches of the Alaska Pipeline and the Richardson Highway, one of Alaska's most scenic roads. At Mile 13, two great waterfalls spill down the slopes into the slate-gray Lowe River. A paved turnout provides access to Horsetail Falls, north of the highway. Farther along, the lovely Bridal Veil Falls tumble down into a deep, rainbow-flanked pool.

North of Valdez, the Worthington Glacier – protected in the Worthington Glacier State Recreation Site – flows steeply down the icy peak of the 6,130-ft- (1,840-m-) high Girls Mountain in a series of fingers that extend to within 430 yards (400 m) of the road. Visitors can admire the scene from below or follow the challenging Ridge Trail up the glacier's lateral moraine and right to its face. The recreation site has an information desk and a small shop.

EXXON VALDEZ OIL SPILL

On March 23, 1989, the tanker *Exxon Valdez* struck Bligh Reef and started leaking oil. Up to 11 million gallons (42 million liters) of oil spilled into the sound, contaminating 1,500 miles (2,400 km) of coastline, killing fish, whales, seals, sea otters, and birds. Nearly 10,000 workers were employed to count dead wildlife and clean up the sound and surrounding areas.

↑ Photographing the stunning glaciers of College Fjord from a cruise tour boat

EXPERIENCE MORE

② Ⓜ³ College Fjord

A E4 🚢 **Tour from Whittier**

The College Fjord arm of Prince William Sound and the neighboring Harriman Fjord include an impressive concentration of easily accessible tidewater glaciers, as well as myriad valley glaciers and hanging glaciers.

In 1899, New York railroad magnate Edward Harriman launched a scientific expedition along the Alaska coast, including to College Fjord, where he named the glaciers after the Ivy League colleges attended by the scientists on board his ship, the *George W. Elder*. As one travels into the fjord, the glaciers on the left are named for women's colleges and those on the right for men's schools. Harvard Glacier is the largest of those in College Fjord, and indeed is the second-largest tidewater glacier in Prince William Sound. Chunks as large as a house often calve (break off) from the massive 300-ft- (90-m-) high glacier faces.

③ Blackstone Bay

A E4 🚢 **From Whittier**

One of Alaska's most dramatic sights, the 18-mile- (29-km-) long Blackstone Bay lies at the foot of three calving tidewater glaciers – Blackstone, Beloit, and Northland. These choke the upper portion of this spectacular fjord with growler ice (small chunks of ice that "growl" as they melt and release air) and bergy bits (large chunks of ice or small icebergs).

In the middle of the fjord is Willard Island. From the unofficial campground at its southern end, campers have a front-row view of nature's intriguing displays, as well as a minor lesson in physics. As chunks calve off the glaciers, three types of waves appear. First, light waves make the calving visible to observers. Several seconds later, a sound wave arrives, carrying the thunder-like crack of the breaking ice. Finally, after a minute or so, the waves created by the big splash roll onto the shore.

Most visitors to Blackstone Bay arrive on day cruises from Whittier, but it is also popular as a venue for ocean kayaking (*see 266–7*). Kayakers typically take two days to reach Willard Island. Although it can be

---

KITTIWAKES

The towering cliffs across Passage Arm from Whittier are home to a colony of thousands of black-legged kittiwakes (*Rissa tridactyla*). During the summer nesting season they can be seen wheeling around the precarious cliff faces where they nest, breed, and hatch their chicks. With a relatively rapid wingbeat, kittiwakes are highly maneuverable and are able to land on narrow cliff ledges even in strong winds. In the winter, these pelagic gulls spend most of their time on the open ocean, feeding on small fish and plankton.

One of Alaska's most dramatic sights, the 18-mile- (29-km-) long Blackstone Bay lies at the foot of three calving tidewater glaciers - Blackstone, Beloir, and Northland.

enjoyable to paddle around between the bergs, visitors should be careful not to approach the glacier faces or get caught on an incoming tide. Pieces of ice, pushed by the forceful current, can crush a kayak.

---

④

Whittier

Ⓐ E4 Ⓐ 59 miles (95 km) SE of Anchorage Ⓡ From Anchorage via Portage Ⓢ From Valdez and Cordova Ⓦ whittieralaska.gov

Whittier's name came from the adjacent Whittier Glacier, named after the American poet John Greenleaf Whittier. Founded in 1943, when the US Army used this ice-free port to build an Alaska base, the town was made accessible by the 3-mile- (5-km-) long Anton

Anderson road-rail toll tunnel, which connects Turnagain Arm with Passage Canal, an arm of Prince William Sound. The tunnel is open for 15 minutes per hour in each direction.

Despite its spectacular setting, surrounded as it is by glaciers and thundering waterfalls, Whittier is probably one of Alaska's oddest towns. The army, not especially concerned with aesthetics, housed their personnel in Soviet-style high-rise apartment buildings. After the army left in 1960, the few hundred residents who stayed behind continued to live in two towers, one of which, the 14-story Begich Towers, has now been converted into condominiums. The town's other occupied building is the less obtrusive Whittier Manor. Most residents are accustomed to unflattering remarks about these buildings, and even seem proud of the undeniably quirky architecture.

One of Whittier's main attractions is a large colony of black-legged kittiwakes in the cliffs across Passage Arm, which can be viewed on sea kayaking trips. Lovers of the outdoors will also enjoy the 26 Glacier Cruise run by **Phillips Cruises and Tours**. The cruise boats travel deep

into Barry Arm and College Fjord, offering close-up views of wildlife and glaciers.

Phillips Cruises and Tours
Ⓐ Cliffside Marina Ⓞ May–Sep: 12:30pm daily Ⓦ phillips cruises.com

---

EAT

The Inn at Whittier
Whittier's only high-end restaurant offers a wide menu featuring fresh seafood from the Sound.

Ⓐ E4 Ⓐ 5A Harbor Loop Road, Whittier Ⓦ innat whittier.com

$$$⑨$

SHOP

Sound Ideas - Whittier Fudge
Head here for Alaska- and ocean-themed gifts and homemade fudge.

Ⓐ E4 Ⓐ 1A Harbor Loop Rd, Whittier Ⓒ 907-472-2535

Whittier's harbor, the launch point for numerous cruise tours

5

Copper River Highway

🅰F4 ℹ www.fs.usda.gov/chugach

There is little to prepare visitors for the arresting beauty of the 48-mile (77-km) drive along the Copper River Highway between Cordova and the end of the road at the Million Dollar Bridge. Along the way, a number of short hiking trails and roadside views, as well as abundant wildlife and a few obligatory sights, will easily fill up a full day.

The gravel road, which is always open for visitors, and usually free of snow by late April, follows the roadbed of the historic Copper River and Northwestern Railway. At Mile 4, a marker provides information on its construction and history. At Mile 5.7, the road passes the Forest Service's Eyak River Trail, a short, 2-mile (3-km) hike that includes a long boardwalk over muskeg. The variety of birdlife found here makes it a favorite walking trail of birders.

About 7 miles (11 km) north along a side road from Mile 13.7, a short walk leads onto the terminal moraine of

↑ The Million Dollar Bridge, in place across the Copper River since 1920

Sheridan Glacier, with fine views of its blue ice. The steep 3-mile (5-km) Sheridan Ridge Trail climbs to a good view. Another 4 miles (6 km) along the highway, a rugged side route leads south to Alaganik Slough, which has a picnic site and a 990-ft (300-m) elevated boardwalk over a wetland. Vast watery views are on offer, replete with colorful wildflowers such as irises. Every summer, thousands of waterfowl, including 7 percent of the world's trumpeter swans, descend on this spot to nest, and countless shorebirds screech overhead.

Beginning around Mile 25 for 10 miles (16 km), the view from the road takes in more water than land as the route crosses the Copper River Delta over a series of bridges and causeways. One of these

bridges was severely damaged in 2011, and, due to the state's budget crisis, has not yet been repaired. This has left the Copper River Highway completely inaccessible from Mile 36 onward.

→

A tourist dinghy approaching Columbia Glacier, home to (inset) many harbor seals

Columbia Glacier

🏔 E4 🚢 Boat tours from Valdez

During the 1980s, the 40-mile- (64-km-) long and 2,000-ft- (600-m-) thick Columbia Glacier was a highlight on the Alaska Marine Highway route between Whittier *(p119)* and Valdez *(p116)*. Ferries would typically stop in this area amid the rafts of sea otters and icebergs laden with harbor seals, and blast their horns in the hope that the sound vibrations would cause the glacier to calve.

However, in the early 1980s, Columbia Glacier began to surge at a pace as great as 115 ft (35 m) per day, calving icebergs into Prince William Sound much faster than snow compression on the ice field could replace it. It is thought that the melting ice created a cushion of water beneath the main ice sheet, allowing the glacier to progress without being impeded by the friction of ice against rock. It calved so much ice that it choked the surrounding waters with large icebergs that froze together. As a result, the glacier face has receded about 13 miles (21 km) since 1982 and can no longer be reached by ferry, although there are hopes that this may eventually stabilize. Currently, this active glacier is most readily accessed on day cruises, such as those run by **Stan Stephens**, and on private tour boats from Valdez.

Stan Stephens

🏠 112 North Harbor Dr, Valdez 🌐 stephenscruises. com

↑ Scenic Cordova Harbor, overlooked by the towering Chugach Mountains

Cordova

E4 50 miles (80 km) SE of Valdez 🛫🚢 From Valdez, 404 1st St; www.cityof cordova.net

Smaller than nearby Valdez, rainy little Cordova offers a slice of the independent, self-sufficent character of "old Alaska" that has faded in more accessible places along the road system. There is a quiet charm in wandering its steets or strolling past the fish canneries. This scenic town is linked to the outside world only by plane or the ferries of the Marine Highway.

Initially a Gold Rush town, Cordova became the Copper River and Northwestern Railway railhead, linking the copper mines at Kennecott *(p186)* with the coast. The railroad functioned until the mines closed down in 1938. Although Cordova was badly damaged by the 1964 earthquake *(p31)*, it bounced back as a fishing town and is known for its prized Copper River red

INSIDER TIP
Orca Beach

Cordova's Orca Beach is a wonderful place to view wildlife in the area. A ten-minute drive from downtown, the rocky beach overlooks Orca Inlet. Take one of the roadside pullouts to look for seabirds, whales, otters, and harbor seals.

salmon *(p121)*, which are shipped fresh to restaurants both inside and outside Alaska.

The town is also home to several museums, including the small **Cordova Historical Museum**. Housed inside the Cordova Center, it features several interesting exhibits. In addition to works by a range of Alaskan artists, including painter Sydney Laurence, the museum houses an old skin-covered canoe and a collection of antique photographs. One exhibit explains the effects of the 1964 earthquake and another showcases Cordova's Iceworm Festival *(p54)*, held in

↑ Canoes on display in the intriguing Cordova Historical Museum

SHOP

Cordova Historical Society Gift Shop
Take in the locally made crafts at this museum gift shop, which include a selection of art and re-used fishing materials that lend support to the museum's mission to promote life in Cordova.
🅰E4 🅰622 Main Street, 99574 📞907-424-6655

Ilanka Culture Center
This fantastic gathering place celebrates the cultures of Cordova, with the art and Native crafts for sale echoing this mission. Products range from salves made using foraged herbs to beautiful carvings.
🅰E4 🅰110 Nicholoff Way, 99574
🆆nveyak.com

February to relieve the stress of wintertime cabin fever. There is a thoughtful display on the Copper River and Northwestern Railway, along with examples of copper jewelry and tools.

Visitors can also discover more about local history at the **Ilanka Cultural Center**, founded to preserve the culture of the Eyak group – in fact, the last Native speaker of the Eyak language died in 2008. The Eyak people's stories are told through an interesting collection of artifacts and photographs. Other exhibits include a complete orca skeleton and a contemporary shame pole. The work of carver Mike Webber, this totem pole follows a coastal Native tradition of publicly

> **Little Cordova offers a slice of the independent, self-sufficient character of "old Alaska" that has faded in more accessible places.**

shaming someone – in this case the Exxon Corporation – for not repaying a debt. The center also provides studio space for Eyak artisans.

Founded immediately after the 1989 oil spill *(p117)*, the **Prince William Sound Science Center** at the entrance to Cordova's harbor is home to teams of research scientists studying the Prince William Sound ecosystem. The center offers a fine view from the deck overlooking the water. The researchers here can answer questions and provide insights into the long- term effects of the *Exxon Valdez* oil spill *(p116)*. The center also offers numerous educational programs. These include holding field trips and science projects for families and adults, informative scientific seminars in isolated communities around Prince William Sound, and summer camps for local schoolchildren.

Cordova Historical Museum
🅰🅰622 1st St 📞424-6665 🕒Late May–early Sep: 10am–5pm Tue–Sat

Ilanka Cultural Center
🅰110 Nicholoff Way 🕒Summer: 10am–5pm Mon–Fri; winter: 10am–5pm Tue–Fri 🆆nveyak.com/ilanka-cultural-center

Prince William Sound Science Center
🅰300 Breakwater Ave, Cordova Harbor 🕒8:30am–5:30pm Mon–Fri 🆆pwssc.org

→

Mike Webber's Shame Pole in the Ilanka Cultural Center

Totem Bight State Historical Park near Ketchikan

SOUTHEAST ALASKA

The narrow panhandle of Southeast Alaska is in some respects the cornerstone of Alaska's governmental and economic history. Long occupied by Tlingit, Haida, and Shimshian coastal Native groups, the region was all but invaded in the late 1700s by Russian fur traders, drawn by the large numbers of sea otters that brought high prices for their fur. Conflict ensued when the town of Sitka was established as a headquarters for the Russian-American Company in 1799, much to the detriment of the local Tlingit community.

Settlement elsewhere in Southeast Alaska was driven not by furs, but by gold. As signs of the precious metal were found at Gold Creek, a small community there grew exponentially, eventually becoming the town of Juneau. Skagway, located at the head of Lynn Canal, became the jumping-off point for miners headed up the treacherous Chilkoot Pass on their way to the Klondike gold-fields in the Yukon Territory. It was a place of debauchery and crime, managed by Jefferson Randall "Soapy" Smith and his gang.

When the rushes waned near the end of the 19th century, it became clear that another industry was needed to keep the economy buoyant. Commercial fishing was the answer, and canneries sprang up in towns such as Ketchikan, Petersburg, and Wrangell along the coastline, and on Prince of Wales Island. With glacial ice available to keep the fish frozen, and plenty of manpower on hand for the demanding work, fishing amply sustained the economies of the region. It was later joined by other industries such as logging, which until the 1980s was a key generator of jobs. Today, Southeast Alaska is the favored venue for most Alaska cruises, with local economies being increasingly driven by tourism.

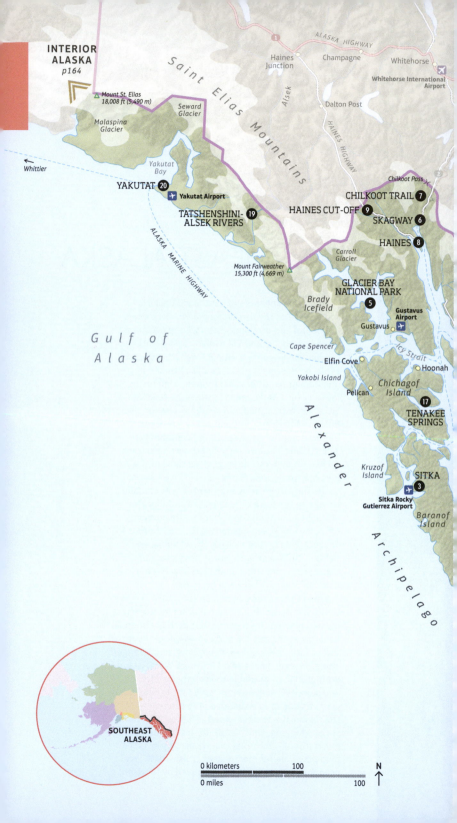

INTERIOR
ALASKA
p164

Saint Elias Mountains

△ Mount St. Elias
18,008 ft (5,490 m)

Seward
Glacier

Malaspina
Glacier

Yakutat
Bay

← Whittier

YAKUTAT ❷⓿ ✈ Yakutat Airport

TATSHENSHINI-
ALSEK RIVERS ❶❾

ALASKA MARINE HIGHWAY

Mount Fairweather
15,300 ft (4,669 m) △

Brady
Icefield

G u l f   o f
A l a s k a

Cape Spencer

Elfin Cove

Yakobi Island

Pelican

Gulf of Alaska

ALASKA HIGHWAY ①

Haines
Junction   Champagne   Whitehorse

Whitehorse International
Airport

Dalton Post

HAINES HIGHWAY

Alsek

Chilkoot Pass

CHILKOOT TRAIL ❼

HAINES CUT-OFF ❾

SKAGWAY ❻

HAINES ❽

Carroll
Glacier

GLACIER BAY
NATIONAL PARK

⑤

Gustavus
Airport ✈

Gustavus

Icy Strait

Hoonah

Chichagof
Island

TENAKEE
SPRINGS ❶❼

Kruzof
Island

SITKA

❸ ✈

Sitka Rocky
Gutierrez Airport

Baranof
Island

A l e x a n d e r   A r c h i p e l a g o

SOUTHEAST
ALASKA

0 kilometers   100

0 miles   100

N
↑

SOUTHEAST ALASKA

Must Sees
1 Prince of Wales Island
2 Ketchikan
3 Sitka
4 Juneau
5 Glacier Bay National Park
6 Skagway
7 Chilkoot Trail
8 Haines
9 Haines Cut-Off

Experience More
10 Hyder
11 Metlakatla
12 Misty Fiords National Monument
13 Wrangell
14 Anan Creek Wildlife Observatory
15 Mitkof Highway
16 Petersburg
17 Tenakee Springs
18 Admiralty Island National Monument
19 Tatshenshini-Alsek Rivers
20 Yakutat

ROCKY MOUNTAINS

Wolf Lake

Johnsons Crossing

Jakes Corner

Teslin

Carcross

Atlin

Teslin Lake

Atlin Lake

CANADA

Meszah Peak
7,100 ft (2,164 m)

Telegraph Creek

Strike

Juneau Icefield

Mendenhall Glacier

Juneau International Airport

4 JUNEAU

Douglas

18 ADMIRALTY ISLAND NATIONAL MONUMENT

Angoon

Admiralty Island

Coast Mountains

Mount Ratz
10,289 ft (3,136 m)

37

Kake
Kake Airport

Kupreanof Island

Kuiu Island

Petersburg Airport

16 PETERSBURG

MITKOF HIGHWAY
15

Wrangell Airport

13
WRANGELL

Point Baker

Wrangell Island

Mt Willibert
6,759 ft (2,060 m)

Mount Pattullo
8,953 ft (2,729 m)

Meziadin Junction

Port Alexander

Christian Sound

Coronation Island

Noyes Island

Baker Island

Coffman Cove

Cleveland Peninsula

14 ANAN CREEK
WILDLIFE OBSERVATORY

Stewart

HYDER 10

Cranberry Junction

37

Klawock Airport

Thorne Bay

Revillagigedo Island

12 MISTY FIORDS
NATIONAL MONUMENT

Klawock
Craig
Hollis

1 PRINCE OF
WALES ISLAND

Hydaburg

2 KETCHIKAN

Ketchikan Airport
Saxman

11
METLAKATLA

Terrace

Dall Island

Cape Muzon

Cape Chacon

Prince Rupert

Skeena

16

A bird's-eye view of the densely forested Prince of Wales island

1

PRINCE OF WALES ISLAND

🅰 G7 🏠 50 miles (80 km) NW of Ketchikan ✈ From Ketchikan ⛴ From Ketchikan or Wrangell ℹ www.visitpow.com

Prince of Wales Island, the third-largest in the US after Hawaii and Kodiak, lies mostly within the Tongass National Forest. It is home to both the Haida and Tlingit peoples, as well as a number of outsiders attracted by its beauty and solitude. One of the most pleasurable activities here is simply to drive through the forests and muskeg of the interior.

①
Craig

🏠 90 miles (145 km) W of Ketchikan ✈ Charter floatplane ⛴ To Hollis ℹ USFS, 900 9th St; www.princeofwalescoc.org

The largest town on the island, Craig is also its only community without a Native majority. It was named for Craig Millar who, with the help of local Haida, set up the first saltery on Fish Egg Island in 1907, followed by a sawmill and a salmon cannery. Due to poor salmon runs, fishing declined in the 1950s, but in 1972, the Head Sawmill, north of Craig, boosted the town's faltering economy. Today, Craig is the island's service center, with a bank, hotel, and several restaurants.

②
Klawock

🏠 5 miles (8 km) N of Craig ✈⛴ To Hollis ℹ 6488 Klawock-Hollis Hwy; www.princeofwalescoc.org

Named for the first Tlingit settler, Kloo-wah, the village of Klawock was originally a summer fishing camp. A trading post and saltery were set up here in 1868, and a decade later it became the site of Alaska's first salmon cannery. Today, the town boasts a hatchery on the shores of Klawock Lake, a sawmill, a log-sorting yard, and a dock for loading timber. In keeping with the timber theme, electricity is provided by a wood-fired generator.

Klawock Totem Park, next to the library, has about 20 restored poles from Tuxekan, a Tlingit winter village to the north. Across the Hollis-Craig Highway from the Chamber of Commerce is the Gaan Ax Adi Clan House, with a carving shed where visitors may sometimes see new totems being carved. The airport, the only one on the island, has an unattended 6,000-ft (1,800-m) paved runway with pilot-controlled lighting – remarkable given its location.

③
Hydaburg

🏠 45 miles (72 km) SE of Craig ✈ Charter floatplane

As rural Alaska towns go, the little Haida village of Hydaburg is as picturesque as it gets. Although the town was only founded in 1912, when the three villages of Sukkwan, Howkan, and Klinkwan combined, Haida peoples

💬 **INSIDER TIP**
Inter-Island Ferry

The Inter-Island Ferry *(www.interislandferry. com)* travels year round between the city of Hollis and Ketchikan, and is a wonderful way to enjoy the wildlife and scenic landscape.

have occupied the area since the 18th century, when they migrated here from British Columbia. Today, the town has the largest Haida population in Alaska.

Hydaburg's Totem Park is well worth a visit. Its collection of restored totems, with their unique emphasis on pastel colors, stands apart from others in the region.

④
Thorne Bay

🏠 **39 miles (63 km) NE of Craig** ✈ **Floatplane from Ketchikan**

During its heyday in the mid-20th century, Thorne Bay was North America's largest

logging camp, but the mill closed in the 1990s and the local economy now depends on fishing. A popular visitor attraction here is the Honker Divide Canoe Route, a three-to four-day trail that begins at Coffman Cove Road and winds through a chain of lakes down to Thorne Bay.

⑤
Kasaan

🏠 **49 miles (79 km) E of Craig** ✈ **Charter floatplane**

Deriving its name from the Tlingit word for "pretty town," Kasaan does indeed have a lovely setting between forested mountains and the sea. In the 1930s, the Haida Chief Sonihat built the Whale clan house, and the various totems around the village were transferred to the same site, forming the Kasaan Totem Park. A 15-minute trail through beachside woods leads to the picturesque park, where the decaying poles and clan house are almost swallowed by the undergrowth. Be aware that during salmon runs, black bears are known to frequent the trails.

⑥
El Capitan Cave

🏠 **Mile 50, N Prince of Wales Rd** ✈ 🕐 **By guided tour only: 9am, noon, & 2:30pm** 🌐 **fs.usda.gov/recmain/tongass/recreation**

Sited northwest of Whale Pass, El Capitan Cave is the largest and longest of the limestone caves dotted around the karst region of northern Prince of Wales Island. Inside these caves, paleontologists have uncovered human remains dating back about 9,500 years, the oldest found in the region. Over 2 miles (3 km) of passageways in El Capitan Cave have been surveyed. Reservations for tours must be made two days in advance, but occasionally, walk-ins are allowed. Helmets and headlamps need to be worn and children must be at least 7 years old. The tour begins with a steep climb up 367 steps.

FORESTRY IN SOUTHEAST ALASKA

Since the late 19th century, forestry and forest products have been an economic factor in the Tongass National Forest. From the 1940s to 1990s, they were the mainstay of the economy. The western hemlock and Sitka spruce of Southeast Alaska were exported, while lower-quality timber was reduced to pulp for the paper industry. In the 1990s, economic and environmental pressures caused the closure of the Sitka and Ketchikan mills. Today the industry plays only a minor role in Alaska's economy.

0 kilometers 50
0 miles 50
N

Creek Street and *(inset)* totem poles at the Southeast Alaska Discovery Center ↑

2

KETCHIKAN

🏠 G7 🏠 235 miles (378 km) S of Juneau ✈🚌 Bellingham–Skagway
ℹ Front St and Cruise Ship berths; www.visit-ketchikan.com

Situated on the southwestern end of Revillagigedo Island, Ketchikan thrives as a major stop for cruise ships and as a regional service center. It likes to call itself Alaska's First City, because it is the first city that visitors see when arriving in Alaska on a cruise ship or ferry.

↑ An energetic display of sawing in the Great Alaskan Lumberjack Show

Originally a Tlingit fish camp called Kitschk-Hin (meaning "thundering eagle wings creek"), the city began to grow in 1885 when Irishman Mike Martin staked a claim near Ketchikan Creek and set up a fish cannery. By the 1930s, Ketchikan's dozen canneries had earned it the title Salmon Capital of the World. Its other big economic resource, the Ketchikan Pulp Company's paper mill at Ward Cove, operated for over 40 years until it shut down in 1997.

A fun way to find out about the importance of the timber trade to the city is to see the Great Alaskan Lumberjack Show, held in an amphitheater on the site of the old Ketchikan Spruce Mill. The show includes displays of sawing, tree-climbing, and log-rolling. For more background information on the economy, history and culture of the region, visit the Southeast Alaska Discovery Center, both a museum and a visitor center for the 26,000-sq-mile (68,000-sq-km) Tongass National Forest, the lush temperate rain-forest which covers the region.

Covering the seedier side of Ketchikan's history is Dolly's House, a former bordello located on the once notorious Creek Street, the city's red-light district for half a century. Visitors learn interesting facts here, such as how Creek Street's construction lent itself to surreptitious trapdoor deliveries of alcohol after it was banned by the 1917 Bone Dry Law.

TOTEM POLES

The coastal groups of Tlingit, Haida, and Tsimshian have long used totem poles to tell stories and honor individuals, as well as to provide structural support for buildings. Never meant to be objects of veneration, they are cultural symbols of clan identification, most often carved from western red cedar and painted in symbolic colors.

Around Ketchikan

Founded in 1894, the Native village of Saxman (3 miles/4.5 km southeast of Ketchikan) has the finest display of totem poles in Southeast Alaska. Begun in the late 1930s as a Civilian Conservation Corps (CCC) project, Saxman Totem Park is today a popular attraction housing the workshops of Alaska's best totem carvers.

Renovated totem poles can also be seen at Totem Bight State Historical Park, 10 miles (16 km) northwest of Ketchikan. As Europeans established permanent settlements in this region, many Natives joined them, and their traditional villages fell into ruins. In 1938, the CCC launched a project to restore old totem poles that lay rotting in abandoned villages. By 1942, 15 poles and a clan house had been completed. Today, a walkway between the totems leads to the water and a replica clan house that would have held 30 to 50 people.

3

SITKA

A F7 **A** 96 miles (155 km) NW of Petersburg ✈🚌
i 104 Lake St; www.sitka.org

One of Alaska's most beautiful towns, Sitka sits beside an island-studded sea on the west coast of Baranof Island. It began life in 1799 as a fort named Redoubt St. Michael, set up by Russians hunting for sea otter pelts. After local Tlingit destroyed the fort in 1804, the Russians established the fortified town of Novo Archangelsk. By 1808, this was the capital of Russian America and was flourishing economically and culturally. When the US bought Alaska in 1867, the town's name was changed to Sitka, a contraction of Shee Atiká, the Tlingit name for the settlement.

① 🎨 🏛

Sitka History Museum

A 330 Harbor Dr **⏰** May-Sep: 8am-4:30pm Mon-Fri
w sitkahistory.com

Housed in the Harrigan Centennial Hall, this museum outlines Sitka's history from the Russian era to the present, including exhibits on mining, forestry, and World War II. In addition to a model of Sitka at the time of its transfer to the United States, the museum's highlights include Tlingit art, tools, and spruce baskets. There are also trade beads, Russian weapons, historical photographs, and a unique "tea brick." These blocks of compressed Cantonese tea were acquired by the Russians from the Chinese in exchange for the sea otter pelts that formed the basis of Russian Alaska's economy.

Outside, a large Haida ceremonial canoe is on display beneath a canopy. In the summer, the New Archangel Dancers perform in traditional Russian costume for tourists.

② 🎨 🏛

Sheldon Jackson Museum

A 104 College Dr
⏰ May-Sep: 9am-4:30pm daily; Oct-Apr: 10am-4pm Tue-Sat **w** museums.alaska.gov

From 1888 to 1898, the Presbyterian Reverend Sheldon Jackson traveled around Alaska representing the US educational system. In the course of his travels, he collected the Indigenous artifacts that are displayed here, including hunting tools, masks, kayaks, and reindeer sleighs. During the summer months, Native artisans come to the museum to demonstrate crafts such as weaving and carving. The museum shop offers a nice variety of Native handcrafted goods and artwork.

> **In the summer months, Native artisans come to the museum to demonstrate crafts such as weaving and carving.**

←

A view of Sitka harbour, with the Gavan Hill and Sisters Mountains in the background

was sadly lost. One surviving artifact, an icon known as the Madonna of Sitka, has been credited with miraculous healing powers. The reconstruction, this time in fire-resistant materials, took place from 1967 to 1972, and the new cathedral was consecrated in 1976. Visitors are welcome to attend services held here.

③ ✍

St. Michael's Russian Orthodox Cathedral

🏛 240 Lincoln St ⏰ May–Sep: 9am–4pm Mon–Fri, or when cruise ships are in port; winter: by appt 🌐 oca.org/parishes/oca-ak-sitsmk

This onion-domed cathedral is the quintessential Sitka landmark. The cornerstone was laid by Bishop Veniaminov, St. Innocent of Alaska, in 1844, and construction was completed a few years later in 1848. The present church is a replica of the original, which burned down in a fire in 1966. Although locals managed to rescue the paintings, icons, chandelier, and the partially melted bronze bells, the large library of works in Russian, Tlingit, and Aleut languages

📷 **PICTURE PERFECT**
A View with a Bridge

Sitka's John O'Connell bridge is a cable-stayed structure connecting downtown Sitka on Baranof Island with the town's airport and US Coast Guard station on Japonski Island. Completed in 1971, it is an engineering marvel and the site for many a sunset photo.

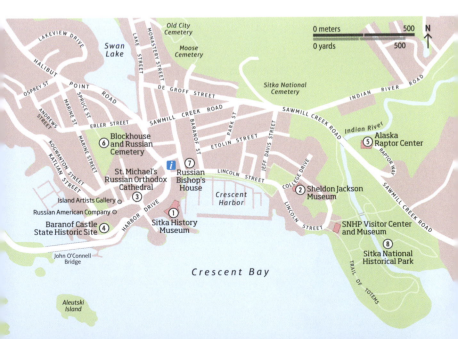

←
Baranof Castle, the site of the official transfer ceremony from Russia in 1867

building lies the somewhat overgrown Russian cemetery, where hundreds of graves recall 18th- and 19th-century Russian Sitka.

(7)

Russian Bishop's House

🏠 Lincoln & Monastery Sts 🚌 Community Ride ⏰ May-Sep: 8:30am-5pm daily; winter: by appt 🌐 nps.gov/sitk

The oldest building in Sitka, this 1843 structure is one of the few surviving examples of secular Russian architecture in the town. The original building was made from spruce by

---

(4)

Baranof Castle State Historic Site

🏠 Harbor Road 🌐 dnr.alaska.gov/parks/aspunits/southeast/baranofcastle

Popularly known as "Castle Hill Park," this historic mound of land standing in the middle of downtown Sitka is one of Alaska's most culturally relevant places. Originally the home of Tlingit groups, it was inhabited by Russians from 1804 to 1867. When the United States took possession of Alaska in 1867 (p57), Castle Hill was the site of the transfer ceremony. Also a National Historic Landmark, the park has a range of walking paths, interpretive signs, and special events held on Alaska Day each October.

---

(5)

Alaska Raptor Center

🏠 1000 Raptor Way 🚌 Community Ride ⏰ May-Sep: 8am-4pm daily; Oct-Apr: 10am-3pm Mon-Fri 🌐 alaskaraptor.org

One of the state's best raptor hospitals and rehabilitation centers, the non-profit Alaska Raptor Center treats injured ravens and raptors such as eagles, falcons, owls, and hawks, and tries to readapt them to life in the wild. Seriously wounded birds become Raptors-in-Residence and are used in educational programs for visitors.

---

(6)

Blockhouse and Russian Cemetery

🏠 Kogwantan & Marine Sts ⏰ Blockhouse: late May-early Sep: noon-4pm Sun; cemetery: 24 hrs daily

North of St. Michael's Russian Orthodox Cathedral sits a reconstruction of an octagonal two-story blockhouse that was used by the Russians to shield their redoubt from the Tlingit. Just behind the

←
A rescued bald eagle at the Alaska Raptor Center

Finnish woodworkers, who introduced a Baltic-style opulence to Russian America. Despite the building's flamboyance, its first occupant, Bishop Veniaminov, lived a very simple monastic life.

Over the years, the building has served as an orphanage, seminary, and school. The last Russian bishop moved out in 1969 and the building was purchased in 1972 by the US National Park Service for restoration. On the main floor is a model of Novo Archangelsk as it looked in 1845 and a collection of icons and relics. To see the library, chapel, and bishop's quarters, it is necessary to join a guided tour.

⑧ Ⓜ 🛍

Sitka National Historical Park

🏠 103 Monastery St
🕐 May–Sep: 6am–10pm daily; Oct–Apr: 7am–8pm daily 🗓 Federal hols
🖥 nps.gov/sitk

Alaska's oldest federal park was established in 1910 to commemorate the 1804 Battle of Sitka. In 1802, Tlingit warriors of the Kiks.ádi group attacked the Russian redoubt, killing most of the Russian and Aleut personnel. Two years later, the Russians returned with four ships and beseiged the Tlingit fort at the mouth of the Indian River. After much bloodshed, the Russians broke into the fort to find that it had been abandoned by the Tlingit. Today, the battleground and fort site form part of the park. They are accessed from the visitor center and museum via trails that lead through rainforest past nearly a dozen Northwest Coast totem poles. To the north, across the creek, is the Russian Memorial.

→

A totem pole at the entrance to a trail in Sitka National Historical Park

4

JUNEAU

F6 ⬆ 95 miles (153 km) NE of Sitka ✈ ⛴ Auke Bay Terminal ℹ 470 S Franklin St; www.traveljuneau.com

Often described as a little San Francisco owing to its hilly setting, Alaska's capital is located between Mount Juneau and Mount Roberts along Gastineau Channel. The 1880 discovery of gold here by Joe Juneau and Dick Harris and Juneau's strategic location on the route to the Klondike goldfields established the town's importance and led to it taking over the role of Alaska's capital from Sitka in 1900. In the mid-1970s, Alaskans voted to move the state capital to Willow, but owing to projected costs, they reversed the decision in 1982.

↑ The imposing entrance to the Alaska State Capitol Building

① Alaska State Capitol Building

🏛 4th & Main Sts 🕐 7am-5pm Mon-Fri

Designed to serve as the seat of the Territorial Government, this marble Art Deco building was completed in 1931. Today it houses the Alaska State Legislature and the offices of the Governor and Lieutenant Governor. A state map made from a slice of the Trans-Alaska Pipeline is on display near the staircase, and decorative details showcase aspects of Alaska's culture. There are free tours daily in summer.

② Alaska State Museum

🏛 395 Whittier St 🕐 May-Sep: 9am-5pm daily; Oct-Apr: 10am-4pm Tue-Sat 🌐 museums.alaska.gov

The Alaska State Museum has an impressive collection reflecting many facets of Alaska history, ranging from prehistoric times to modern days. On the ramp to the second floor is a mock rainforest, complete with recorded birdsong and a replica bald eagle nest. Displayed along the walls of the ramp are a range of Native artifacts, including dolls, masks, baskets, and models of traditional canoes. There is also a collection of Native ivory "billikens" upstairs. These charming elf-like figurines have now become mainstays of Alaska's tourist trade. Russian America is represented

South Franklin Street, one of Juneau's most popular shopping streets ↑

Must See

by a collection of icons and samovars, while mining tools bring the Gold Rush to life. Other highlights include a mineral collection, the pen used by President Dwight Eisenhower to sign the bill that gave Alaska its statehood, and a children's area.

③

Wickersham State Historical Site

📍 213 7th St 🕐 Late-May-late Sep: 10am–5pm Sun-Thu; late Sep–late May: by appt 🌐 dnr.alaska.gov/parks/units/wickrshm.htm

The historic Wickersham house, built in 1898, was once the home of Judge James Wickersham, who served as the voice of the law in more than half of Territorial Alaska. As a delegate to Congress, the judge introduced an Alaska Statehood Bill in 1916, planting the seeds of an idea that would come to fruition in 1959. After his death in 1939, his niece Ruth Allman opened the house to the public. In 1984, the house and its relics were purchased by the state and turned into a museum, with photos, furnishings, and other memorabilia providing a unique insight into Alaska's early frontier days. Entry to the house is free, but donations are welcome.

SHOP

Alaska State Museum Gift Shop
Outstanding art, jewelry, and crafts.

📍 395 Whittier Street
📞 465-2901

Treetop Tees
T-shirts, beanies, and blankets with graphics unique to Juneau.

📍 110 Franklin Street
🌐 treetoptees.com

Hearthside Books and Toys
A bookstore featuring a wide range of titles authored by Alaskans. Also good for toys.

📍 2 Marine Way, Ste 119
🌐 hearthsidebooks.com

The retro bar of the famed Red Dog Saloon and *(inset)* its easy-to-spot entrance

Red Dog Saloon

- 278 S Franklin St
- 11am–11pm daily
- reddogsaloon.com

During Juneau's mining heyday in the late 19th century, this Saloon offered alcohol, entertainment, and dancing to travelers and local miners. The Harris family bought the place in 1973 and turned it into a bar. Popular with visitors, it has become a bit of a tourist trap, offering food, drinks, and live music in a retro setting.

⑤ Last Chance Mining Museum

- 1001 Basin Rd 586-5338 Mid-May–late Sep: 9:30am–12:30pm & 3:30–5:30pm daily

The only remnants of the Juneau goldfields are the old buildings and relics of the Last Chance Mining Museum. It is located in the mine's old service center, which once housed dormitories, assay offices, and machine repair shops. The museum displays what was once the world's largest air compressor, a variety of different mining tools, and a three-dimensional representation of the mine tunnels that wind through the adjacent mountain.

⑥ Juneau-Douglas City Museum

- 114 W 4th 3, 5
- Summer: 9am–6pm Mon-Fri, 10am–4:30pm Sat & Sun; winter: 10am–4pm Tue-Sat beta.juneau.org/library/museum

Housed just across the street from the Capitol and standing on the site of the official statehood ceremony in 1959, this museum captures the spirit of Juneau and the tiny community of Douglas, across Gastineau Channel from downtown. Look for interactive displays about Juneau's early history, the mining industry, and an excellent timeline of Alaska's march to statehood. There are also fascinating exhibits about centuries-old Tlingit groups in the area, and Southeast Alaska's connection to the sea. Children will particularly enjoy a visit to this large museum, which is full of kid-friendly displays that bring the exhibits to life. The store here sells a fine collection of Juneau memorabilia and art.

WALKING TOUR OF JUNEAU

The city has made it easy for visitors to explore on foot. Grab a walking tour map from one of the visitor centers or download one at Travel Juneau (www.traveljuneau.com) and start strolling. See the dockside memorials to fishermen, spy mountain goats with one of the provided telescopes, then head toward historic Franklin Street, Juneau's main shopping artery. A bracing walk uphill will take you to Seward Street and the historic homes built with views of Gastineau Channel. Finally, swing uphill to peaceful Cope Park.

⑦ 🎨 🏛️

Sealaska Heritage Institute

🏠 105 S Seward Street
🕐 Summer: 9am-8pm daily
🌐 sealaskaheritage.org

Housed in a beautiful cedar building in Juneau's downtown core, the Sealaska Heritage Institute is a collective facility explaining the cultures of Southeast Alaska's Tlingit, Haida, and Tshimshian people. Visitors can walk into a life-sized clan house, admire Native art and woodworking, and explore the craftwork of juried artisans on display throughout the year. A place worthy of lengthy exploration, the institute is a must-stop for anyone interested in the tribal hierarchy, traditions, and ways of life of Southeast Alaska Natives. There's also the chance to buy crafts and exquisitely carved jewelry.

⑧ 🎨 🍴 🖥️ 🏛️

Mount Roberts Tramway

🏠 490 S Franklin St
🕐 May-Sep: 8am-9pm daily 🌐 mountroberts tramway.com

The tramway that ascends the slopes of Mount Roberts offers panoramic views of Gastineau Channel and across to Douglas Island. At the summit, the Mountain House has a gift shop, a restaurant, and the Chilkat Theater, which screens a film on Tlingit culture. The short Alpine Loop trail winds through meadow and forest, past several Tlingit carvings, with a short side trip to Father Brown's Cross. If you are looking for a spot of exercise, it is also possible to hike up or down and only take the tram one way, but hikers should be prepared for steep trails and varying weather patterns.

EAT

Tracy's King Crab Shack

Boasting "the best legs in town," Tracy's is a hub for king crab lovers. From crab rolls to an exquisite king crab bisque, this is the top place to savor the flavor and delicate texture of king crab.

🏠 432 S Franklin Street
🌐 kingcrabshack.com

$$ ⑤ ⑤ ⑤

Deckhand Dave's Fish Tacos

From Dave's tiny food truck - a Juneau staple - come crunchy salads, excellent smoked salmon chowder, and the freshest tacos made with Alaska salmon.

🏠 139 S Franklin Street
🌐 deckhanddaves.com

$$ ⑤ ⑤ ⑤

SALT

A sleek, modern establishment that took Juneau by storm several years ago, SALT is a place to celebrate Alaska's leap into the world of fine dining. Dishes inspired by Southeast Alaska's ingredients make dinner an experience, not a process. Look for reserve spirits and wines, too.

🏠 200 Seward Street
🌐 saltalaska.com

$$ ⑤ ⑤ ⑤

← The Mount Roberts Tramway, offering dizzying views over Juneau's fabulous setting

BEYOND JUNEAU

⑨ 🏛

Shrine of St. Therese of Lisieux

🏛 21425 (Mile 22) Glacier Hwy ⏰ Apr–Sep: 8:30am–10pm daily; Oct–Mar: 8:30am–8pm daily 🌐 shrine ofsainttherese.org

This peaceful pilgrimage site lies on Shrine Island at the end of a 400-ft (120-m) pedestrian causeway. Built of beach stone, the Catholic chapel occupies a lovely forested spot with views across the sea to the peaks of the Chilkat Range. It is dedicated to the 19th-century French saint Therese de Lisieux, who is the patron saint of the state.

⑩ 🏛

Juneau Icefield

📍 Accessible by flightseeing or helicopter tour only

The impressive Juneau Icefield sprawls across 1,500 sq miles (3,885 sq km) of the Coast Range. Its highest peak is the very steep 8,584-ft (2,616-m) Devil's Paw, which straddles the US-Canada border.

The icefield feeds about 40 large and 100 small glaciers. Of these, only Taku Glacier continues to advance and calve into Taku Inlet.

The most readily accessible portion of the icefield is the retreating Mendenhall Glacier. A hike to the rest of the vast white wilderness of the icefield can be quite challenging. Helicopter or flightseeing tours are possible, as well as summer dog-sled rides across the ice. Ice-climbing classes are also available.

⑪ 🏛 🏛 🏛

Mendenhall Glacier

🏛 8150 Mendenhall Loop Rd ⏰ May–Sep: 8am–7:30pm daily; Oct–Apr: 10am–4pm Fri–Sun 🌐 fs.usda.gov/main/tongass/home

Spilling into the Mendenhall Valley from the vast Juneau Icefield, the large Mendenhall Glacier was first called Auke Glacier after the nearby Tlingit village, Aak'w Kwaan. In 1892, it was renamed in honor of physicist Thomas Mendenhall, who surveyed the international border between Canada and Southeast Alaska.

Several trails access the glacier. The East Glacier Loop follows the glacial trimline, while the West Glacier Trail goes up to the glacier's west face. The Moraine Ecology Trail has information panels explaining the regeneration of vegetation on deglaciated areas. The Photo Point Trail is lined with benches and interpretive panels, and provides the best vantage points to capture panoramic shots of the glacier.

At Mendenhall Lake, which is often choked with icebergs calved from the glacier, the huge curving glass wall of the Mendenhall Glacier Visitor Center offers fabulous views of the glacier across the lake. An exhibit hall has information on glaciers, and a theater shows films on icefield geology. A salmon-viewing platform and a fish-cam provide views of spawning salmon moving up Steep Creek from mid-July to mid-September.

Dobson Landing

⑨ Shrine of St. Therese of Lisieux

⑩ Juneau Icefield

Mendenhall Glacier ⑪

Suicide Glacier

Peterson Lake

GLACIER HIGHWAY

Mendenhall Lake

Bullard Mountain ▲ 4,226 ft (1,288 m)

Auke Bay

Mendenhall Valley

Auke Bay

Coghlan Island

⑫ Glacier Gardens

Alaskan Brewing Company

Juneau International Airport

Lemon Creek

⑬ Macaulay Salmon Hatchery

See Juneau map on p137

Douglas Island

Douglas

0 km 5
0 miles 5

N

↑ Walking through an ice cave in an iceberg on Mendenhall Lake

DRINK

Alaskan Brewing Company

The state's oldest microbrewing company, Alaskan Brewing has been in operation since 1986 and started the trend of small-batch beer with local flavors. Stop by for a series of samples and take a tour of the company's unique system, which uses leftover spent grain to power the vats for "beer-powered beer." Located a few miles out of downtown; a shuttle transports visitors from the downtown brewing depot.

🅐 5364 Commercial
🅦 alaskanbeer.com

Devil's Club Brewing Company

Brewing Belgian-style ales and offering sandwiches and snacks to fill up hungry visitors, the brewery does a brisk business all year long. Be sure to check out the latest seasonal specials.

🅐 100 North Franklin Street
🅦 devilsclub brewing.com

Amalga Distillery

Amalga is Juneau's inaugural distillery, and its stillhouse is conveniently located next door to its tasting room. Try the Juneauper Gin, or the exquisite, newly released single-malt whisky.

🅐 134 N Franklin Street
🅦 amalgadistillery.com

⑫ 🗺 Ⓜ 🏛

Glacier Gardens

🅐 7600 Glacier Hwy
🕐 May-Sep: 9am-6pm daily
🅦 glaciergardens.com

Nearly surrounded by the Tongass National Forest, the 52-acre (21-ha) Glacier Gardens are a pleasant blend of groomed gardens and natural rainforest, including a series of artificial streams and ponds flanked by lovely plantings. A collection of upended tree stumps dubbed "Flower Towers," salvaged from a devastating 1984 mudslide, form unusual planters for colorful hanging gardens of petunias, begonias, fuschias, and much else.

From the greenhouse, a succession of rainforest trails leads to boardwalks and a platform offering dramatic views of Gastineau Channel. For those who do not want to climb the steep hillside, the admission price includes transport by an electric golf cart through the woods, with an onboard commentary on the lush rainforest environment. Keep an eye out for the resident bald eagles that nest in the gardens in summer.

⑬ 🗺 Ⓜ 🏛

Macaulay Salmon Hatchery

🅐 2697 Channel Dr, 3 miles (5 km) N of downtown Juneau 🕐 May-Sep: 10am-6pm Mon-Fri, 10am-5pm Sat & Sun 🅦 dipac.net

A working hatchery that provides fry to stock streams in many areas of Southeast Alaska, the highly interesting Macaulay Salmon Hatchery raises around 130 million chum, king, and coho salmon each year. It also has over 100 species of local sealife on view in a number of large saltwater aquariums. Outside the building, walkways lead past several tanks where fry of various ages are fed and reared until they are ready for release into the surrounding waterways. Small salmon are also released into nearby Twin Lakes for recreational anglers.

Between June and October, a 450-ft (135-m) fish ladder provides easy access for pink and chum salmon returning to the hatchery to spawn and produce their fry. Visitors can also purchase a variety of local salmon products in the hatchery shop.

5 〽️ 🍴 🛍️

GLACIER BAY NATIONAL PARK

🅰️F6 📍75 miles (105 km) NW of Juneau ✈️🚢From Juneau 🚌Gustavus-Bartlett Cove shuttle bus 🕐May & Sep: 8am–5pm daily; Jun–Aug: 7am–7pm daily
ℹ️NPS Visitor Center, Glacier Bay Lodge, Bartlett Cove; www.nps.gov/glba

A UNESCO World Heritage Site, Glacier Bay National Park comprises 5,000 sq miles (13,000 sq km) of pristine mountains and waterways. It is a living laboratory for scientists and a picturesque retreat for visitors.

Best known for its tidewater glaciers and deep fjords, Glacier Bay is a biosphere for scientists studying climate change, with some of the purest air on the planet. Its forests and alpine peaks are habitats for bears, wolves, moose, and mountain goats, and the water is home to humpback whales and the occasional orca. Home to Huna Tlingit groups for centuries, the bay has been a prime destination for visitors since naturalist John Muir made his way here in the 1800s.

Ancestral Homeland

For many years, however, the Huna Tlingit were barred from engaging in subsistence practices here owing to the National Park protections, and the relationship between the National Park Service and local Huna Tlingit groups was extremely strained. When Glacier Bay was made a national monument by President Calvin Coolidge in 1925, the Huna Tlingit were not consulted. Understandably angry at this designation by a distant United

States government, the Huna felt the nation took advantage of their lack of English language knowledge. The park service continued to limit Huna Tlingit tribal access, first by restricting firearm use under the guise of protecting brown bears, then through outlawing all hunting and trapping. By 1976, even the trapping of seals was illegal, and the Huna had no way of practicing the subsistence lifestyle that had sustained them for centuries. Bowing to repeated calls to respect the Alaska Natives' right to subsist in their ancestral home, the National Park Service began constructive talks in 1997, and in 2016 the Huna Tribal House was dedicated to provide a meeting place where the Huna Tlingit can reconnect with their homeland. Visitors to Bartlett Cove, known as the entrance to Glacier Bay National Park, are able to view a presentation and see dancing and drumming in the Huna Tribal House, which celebrates a hard-won piece of Alaska culture.

↑ The Huna Tribal House, located at Bartlett Cove

← Hiking along a boardwalk trail through lush forest near Bartlett Cove

↑ Margerie Glacier, one of the seven tidewater glaciers at Glacier Bay

EXPLORING GLACIER BAY NATIONAL PARK

Most visitors to the park arrive via cruise ship or organized boat tour, which are strictly regulated by a National Park Service agreement. However, it is also possible to explore the waters independently by kayak or small boat, as well as hike or camp on land, provided that you obtain a permit from the National Park Service. The park's headquarters are at Bartlett Cove, which is also the location of the Huna Tribal House *(p143)*. There are several short hiking trails that loop through the forest here, and the beach is an excellent place to see

The best views of Glacier Bay are from the water, surrounded by the evocative sounds of calving glaciers.

a wide variety of birds. The best views of Glacier Bay are from the water, surrounded by the evocative sounds of calving glaciers, blowing whales, and the wind whistling through alpine meadows.

*Of the seven tidewater glaciers that calve icebergs into the bay, **Margerie Glacier** is the most visited. It was once a tributary of the Grand Pacific Glacier, which has retreated 70 miles (112 km) in the past 200 years.*

*The forbidding **Fairweather Range**, which culminates at the 15,300-ft- (4,663-m-) high Mount Fairweather, was the source of the ice that created the park's deeply indented fjords. The range continues to feed the glaciers on the western peninsula of the park.*

Mount Barnard
8,214 ft (2,504 m)

Rendu Glacier

Tarr Inlet

Margerie Glacier

Mount Fairweather
15,300 ft (4,663 m)

Fairweather Glacier

Lamplugh Glacier

Fairweather Range

Mount Abbe
8,750 ft (2,667m)

Reid Glacier

Lituya Glacier

North Crillon Glacier

Mount Crillon
12,726 ft (3,879 m)

Brady Icefield

Crillon Lake

Mount La Perouse
10,728 ft (3,270 m)

La Perouse Glacier

Brady Glacier

Icy Point

Cape Spencer

← *The majestic peaks of the Fairweather Range, which dominate the western side of the park*

Looking for whales and other marine mammals on a cruise through Glacier Bay

Takhinsha Mountains

Muir Glacier

Cushing Glacier

Mount Brock
4,990 ft (1,521 m)

Sitth-gha-ee Peak
5,870 ft (1,789 m)

Carroll Glacier

Casement Glacier

Mount Rice
5,658 ft (1,725 m)

Mount Merriam
5,083 ft (1,549 m)

Muir Inlet

Mount Wright
5,139 ft (1,566 m)

Beartrack Mountains

Glacier Bay

Drake Island

Excursion Ridge

Excursion River

Willoughby Island

Bartlett River

Wood Lake

Dundas River

Barlett Cove

Gustavus

Lemesurier Island

Inian Island

Cross Sound

Black-and-white killer whales (orcas) and humpback whales can frequently be spotted in **Glacier Bay**, along with sea otters, sea lions, and harbor porpoises. Boats are not allowed within 500 yards (450 m) of the whales, so bring binoculars.

The village of **Gustavus**, outside the southeast corner of the park, prospered in the 1920s as an agricultural homestead area. It offers lodging and visitor services, and operators run tours and rent kayaks for private trips.

0 kilometers   20

0 miles   20

N

Several easy hikes are available around **Bartlett Cove**, the only developed area within the park. It has a visitor center, park headquarters, a lodge, a campground, and the lovely Huna Tribal House.

↑ The Gustavus Inn, one of several cosy accommodation options in Gustavus

6

SKAGWAY

A F6 **A** 15 miles (24 km) N of Haines **X** From Juneau and Haines **R** From Fraser and Bennett Lake, BC (Canada) **B** From Fraser, BC (Canada) **S** From Haines and Juneau **i** Broadway, between 2nd & 3rd Aves; www.skagway.com

Skagway was founded as a gateway to the goldfields in the late 1890s, with over 30,000 prospectors passing through in its first year. It later became an Alaska Highway construction staging camp in the 1940s, and today has an economy driven mainly by tourism.

①

Arctic Brotherhood Hall

A 245 Broadway

The unusual Arctic Brotherhood Hall – once the meeting place for a fraternity of gold miners and now housing the Skagway Convention and Visitors Bureau – is thought to be the most photographed structure in Alaska. The unique facade is made of 8,000-plus pieces of driftwood, installed in 1899 by the miners, and refurbished in 2005 after around 40 percent of the original siding had rotted away. The Arctic Brotherhood that met here was set up by a group of 11 gold prospectors; the hall – known originally as Camp Skagway No. 1 – was a place where miners could meet and support each other. The society spread to other gold mines, and at its height the fraternity membership numbered around 10,000 gold miners.

②

White Pass Yukon Route Railroad Depot

A 231 2nd Avenue Klondike Gold Rush

This historic building was constructed to accommodate the rush of businessmen and miners who arrived in the late 1890s with the hope of finding gold. Replacing an old shack, the structure stood as the main depot until the 1950s.

→

A monument celebrating the role of Native Tlingit guides in the Klondike Gold Rush

Klondike Gold Rush National Historical Park Visitor Center and Museum

🕐 Summer: 8:30am–5:30pm daily; winter: 8am–3pm Mon–Fri 🔗 nps.gov/klgo/planyourvisit/visitorcenter

③ 🖼️ 🍴

Red Onion Saloon

🏠 201 Broadway
🕐 10am–10pm daily
🔗 redonion1898.com

Not just a saloon, but a museum as well, the Red Onion relays the story of Skagway's colorful Gold Rush characters in the restored Brothel Museum above the pub. In the late 1880s, as men rushed into the territory to strike it rich, women arrived as well to offer their services to hardworking, hard-living miners. The saloon serves food and drink to visitors, including pizzas, cocktails and locally brewed beer, and the fun 20-minute museum tour, guided by a "Good Time Girl," explains the history and culture of Skagway at the turn of the 20th century. Visitors might even catch a glimpse of the resident ghost, Miss Lydia. The recommended age for tours is 14; no one under 21 is admitted without an adult guardian.

WHITE PASS AND YUKON ROUTE RAILROAD

The White Pass and Yukon Route Railroad (WP&YR) was built in 1898 to link Skagway with the Klondike, opening up the Interior to the outside world. Although the Gold Rush has long since ended, it is still possible to follow the trail of the prospectors on the railroad's hugely popular Summit Tour *(wpyr.com)*, a scenic, sometimes hair-raising journey to the White Pass Summit.

↑ Colorful timber buildings lining Skagway's main shopping street

It supported military efforts between Canada and the US during World War II, and operated as a major force in the success of the Alaska Highway and Trans-Alaska Pipeline construction processes. Now the headquarters of the Klondike Gold Rush National Historical Park (US Park Service), the building houses a number of interesting interpretive displays and makes a good starting point for exploring Skagway's historic downtown area.

Also inside the depot is the **Klondike Gold Rush National Historical Park Visitor Center and Museum**, full of exhibits documenting the colorful history of this Gold Rush town. A good first stop for visitors to Skagway, the center has ranger presentations, interactive exhibits on the Klondike Gold Rush, a theater, 3D maps, and a number of activities just for children, including the popular Junior Ranger program.

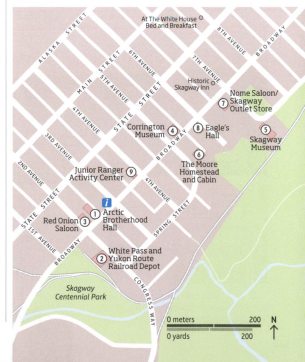

At The White House Bed and Breakfast

Alaska Street · 6th Avenue · 7th Avenue · 8th Avenue · Broadway

Main Street · 5th Avenue · State Street

4th Avenue

Historic Skagway Inn

Nome Saloon/Skagway Outlet Store ⑦

3rd Avenue

Corrington Museum ④ · ⑧ Eagle's Hall · ⑤ Skagway Museum

⑥ The Moore Homestead and Cabin

2nd Avenue

Junior Ranger Activity Center ⑨

4th Avenue · Spring Street

ℹ Arctic Brotherhood Hall

State Street · 1st Avenue · Broadway

Red Onion Saloon ③ · ①

② White Pass and Yukon Route Railroad Depot

Skagway Centennial Park

Congress Way

0 meters 200
0 yards 200

N

STAY

At The White House Bed and Breakfast

Located in a historic building, right at the heart of downtown. It features cosy quilts under which to snuggle at night and serves freshly baked goods for breakfast each morning.

🏠 **475 8th Avenue**
🌐 **atthewhite house.com**

$ $ $

Historic Skagway Inn

This charming inn was built in 1897 and has an adjacent restaurant - Olivia's - where guests are treated to fine dining in a delightfully quaint atmosphere.

🏠 **655 Broadway**
🌐 **skagwayinn.com**

$ $ $

> **Captain William Moore and his adult son Ben arrived in the quiet forest valley in anticipation of a "future Gold Rush" in 1887, building a log cabin that still stands**.

④

Corrington Museum

🏠 **575 Broadway** 📞 **907-983-2579** 🕐 **Hours vary, call ahead**

Constructed in 1975, the Corrington Museum may not be of great historical interest but is a good place to see Native basketry, ivory, and an impressive mammoth tusk.

---

⑤

Skagway Museum

🏠 **700 Spring Street**
🕐 **Summer: 9am-5pm Mon-Sat, 10am-4pm Sun**
🌐 **skagway.org/museum**

Established in 1961 as a community resource, this little museum holds a wealth of information about Skagway's early role as a transportation corridor. Exhibits also showcase some of Skagway's most notorious characters, such as Soapy Smith, and outline the cultural traditions of local Tlingit groups. Housed in the faux-Gothic McCabe College building, the museum's property was also used as a private school, a town hall, and a federal courthouse before transitioning to its current state.

---

⑥

The Moore Homestead and Cabin

🏠 **400 Spring Street**

Not every settler came to Skagway after the Gold Rush began. Captain William Moore and his adult son Ben arrived in the quiet forest valley in anticipation of a "future Gold Rush" in 1887, building a log cabin that still stands today. The family grew to include Ben's wife and children and was a stalwart force for the clearing of land for the White Pass trail. A petite frame house is also located on the

↑ An exhibit inside the Skagway Museum, housed (inset) in a stone building that was once a school

SOAPY SMITH

Born Jefferson Randolph Smith in Georgia in 1860, Soapy earned his nickname after a swindle involving soap. In 1896, he arrived in Skagway, opened a saloon, and set himself up as an underworld boss and local philanthropist. His most notorious scams included a phony freight company and a fake telegraph office that would "wire" money across non-existent wires. In 1898, this uncrowned "king" of Skagway was killed after a shootout with city surveyor Frank Reid.

homestead as a sign of the family's prosperity and efforts to grow Skagway. Both the cabin and home are operated by the National Park Service.

⑦ Nome Saloon/ Skagway Outlet Store

🏠 **678 Broadway**

Built in the fall of 1899, the two-story Nome Saloon was one of several lining Sixth Avenue. With a dance hall and gambling room, and later a variety theater, the place was always busy as men stopped in to wet their whistle and gamble their fortunes away.

The building is currently part of the Skagway Outlet Store complex, but it is still possible to get a sense of its character once you get past the merchandise displays.

⑧ Eagle's Hall

🏠 **601 Broadway**

Only members and their guests may go inside the Eagle's Hall, but the exterior of this historic building, dating from 1898, merits a look. It is best known for the Days of '98 Show, hosted here each summer. Produced by the local arts council, the show

re-creates the famous fatal shootout between Frank Reid and Soapy Smith.

⑨ Junior Ranger Activity Center

🏠 **291 Broadway** 🕐 **Mid-May–mid-Sep: 10am–noon & 1–3pm Mon–Fri** 🌐 **nps.gov/klgo/learn/kidsyouth/jrac**

The nation's only dedicated space for young ranger explorers, this activity center, located in the former Pantheon Saloon, features hands-on displays and exhibits created for kids – although visitors of all ages will enjoy the activities. Park Service rangers are on hand to provide information, play games, and lend materials to visiting families.

⑦
CHILKOOT TRAIL

🅰F6 ⛺ Trail starts at Dyea, 4 miles (6 km) N of Skagway

The 35-mile (56-km) Chilkoot Trail is the most famous of several trails that were created to link the coast with the Yukon goldfields in the late 1890s. Designated a US National Historic Landmark in 1978, it provides an immersive glimpse into Gold Rush history.

The Chilkoot Trail starts at the site of Dyea, which was a bustling town during the Gold Rush days, attracting thousands of prospectors. The first part of the trail winds its way through coastal rainforest, then climbs steadily up through beautiful, rocky alpine scenery until it reaches Chilkoot Pass. It then descends to Bennett Lake in Canada's British Columbia. There are campgrounds all along the way. Hikers can return by the narrow-gauge 1898 White Pass and Yukon Route Railroad, which runs between Skagway and Whitehorse in Canada, past vertical cliffs, through tunnels, and over old bridges; the section from Skagway to White Pass rises from sea level to 2,865 ft (860 m) in just 20 miles (32 km). Alternatively, you can drive back along the picturesque Klondike Highway, which passes spectacular scenery on the opposite side of the Skagway River from the railroad. This route also makes a very good alternative to hiking if you're short of time.

← St. Andrew's wooden church, overlooking Bennett Lake

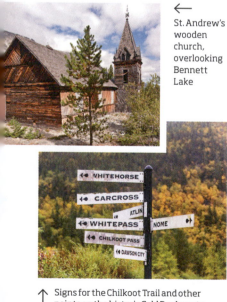

↑ Signs for the Chilkoot Trail and other points on the historic Gold Rush route

Dyea

Although it rivaled Skagway as Alaska's largest town during the Gold Rush *(p58)*, nothing remains of Dyea other than a few harbor pilings, a cemetery, and the wooden frontage of a land office. Thousands of prospectors, also called stampeders, set off from Dyea for the Klondike. Today, it is the trailhead for the Chilkoot Trail.

Canyon City

◄ In 1898, Canyon City had 1,500 residents and 24 businesses, but the town had disappeared within two years. Today, the only evidence that it existed is the remains of a boiler once owned by a transportation company.

Chilkoot Pass

▶ After struggling up to the 3,525-ft (1,058-m) Chilkoot Pass on the US-Canada border, hikers can look forward to a downhill run all the way past Lindeman Lake to Bennett Lake. During the Gold Rush, stampeders crossing the border had to stop here to pay customs duties to the Royal Canadian Mounted Police.

Lindeman

Now a campground, Lindeman was a bustling tent town of 4,000 during the Gold Rush. While stampeders and their gear were carried by a steamer and barges across Lindeman Lake in the summer, in the winter they had to walk across the frozen lake.

Bennett Lake, British Columbia

In the winter of 1897, a town of over 20,000 people sprang up at Bennett Lake, as stampeders waited for the ice to break up. In May 1898, in the week after the thaw, about 7,000 boats set off for the goldfields. For today's hikers, the lake is the end of the trail.

💬 **INSIDER TIP**
Hiking Practicalities

The Chilkoot Trail takes three to five days to hike. Hikers need permits from the Chilkoot Trail Center (*www.nps.gov/klgo*). Because the route crosses into Canada, hikers must carry passports and clear customs at the Trail Center in advance.

←
Trekkers arriving at Bennett Lake, the end of the Chilkoot Trail

HAINES

A F6 **🏔** 75 miles (120 km) NW of Juneau ✈ 🚢 **ℹ** 122 2nd Ave; www.visithaines.com

With a mild climate and a spectacular setting, Haines has drawn many artists and entrepreneurs over the years, and counts several galleries and a renowned microbrewery among its varied attractions.

Founded in 1881 by Presbyterian missionaries, Haines sits on a site known to Indigenous peoples as Dei-Shu, or "end of the trail." Early residents were quick to take advantage of the plentiful fish in the adjacent Lynn Canal, the country's deepest and longest fjord. By 1900, commercial fishing and canning had grown into major enterprises. In 1939, a sawmill was developed to support a nascent timber industry.

A good place to start exploring the town is Fort Seward. Built in 1903, the fort was the state's first permanent army post and the mainstay of Haines' economy. Today, it houses art galleries, restaurants, a replica Tlingit clan house, and a center for Native arts. More of the town's history can be explored at the Sheldon Museum on Main Street. Based on a private collection of artifacts from

BALD EAGLES

The national bird of the United States, the bald eagle (*Haliaeetus leucocephalus*) is the only eagle that's unique to North America. In this case, the word "bald" means not hairless, but white, a reference to the bird's distinctive head color. Currently, North America is home to roughly 100,000 bald eagles – about half of which live in Alaska. Indigenous peoples are allowed to use eagle feathers in their traditional dresses and ceremonies.

the early days of European settlement in the upper Chilkat Inlet area, it also displays relics from the Gold Rush era and the fishing and timber industries. On the other side of the street, the Hammer Museum is Alaska's contribution to the world's quirkiest museums. Over 2,000 hammers of varying sizes are on display, including an 800-year-old Tlingit slave-killing hammer found on a Southeast Alaska beach.

Around Haines

There are excellent hiking trails around town, including the easy 2-mile (4-km) Battery Point Trail and the more arduous Mount Ripinsky and Mount Riley trails. Rising above Haines, the 3,610-ft (1,083-m) Mount Ripinsky affords the best view over the town and its stunning hinterlands. The trailhead is north of the town center, at Young Road; hikers should carry bear spray and plenty of water, and allow at least seven hours for the strenuous round trip. The Mount Riley trail lies east of town on Mud Bay Road, and offers an easier hike to a height of 1,760 ft (528 m).

In the summer, Haines hosts a modest population of bald eagles that can be seen at the waterfront or along streams. In October and November, however, cottonwood trees in the Chilkat Bald Eagle Preserve fill with up to 3,500 eagles, which arrive to feed on Alaska's last salmon run after most other waterways have frozen solid. Summer visitors can watch a video of this "Gathering of the Eagles" at the American Bald Eagle Foundation Center in town, dedicated to the protection and preservation of bald eagles.

Along Mud Bay Road, 7 miles (11 km) from downtown Haines, is beautiful Chilkat Lake State Park – a lovely place to spend a few hours or a few days. Launch a boat toward Chilkat Inlet, or watch brown bears feed on salmon at the fish weir nearby. The information cabin staff have hiking maps and helpful advice.

DRINK

Port Chilkoot Distillery
This distillery creates masterful spirits using a special blend of Alaska-infused ingredients, and, as they say, "attitude."

🏠 **34 Blacksmith Street**
🌐 **portchilkoot distillery.com**

Haines Brewing Company
This brewery offers tours, tastings, and plenty of space in which to enjoy a refreshing pint or two.

🏠 **327 Main Street**
🌐 **hainesbrewing.com**

SHOP

Alaska Arts Confluence
A wonderful showcase for the work of artists in Haines and around Southeast Alaska.

🏠 **217 Main Street**
🌐 **alaskaarts confluence.org**

Uniquely Alaskan Art
Uncover wood carvings, masks, beaded jewelry, and paintings by talented local artist Tresham Gregg.

🏠 **109-115 2nd Avenue**
📞 **907-766-3525**

←

Haines, with its dramatic mountainscape, and *(inset)* a detail of the replica Tlingit clan house at Fort Seward

The picturesque Haines Highway, bordered by snow-covered forest ↑

Three Guardsmen Lake and Peaks

▽ The imposing Three Guardsmen Lake and Peaks lie in the alpine portion of the route. The highest of the peaks is rocky Glave Peak. The crystal-clear lake is formed by snow melt.

Klukwan

⊿ This traditional Chilkat village is home to the Jilkaat Kwaan Cultural Heritage Center, featuring a tribal house, a trove of Alaska Native art, and live exhibitions (www.jilkaatkwaan-heritagecenter.org).

Chilkat Pass

⊿ The 40-mile (64-km) alpine portion of the route reaches its highest point at 3,510-ft (1,070-m) Chilkat Pass. Much of this stretch may be impassable in the winter months.

9

HAINES CUT-OFF

⬛F6 ⬛ Highway starts at Haines

The breathtaking 146-mile (234-km) Haines Cut-Off, or Haines Highway, races past fields of forest and powdery peaks from the adventure capital of Alaska to Canada's Yukon region. This epic route is open all year round and is usually free of snow by May.

From Haines, the route follows the Chilkat and Klehini rivers northward. Near the Canadian border, the track climbs steeply, gaining 3,000 ft (900 m) over 18 miles (29 km). For the next 50 miles (80 km), the highway passes through the stunning alpine country of northern British Columbia before dropping into Yukon's lake-studded forests to join the Alaska Highway at Haines Junction. There are a number of good stopping-off points along the way, including an overlook at Mile 78, which affords great photo opportunities, and Dezadeash Lake at Mile 114, which has basic campgrounds.

> **INSIDER TIP**
> **Whitewater Rafting**
>
> There is excellent whitewater rafting at Tatshenshini-Alsek Park at Dalton Post. Check with the National Park Service for details (*www.nps.gov/glba/ planyourvisit/rafting*).

↑ A brown bear cub foraging for food at the side of the highway

Million Dollar Falls

▽ Boardwalk trails and viewing platforms at the Million Dollar Falls campground provide great views of the Takhanne River as it tumbles from a height of 200 ft (60 m).

Haines Junction

▽ The village of Haines Junction appeared in 1942 with the construction of the Alaska Highway, and today is a popular starting point for trips into Canada's Kluane National Park and Reserve.

Klukshu Village

△ Visitors to this Indigenous village can admire the traditional fish traps, shop for Native crafts, and stop by the small museum.

Kathleen Lake

This spectacular glacier-fed lake and campground in Canada's Kluane National Park is well worth a stop. On summer evenings, park rangers often conduct naturalist programs.

Salmon Glacier near Hyder, the largest road-accessible glacier in the world ↑

EXPERIENCE MORE

10

Hyder

🅰 G7 🏠 2 miles (4 km) W of Stewart, BC (Canada) 🚊 Stewart 🚌 Stewart-Terrace 🛈 222 5th Ave, Stewart, BC; (888) 366-5999

Isolated from the rest of Alaska by a roadless range of mountains, Hyder sits on the US border at the end of Canada's Route 37A. Despite running on Canadian time and using a Canadian phone code, the town enjoys a distinctly Alaska atmosphere.

Hyder is an attractive spot, with its historic buildings and good opportunities for wildlife spotting. The scenic but rough Granduc Road heads north from Hyder, following the Salmon River past old gold mines to a grand view of Salmon Glacier.

11

Metlakatla

🅰 G7 🏠 18 miles (29 km) SW of Ketchikan 🚤 Ketchikan 🚢 From Ketchikan 🛈 www.metlakatla.com

Located on Annette Island southwest of Ketchikan, Metlakatla was founded in 1887 by Scottish clergyman Father Duncan. After falling out with the church in Old Metlakatla, Canada, he fled to Annette Island with over 800 of his Tsimshian followers. In 1891, the US Congress gave them possession of the island. Because the Tsimshian rejected the Alaska National Interest Lands Conservation Act in the early 1970s (p60), they retained their sovereignty, and Annette Island is now Alaska's only Native reservation, with an economy dependent on fishing and the timber industry.

Metlakatla's main appeal lies in its quiet, small-town atmosphere. The Duncan Cottage Museum contains an intriguing collection of Father Duncan's educational and medical materials, musical instruments, and an old Edison phonograph. The town's traditional Tsimshian longhouse is well worth a visit; here, you can watch dance performances and totem carvers at work. There's also a pleasant, short hike up Yellow Hill for great Inside Passage views.

An intricately painted totem pole, found in Metlakatla on Annette Island →

12

Misty Fiords National Monument

🅰 G7 🏠 22 miles (35 km) E of Ketchikan 🚤 Charter float-plane from Ketchikan 🛈 www.fs.usda.gov/tongass

Misty Fiords is a hidden gem, not only because it is little-known outside Southeast Alaska, but also because it's often hidden in rain behind a bank of clouds. Home to wild fjords, roaring waterfalls, rainforests, snowy peaks, and soaring granite cliffs, the site was first identified in the 1793 journals of Captain George Vancouver.

Many travelers opt for boat and floatplane tours, such as the boat-in, fly-out trip organized by **Allen Marine Tours**.

Allen Marine Tours

🏠 5 Salmon Landing #215, Ketchikan 🆆 allenmarinetours.com

ALASKA'S TEMPERATE RAINFOREST

Characterized by lush, rain-soaked flora, the forests of Southeast Alaska make up the northern extent of the world's largest temperate rainforest. Much cooler than their tropical counterparts, temperate rainforests have climatic conditions that are marked by average summer temperatures of less than 16° C (61° F), a cool dormant season, and at least 55 inches (140 cm) of precipitation per year.

Alaska's temperate rainforest includes a canopy composed of tall coniferous tree species such as Sitka spruce and western hemlock. Rainforest trees can live up to 1,000 years, and when they fall they decompose into a rich organic material that nourishes vegetation. On the damp, shady forest floor grow ferns and large-leafed plants. Ferns prefer moist conditions with low levels of light and thrive under the temperate rainforest cover, while epiphytic mosses and lichens draw nutrients and moisture directly from the air, using the host trees just for support.

TOP 3 ANIMALS TO SPOT

Black Bears
The most common and widely distributed of North America's three species of bear *(p216)*, black bears are also the smallest.

Sitka Black-Tailed Deer
Endemic to the region, these deer feed on the native hemlock, berries, and lichens.

North American Porcupines
Nocturnal animals, porcupines are second in size only to beavers among Alaska rodents.

↑ A North American porcupine *(Erethizon dorsatum)* in Glacier Bay National Park

Taking a break on a hike through the rainforest to Mendenhall Glacier ↑

13 Wrangell

🗺 G7 🚗 80 miles (128 km)
N of Ketchikan ✈ From
Ketchikan ⛴ From Juneau,
Ketchikan, or Petersburg
ℹ Nolan Center, 293
Campbell Drive; www.
wrangellalaska.org

The original fort on this site was founded as Redoubt St. Dionysius by the Russians in 1833, and was intended to protect Russian fur trading interests from the British and Spanish. The local Tlingit, under Chief Shakes V, recognized the economic benefits of cooperation with the Russians and joined them at the redoubt in 1834. In the same year, combined Tlingit and Russian forces managed to repel the British forces led by Peter Skeen Ogden, who had attempted to establish a fur trading post. In 1868, after Alaska's transfer to the US, the Americans established a military fort that they named after the head of the Russian-American Company, Baron Ferdinand von Wrangel.

Today, Wrangell is a friendly little town, drawing a few adventurous visitors and a handful of small cruise ships in the summer. Attractions here include the **Wrangell Museum**, housed in the same building as the town's visitor

information office. It contains a wonderful collection of artifacts, beginning in the entryway with the original 17th-century houseposts of the Frog Clan from the Tlingit Tribal House on Chief Shakes Island. Electronic lighting on the ceiling of the lobby simulates the undulations of the aurora borealis. Museum displays begin with the natural history of the region and proceed chronologically through exhibits on Native culture, the fur trade, military history, the Stikine Gold Rush, fishing, and forestry. The museum is also a repository for thousands of historical images and numerous audio and video records.

Accessible by a wooden walkway across an arm of the harbor, **Chief Shakes Island** is a park and a repository for Tlingit totems dating from 1840 to 1940. Opened in 1940 and restored in 2013, the large replica Tlingit Tribal House, a National Historic Site, was named Ck! Udatc Hit ("House of Many Faces") in reference to the human visages in its design. Inside are replica houseposts of the Frog Clan, and dotted around the park are several distinctive totems. The peaceful park overlooks the picturesque harbor, and its green lawns provide a perfect place to relax on sunny days.

← A striking totem pole on display within the Wrangell Museum

↑ Visitors' platform at Wrangell's Petroglyph Beach State Historic Site

Archeologists believe that an ancient culture already occupied the Wrangell area before the modern-day Tlingit arrived. Evidence found at the **Petroglyph Beach State Historic Site** suggests that these early groups were here around 10,000 years ago, at the end of the last Ice Age, and that they established subsequent settlements roughly 5,000 and 3,000 years ago. It is thought that these early people made some of the 40 petroglyphs that adorn the rocks of the beach, but the artwork reveals little information about their culture. Interestingly, however, some spiral and sun designs match petrogylphs found as far away as South America. The petroglyphs of wolves, bears, and orcas found here were probably carved by the Tlingit. Most of the petroglyphs, carved on boulders scattered along the beach, have been eroded over time by the sea. A visitors' platform provides access to the beach, where the state has reproduced the most interesting petroglyphs to allow visitors to make rubbings of the carvings.

Keen golfers might be interested in playing a round at **Muskeg Meadows Golf Course**, a nine-hole, par 36

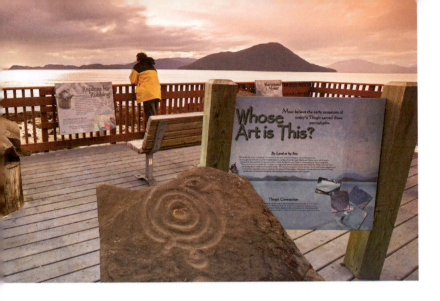

course carved from the muskeg bog for which it was named. From 1995 to 1998, volunteers from the non-profit Wrangell Golf Club worked to create a beautiful course set amid spruce and cedar rainforest. This is the world's only golf course with a "Raven Rule," which states that if a raven steals a golf ball, it can be replaced without penalty, provided the golfer has a witness.

The real draw for most visitors to Wrangell, however, is the glacier-fed Stikine River, just outside town. Originating in the mountains of British Columbia in Canada, the river flows through 30 miles (48 km) of the Stikine-LeConte Wilderness on the Alaska mainland to its mouth across the narrows near Wrangell. Several companies organize jetboat tours, which head upstream through spectacular mountain scenery and past waterfalls and the iceberg choked face of Shakes Glacier. There are good opportunities to see harbor seals, black bears, spawning salmon, and the world's largest summer concentration of bald eagles. A popular destination is Chief Shakes Hot Springs, where open-air hot tubs offer soaking in a wild setting.

Other top excursions from Wrangell include Anan Creek and outlying parts of Wrangell Island, both popular for wildlife viewing. From the town, forest roads lead to free campgrounds, the best of which are at Nemo Point, with its wonderful high-altitude views over Zimovia Strait.

Wrangell Museum
🅰️🅰️🅰️ 🅰️ Nolan Center, 296 Campbell Drive 📞 874-3770 🅰️ Apr-Sep: 10am-5pm Mon-Sat; Oct-Mar: 1-5pm Fri-Sat

Chief Shakes Island
🅰️ Shake St

GARNET MARKET
Kids in Wrangell don't sell lemonade to raise money - they're too busy hawking garnets. Founded in 1881, the Wrangell garnet ledge was purchased by Fred G. Hanford in 1962 as a gift for the Boy Scouts of America, on the condition that the land be used only by the town's children to mine "in reasonable quantities." Today's Wrangell youth pry loose the rough gems, polish them up, and sell them to tourists.

Petroglyph Beach State Historic Site
🅰️ 0.5 miles (1 km) N of Wrangell 🅰️ 24 hrs daily

Muskeg Meadows Golf Course
🅰️🅰️🅰️ 🅰️ Mile 0.5, Ishiyama Dr 🅰️ Apr-Nov: 9am-6pm 🌐 wrangellalaskagolf.com

SHOP

The Nolan Center Museum Gift Shop
This museum gift shop offers an excellent array of Alaska Native art, jewelry, and other items relating to Wrangell's local culture.

🅰️ 296 Campbell Dr, Wrangell 📞 874-3770

Angerman's
This family-owned store has long been Wrangell's go-to for everything from rubber boots to fishing tackle.

🅰️ 2 Front St, Wrangell 📞 874-3640

↑ A bear catching salmon, seen from the Anan Creek Wildlife Observatory

EAT

Coastal Cold Storage, Inc.

Open daily for the best fish and chips in perhaps all of Alaska. This is where the locals go for simple dishes full of freshness and flavor.

⚠ G7 🏠 306 N Nordic Dr, Petersburg 🌐 coastal coldstorage.com

💲💲💲

The Salty Pantry

Part bakery, part gift shop, and part restaurant, this is an excellent place to stop for a tasty bite.

⚠ G7 🏠 14 Harbor Way, Petersburg 📞 772-2665

💲💲💲

Glacier Express Café

A trendy little spot serving up delicious smoothies, excellent coffee, and baked goods.

⚠ G7 🏠 400 N Nordic Dr, Petersburg 📞 772-4141

💲💲💲

⑭ Anan Creek Wildlife Observatory

⚠ G7 🏠 31 miles (50 km) S of Wrangell ✈ By floatplane 🚤 Boat tours 🛈 www.fs.usda.gov/tongass

Located on the Cleveland Peninsula, Anan Creek is the site of one of Alaska's greatest pink salmon runs. The fish are slowed by a waterfall half a mile (1 km) inland, which attracts large numbers of hungry brown and black bears. Adjacent to the falls, a wildlife observatory – which is actually a large viewing platform – allows visitors close-up views of the feeding bears. During the salmon run, sea otters, harbor seals, and bald eagles can also be spotted along the shore near the mouth of Anan Creek.

While wildlife is usually visible all summer, permits are needed to visit the observatory in July and August. Only 60 permits are issued for each day, and these can be booked through authorized guiding companies (see website for further information). Four permits are also available for those staying at the nearby Anan Bay public-use cabin – the only accommodations available in the area.

⑮ Mitkof Highway

⚠ G7 🛈 12 N Nordic Dr; www.fs.fed.us/r10/tongass/districts/petersburg

The scenic Mitkof Highway follows the coastline from Petersburg to the southern end of Mitkof Island. At Mile 14.5, a lovely boardwalk trail crosses the muskeg to access some picnic spots and the salmon run at Blind River Rapids. Wintering trumpeter swans can be seen from mid-October to December at the Swan Observatory at Mile 16. Not far ahead, at Mile 18, the Crystal Lake Hatchery and Blind Slough Recreation Area offer scenic picnic sites.

The pretty Man Made Hole at Mile 20 was once a quarry that has filled with water to form a lake, with a gentle trail around its perimeter. At Mile 22, Ohmer Creek Campground offers visitors free camping at the island's only public site.

→ The pleasant Bojer Wikan Fishermen's Memorial Park in Petersburg

Petersburg

Ⓐ G7 🚗 32 miles (51 km) N of Ketchikan ✈️ From Ketchikan, Wrangell, & Juneau ⛴️ From Ketchikan, Sitka, Wrangell, & Juneau ℹ️ 1st & Fram St; www. petersburg.org

Named for Norwegian settler Peter Buschmann, Petersburg nestles on sheltered Mitkof Island. Buschmann, who arrived to homestead in the area in 1890, initiated the development of the town. By 1900, realizing that glacier ice could be used to preserve fish, he set up the Icy Strait Packing Company cannery. Business soon flourished, and Petersburg now has crab,

---

LITTLE NORWAY

Peter Buschmann's success in Petersburg inspired many of his countrymen to follow him to Alaska in search of fjords, fishing, and opportunity. Nicknamed Little Norway, the town reflects its Norwegian heritage in the decorative details on buildings and the souvenirs on offer. On the weekend nearest Norwegian Independence Day on May 17, the town celebrates the Little Norway Festival *(p54)* with feasting, a parade, and a *bunad* (traditional dress) fashion show. A children's dance troupe performs, although all are welcome to try the traditional steps.

---

shrimp, salmon, and herring fisheries, as well as Alaska's largest halibut fleet.

The town enjoys spectacular mountain views that include the precipitous Devil's Thumb, which straddles the Canadian border. The major attractions for visitors are the beautiful hinterlands of Mitkof Island and neighboring Kupreanof Island, which offer superb outdoor pursuits.

Sing Lee Alley, a picturesque boardwalk, is one of the town's oldest streets. At No. 23, the distinctive Sons of Norway Hall, built in 1912, has graceful, decorative scroll paintings called *rosemaling* on its facade. The adjacent Bojer Wikan Fishermen's Memorial Park is home to a replica Viking ship, the *Valhalla*.

The town's compact **Clausen Memorial Museum** showcases the history and culture of the Petersburg and Kupreanof Island area. There is a replica of a 1970s-era fish packer's office and a Tlingit dugout canoe, but the most popular exhibit, representing every angler's dream, is the 125-lb (56-kg) stuffed king salmon.

Outside Petersburg, Sandy Beach Park has a picnic area and opportunities for recreational activities, and the Three Lakes Trail offers the chance to see moose, and beavers.

Clausen Memorial Museum
Ⓐ 203 Fram St 🕐 Apr-Sep: 10am–5pm Mon–Sat; Oct–Mar: 1–5pm Mon–Fri, noon–5pm Sat 🚫 Jan 🌐 clausen museum.com

---

🔍 HIDDEN GEM
Ancient Artifacts

Sandy Beach Park is the site of ancient fish traps that reveal themselves at low tide, ingeniously designed to keep fish in and water out. Take care not to disturb the delicate ecosystem and artifacts as you stroll the sands.

⑰ Tenakee Springs

🅰F6 📍48 miles (78 km) N of Sitka 🚢Sitka–Juneau ℹwww.tenakeesprings ak.com

Situated on the eastern shores of Chichagof Island, the village of Tenakee Springs takes its name from the Tlingit word *tinaghu*, meaning "Copper Shield Bay," after three prized copper shields that were lost in a storm in Tenakee Inlet.

Historically, the town's main attraction was the 42° C (108° F) hot springs, which made the area bearable in all seasons. A bathhouse was built in 1895 to enclose the spring, and Snyder's Mercantile, launched in 1899, still runs as a general store. The bathhouse now largely functions as a social hub, although some residents do not have showers or baths in their cabins and still rely on the venue for bathing.

Today, the picturesque village stretches along a single street, which is limited to pedestrian traffic. The nearby Native village of Hoonah, accessible by ferry, has the lengthy Icy Strait Point zipline, which is a popular attraction on some cruise itineraries.

⑱ 🚴 🅼 Admiralty Island National Monument

🅰F6 📍43 miles (70 km) NE of Sitka ✈Charter float-plane from Juneau 🚢Sitka–Angoon; tour boat Juneau–Pack Creek ℹwww.fs. usda.gov/tongass

Referred to as Kootznoowoo (meaning "Fortress of Bears") by the Tlingit people, Admiralty Island National Monument sprawls across 1,492 sq miles (3,865 sq km). Almost 98 per-cent of this lush rainforest – which lies within the Tongass National Forest – is a desig-nated wilderness area. The main site of interest for wildlife enthusiasts is Pack Creek in the Stan Price State Wildlife Sanctuary at the island's northeast corner. This area is home to the world's densest population of brown bears. Sitka black-tailed deer can be seen along the shore, and Mitchell, Hood, Chaik, and Whitewater bays contain porpoises, seals, and sea lions. Summer access to the tidal estuary and bear-viewing tower is by permit only.

The sole settlement on the island is Angoon, a small Native village accessible via the Marine Highway. Kayakers and canoeists will enjoy the Cross-Island Canoe Route, which connects Angoon with Mole Harbor via a series of lakes, streams, and portages.

Did You Know?

The Southeast Alaskan coast is roughly as long as the west coast of Canada.

⑲ 🚴 🅼 Tatshenshini-Alsek Rivers

🅰G5 ℹwww.env.gov.bc. ca/bcparks/explore/ parkpgs/tatshens

The Tatshenshini River and its tributary, the Alsek – which are considered two of the world's best rivers for white-water rafting and kayaking – rise in the St. Elias Range in British Columbia and the Yukon Territory, respectively. They flow 160 miles (256 km) through canyons and rapids and past glaciers to the coast at the northern end of Glacier Bay National Park *(p142)*. Once a vital Tlingit trade route, the Tatshenshini supports produc-tive salmon runs, and visitors to Klukshu *(p155)* can see how the First Nations once caught salmon with fish traps and dried them for use in winter.

The usual put-in site for the Tatshenshini is Dalton Post, near the border of the Yukon Territory and British Columbia, while Alsek rafters put in near Haines Junction. Rafters on both rivers must get a permit for Glacier Bay National Park, citing a pre-specified take-out time from Dry Bay, which will require a bush flight to Haines or Yakutat. For private trips on the Alsek, rafters also need a permit from Canada's Kluane National Park. Additionally, rafters on the Alsek should be aware that there is a 10-mile (16-km) stretch that presents serious whitewater, and must be bypassed using a pre-organized helicopter portage. There are no services along the route, so river runners need to be fully self-sufficient. Most rafters go with commercial operators and experienced guides.

Yakutat

G5 **225 miles (362 km) NW of Juneau** **Yakutat Chamber of Commerce; www.yakutatalaska.com**

Located on the Gulf of Alaska at the southern edge of Wrangell-St. Elias National

↑ Kayaking the waters of the Admiralty Island National Monument

Park (p182), Yakutat is just 70 miles (110 km) from the 18,008-ft (5,490-m) Mount St. Elias, the second highest peak in the US.

The Russians were among the first outsiders in Yakutat, whose name translates as "where the canoes rest" in the Tlingit language. In 1805, the Russian-American Company built a fur trading post here, but it was destroyed by the Tlingit, who had been denied access to their traditional hunting and fishing lands. In 1886, minor gold deposits were discovered in the beach sands, but the area's economy took off only in 1903, when a cannery, sawmill, and railroad were established. Yakutat also served as a garrison and airstrip during World War II.

Due to its remote location, modern Yakutat sees few casual visitors (although Alaska Airlines does fly here). However, it has been discovered by fly-fishermen, who come for steelhead, and surfers who head to Cannon Beach, a popular place to surf the waves. The town also enjoys good views of a host of peaks and glaciers, including

↑ Cruise ship passengers taking in the Hubbard Glacier near Yakutat

the galloping Hubbard Glacier, one of the few advancing glaciers in Alaska, and the vast Malaspina Glacier, which is one of the largest in North America. Yakutat is a good base for exploring both the southeast corner of Wrangell-St. Elias National Park and the Russell Fjord Wilderness. The latter is a 26-mile (42-km) drive away and includes Harlequin Lake and Yakutat Glacier.

> **INSIDER TIP**
> **Yakutat Tern Festival**
>
> Held each May at the height of a returning migration of Alaska shorebirds, this festival is fast becoming a "must-do" event for birders. The festival is held in and around the Yakutat High School area, with field trips, activities, and plenty of bird-watching education.

INTERIOR ALASKA

Bordering the Alaska Range to the south and the Brooks Range to the north, Interior Alaska has supported human populations for at least 11,000 years. It was first settled around the Yukon River Basin by the nomadic Athabascan people, who traveled between summer and winter camps, utilizing the landscape and wildlife for food, shelter, and clothing.

In 1901, when the steamer of Yukon merchant E. T. Barnette ran aground on the banks of the Chena River, he made the best of his misfortune by establishing the first permanent human settlement the area had ever known. Fortuitously, the Gold Rush brought thousands of miners looking for easy-to-reach riches, and his trading post grew into the thriving city of Fairbanks. Towns such as Dawson City also sprang up in remote areas along the Yukon River, and when the gold began to dwindle many penniless prospectors opted to stay in these communities to homestead.

World War II brought the construction of the Alaska Highway, which not only opened up an access route through the Interior but also boosted the economy of the region. There was a further growth spurt in the 1970s, when the Richardson Highway became the corridor for the Trans-Alaska Pipeline. Fairbanks was chosen as as the pipeline's logistical headquarters, and became an important supply hub for the oil-rich Arctic thanks to its position as the northernmost terminus on the Alaska Railroad. With much of the Interior still largely wilderness, the city continues to play a central role in the fortunes of the region.

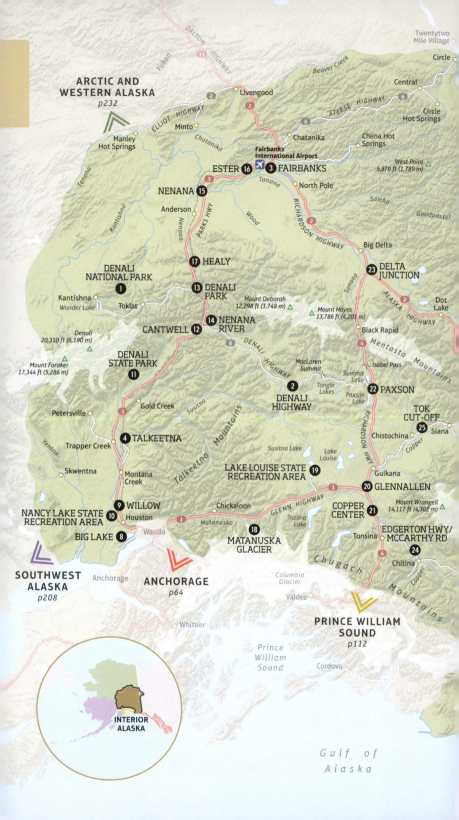

INTERIOR ALASKA

Must Sees
1. Denali National Park
2. Denali Highway
3. Fairbanks
4. Talkeetna
5. Wrangell-St. Elias National Park
6. Kennecott Mines
7. Dawson City

Experience More
8. Big Lake
9. Willow
10. Nancy Lake State Recreation Area
11. Denali State Park
12. Cantwell
13. Denali Park
14. Nenana River
15. Nenana
16. Ester
17. Healy
18. Matanuska Glacier
19. Lake Louise State Recreation Area
20. Glennallen
21. Copper Center
22. Paxson
23. Delta Junction
24. Edgerton Highway/McCarthy Road
25. Tok Cut-Off
26. Tok
27. Tok River State Recreation Site
28. Northway
29. Chicken
30. Fortymile Country
31. Tetlin National Wildlife Refuge
32. Eagle
33. Yukon-Charley Rivers National Preserve

1 ⌖

DENALI NATIONAL PARK

🅐 D3 🅐 125 miles (200 km) S of Fairbanks 🅟🚌 *i* Denali Visitor Center (& Backcountry Information Center) Mile 1.2, Park Rd; www.nps.gov/dena

Alaska's top attraction, the expansive Denali National Park sprawls across 9,420 sq miles (24,395 sq km) and is larger than the entire state of New Hampshire. The park's highlight is the majestic Denali, North America's highest peak, but its remote lakes, glistening glaciers, and carpets of wildflowers will leave you just as awestruck.

As well as being famous for Denali, which dominates the surrounding landscape, Denali National Park is world-renowned for its wildlife viewing; visitors can expect to see a wide variety of animals, including caribou, moose, grizzly bears, wolves, and Dall sheep. In the summer, Denali's tundra regions explode with wildflowers, while in September, they are ablaze with autumnal yellows, reds, and oranges. Just one road penetrates the backcountry. After Mile 15, this route is accessible only in the summer and only via the park's shuttle buses, which cross open tundra, boggy lowlands, taiga forest, and mountain passes to wind up at beautiful Wonder Lake. Visitors can tour the park by bus, by bike, or on foot; alternatively, whitewater rafting is also an option.

> 💬 INSIDER TIP
> **Horseshoe Lake**
>
> Near the main entrance to the park, secluded Horseshoe Lake is inhabited by several families of beaver; it can be reached on a 2-mile (3-km) hike through the trees.

Exploring Denali National Park

Most summer visitors to Alaska have Denali National Park on their itineraries, so a smooth visit requires pre-booking and advance planning. In the June to August peak season, it is not uncommon to have to wait several days for shuttle tickets or campsite bookings. For hikers, the park is divided into 43 backcountry units, each of which accommodates one group per night. Backcountry permits cannot be reserved, so access to high-demand units can require long waits. To get to the most appealing parts of the park, visitors without bookings should stop off at the Denali Bus Depot to organize their visit. Be aware that no private vehicles are allowed on the Denali National Park Road beyond Savage River at Mile 15. While most visitors to Denali National Park focus on activities further along the park's main road (where there is a second visitor center), it is also important to note the wealth of things to do in and around the greater entrance area. Offering everything from beautiful guided walks and strenuous hikes to educational events, Denali's main entrance bustles at any time of the day.

THE WOLVES OF DENALI

It's not very often that visitors to Denali are lucky enough to spy a wolf jogging along the side of the road, or even at a distance, but when they do, it's a special moment. After suffering a decline in numbers in 2010, Denali now has 70 wolves making up ten packs. Park scientists radio collar certain wolves and monitor them to determine size and overall pack health.

← A grizzly bear at colorful Polychrome Pass, Denali

↑ The aptly named Wonder Lake, reflecting the landscape in its clear waters

Cycling up to Grassy Pass along Denali National Park Road ↑

STAY

Camp Denali
The epitome of an Alaska adventure. Has 18 cabins; meals are included.

Ⓦ campdenali.com/ alaska-lodges/camp-denali

Ⓢ Ⓢ Ⓢ

North Face Lodge
Features 15 rooms and sweeping park views.

Ⓦ campdenali.com/ alaska-lodges/north-face-lodge

Ⓢ Ⓢ Ⓢ

Kantishna Roadhouse
A fine blend of luxury and adventure.

Ⓦ kantishnaroadhouse. com/denali-park-accommodations

Ⓢ Ⓢ Ⓢ

---

① 🍴 🛍

Denali National Park Headquarters Area

Ⓐ Mile 3, Denali National Park Road

The headquarters of Denali National Park, located near the main entrance on the eastern edge of the park, are a necessary stop for all visitors. They are reached via a road that passes the Denali Bus Depot, which handles all shuttle bus tickets and campground reservations, and Riley Creek Campground, which has sites for tents and RVs.

The Denali Visitor Center is a good place for information about park history, wildlife, and general activities. It also houses the Backcountry Information Center, where you can get backcountry permits. Visitors exploring off Denali's roads are required to watch a bear-safety presentation.

The Murie Science and Learning Center, a short walk away, is designed for hands-on science education related to the park's geology, wildlife, and conservation efforts. A must-see is the working sled dog kennels, where the National Park Service's only team resides. These hardy dogs spend the winter patrolling the park's backcountry for weeks on end, and enjoy the summer months playing host to scores of visitors.

---

② 🚴

Denali National Park Road

🚌 Late May–mid-Sep: 6am–3pm at half-hour intervals from Denali Bus Depot; reserve well in advance
Ⓦ reservedenali.com

The Denali National Park Road leads 85 miles (136 km) into the heart of the park through a picturesque and wildlife-rich forest and tundra landscape. The area between the Park Headquarters and Savage River, west of the entrance at Mile 15, is moose habitat. In the spring, visitors can look out for cow moose with calves, but should not approach the wildlife. Beyond the river, the road grows more scenic as it climbs into alpine tundra, with herds of Dall sheep often visible on Primrose Ridge to the north.

The road continues above the treeline to Sable Pass. Polychrome Pass at Mile 45 is another highlight: the stunning, vividly colored rocks of Polychrome Mountain were formed by volcanic action about 50 million years ago. Wolves sometimes hunt migrating caribou in this area, and visitors might spot a lone wolf on the road in the summer. Shortly after the road's highest point at the 3,980-ft (1,213-m) Highway Pass, visitors get their first good view of Denali at the Stony Hill Overlook. The road continues west to the Eielson Visitor Center. From here, the route passes the foot of Muldrow Glacier and follows McKinley River to Wonder Lake. Visitors should be careful to always follow park ranger directions.

③
Wonder Lake

🏕 **Mile 85, Denali National Park Road** 🚌 **From Denali Bus Depot**

Wonder Lake, at an altitude of just 2,090 ft (627 m), enjoys an unobstructed view of Denali,

which rises 18,230 ft (5,569 m) above the level of the lake. The colorful region around the lake, characterized by expanses of tundra and blueberry bushes, is favored grizzly habitat, and lucky campers at the Wonder Lake Campground frequently see bears and caribou. In nearby ponds, beavers can often be seen cutting willows, and moose can be spotted dredging for pond weed.

④
Kantishna

🏕 **93 miles (150 km) W of Denali Village** 🚌 **From Denali Bus Depot**

Located 7 miles (11 km) beyond Wonder Lake, tiny Kantishna is one of many Alaska settlements that started as mining camps. In 1985 all mining, including that on private claims, was banned, and today Kantishna is little more than an airstrip and a collection of lodges. The 1906 recorder's and assayer's office and the original 1919 Kantishna Roadhouse can still be seen near the current roadhouse.

↑ A moose wandering out in front of the national park shuttle bus

> ⛰ GREAT VIEW
> **Savage River**
>
> The Savage River Loop Trail is a 2-mile (3-km) hike. Alpine meadow flowers bloom midsummer, and the craggy rocks of the Savage Canyon provide an interesting view as you stroll this riverside loop.

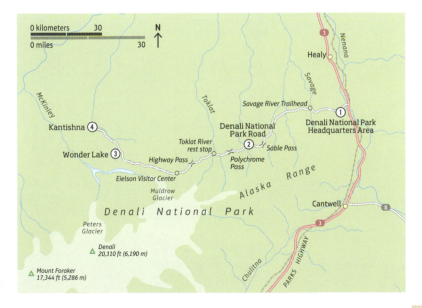

②

DENALI HIGHWAY

⚐E4 🏠Highway starts at Paxson

The spectacular Denali Highway extends for 135 miles (217 km) from Paxson to Cantwell through boundless mountain scenery. A drive along this wild and winding route makes for an unforgettable experience.

Built in 1957, the Denali Highway was the only link between Anchorage and Denali National Park until the completion of the Parks Highway in 1972. The sky-grazing mountains and glaciers of the Alaska Range run along the highway's length, offering sweeping views, while the lower regions of tundra and taiga forests are home to moose, caribou, and grizzlies. Except for the first 21 miles (34 km) westward from Paxson and the last couple of miles, the route is gravel, with the surface ranging from smooth to rough and rutted. Winter snowfalls usually close the road from around mid-October to mid-May.

STAY

Take your time with an overnight stop at one of these cosy lodges en route.

Maclaren River Lodge
🏠Mile 42
ⓦmaclarenlodge.com

$$$

—————

Clearwater Mountain Lodge
🏠Mile 82 (Susitna River) ⓦclearwater-mountainlodge.com

$$$

> Tangle Lakes, the headwaters of the Delta River, are popular for kayaking and fishing. The surrounding 350-sq-mile (900-sq-km) area includes several ancient Native hunting sites.

A caribou, one of around 1,700 that currently inhabit the area

Highlights

Summit Lake

▷ Around Mile 4, several highway turnouts afford great views north to Summit Lake and Gakona Glacier.

Tangle Lakes

Tangle Lakes, the headwaters of the Delta River, are popular for kayaking and fishing. The surrounding 350-sq-mile (900-sq-km) area includes several ancient Native hunting sites.

MacLaren Summit

▽ At 4,086 ft (1,226 m), MacLaren Summit is Alaska's second-highest highway pass. The view north takes in several glaciers, including the Susitna Glacier.

Clearwater Creek Controlled Use Area

Gold was mined in the Clearwater Creek area in the early 20th century. Today, there is plenty of good hunting and fishing available here.

Susitna River

The 260-mile- (416-km-) long Susitna River, popularly called the Big Su, has its headwaters in the Susitna Glacier in the Alaska Range. The river boasts Class III to Class V rapids between the glacier and Talkeetna.

Brushkana River

▷ Denali Highway crosses the Brushkana River at Mile 104.3. The campground near the river bridge is ideal for fishing.

← Denali Highway winding its way through spectacular mountain scenery

3

FAIRBANKS

🏔️ E3 📍 357 miles (574 km) N of Anchorage ✈️
🚌 Anchorage-Whitehorse ℹ️ 101 Dunkel St;
www.explorefairbanks.com

Known as Alaska's Golden Heart City, Fairbanks sprawls across the broad Tanana Valley. The town was founded in 1901 and drew thousands of gold prospectors. Most boomers left when the seam played out in the 1920s, but the town's economy was bolstered by World War II and the construction of the Trans-Alaska Pipeline in the mid-1970s. Today, it continues to thrive as Alaska's second-largest city, hosting the lively Golden Days festival in July.

① 🏅 🏛️
Creamer's Field Migratory Waterfowl Refuge

🏠 1300 College Rd 🚌 Red Line 🕐 Refuge: 24 hrs daily; visitor center: Jun–mid-Sep: 10am–5pm daily; mid-Sep–May: noon–4pm Sat 🌐 friendsofcreamers field.org

This refuge was originally a dairy farm but was sold to the state in 1975. As it had always attracted migratory birds, the Alaska Conservation Society expanded the acreage to turn it into Creamer's Field Migratory Waterfowl Refuge. Today, the site offers good opportunities to view harriers, falcons, and swans. Sandhill cranes can be seen performing their unique dance, consisting of a series of bowing and hopping movements, through much of the summer.

Creamer's Field also has several miles of walking and skiing trails, including an interpretive trail through a boreal forest. The pathways are flat and easy to navigate, bringing visitors of all ages and abilities. The Creamer's Field staff and volunteers often schedule guided nature walks to acquaint visitors with local birds and wildlife.

②
Pioneer Park

🏠 2300 Airport Way. ☎️ 459-1087 🚌 Blue & Red Lines 🕐 Museums: Mar & Apr: 1–5pm Fri–Sun; early May: 1–5pm daily; mid-May–mid-Sep: 11am–8pm daily; late Sep: 1–5pm daily

This historical theme park features gold panning, a reconstructed Gold Rush

---

🔍 HIDDEN GEM
Classic Cars

For a step back in time, visit the Fountainhead Antique Auto Museum (*www.fountainhead museum.com*), with an impressive collection of pre-World War II vehicles that are kept in pristine condition.

An aerial view of Fairbanks, set on the banks of the Chena River

town, the railroad car that President Warren G. Harding used while visiting Nenana in 1923, and the SS *Nenana*, a sternwheeler that operated on the Chena River from 1933 to 1956. The interesting Alaska Native Museum highlights Athabascan culture, while the Alaska Pioneer Museum outlines the lives of early settlers. Don't miss the Pioneer Park Air Museum, with its collection of vintage aircraft and exhibits on Alaska's aviation history.

③ Morris Thompson Cultural and Visitors Center

⌂ 101 Dunkel St ▦ Blue and Red Lines ⊙ Mid-May–mid-Sep: 8am–9pm daily; mid-Sep–mid-May: 8am–5pm daily ⌨ morristhompson center.org

On the Chena River in the heart of Fairbanks, this lovely modern building has state-of-the-art exhibits portraying traditional cultures and the natural world. See artisans at work, watch a dance performance, or enjoy a film on Alaska life. A block away, Golden Heart Plaza's fountain features Malcolm Alexander's sculpture *The Unknown First Family*, depicting an Inuit family and dedicated to the spirit of all Alaskans.

④ University of Alaska Museum of the North

⌂ 907 Yukon Dr, University of Alaska Fairbanks ▦ Blue, Yellow, & Red Lines ⊙ Jun–Aug: 9am–7pm daily; Sep–May: 9am–5pm Mon–Sat ⌨ uaf.edu/museum

Packed with natural history, cultural, and geographical displays, the University of Alaska Museum of the North is well worth a visit. Exhibits include the famous Blue Babe, a mummified Ice Age bison; a large collection of Inuit carvings; and Native costumes. The Rose Berry Gallery of Alaska Art exhibits works by renowned Alaskan artists, while the delightful grounds of the **Georgeson Botanical Garden** display Alaska flora.

Georgeson Botanical Garden

⌂ 117 W Tanana Dr, UAF ⊙ Jun–Aug: 8am–8pm daily ⌨ georgesonbotanical garden.org

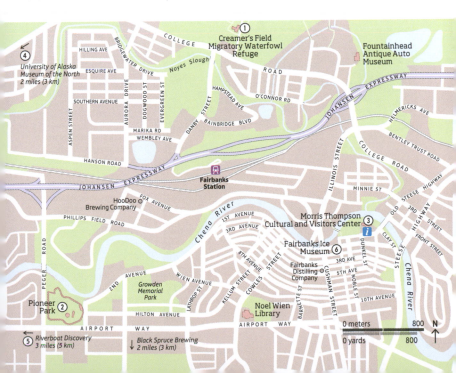

⑤ 🖋️ 🖼️ 🎒

Riverboat Discovery

📍1975 Discovery Dr
🚌Yellow Line ⏱️Mid-May-
mid-Sep: 9am & 2pm daily
🌐riverboatdiscovery.com

Perhaps the town's most
popular attraction, Riverboat
Discovery offers three-hour
sternwheeler riverboat cruises
down the Chena River on the
Discovery I, *Discovery II*, or
Discovery III. En route, a bush
pilot displays field take-offs
and landings from a grass
runway on the bank, and
there are visits to the kennels
of the late Iditarod Trail Sled
Dog Race champion Susan
Butcher and to a reconstructed
Athabascan village, where
guides explain Native traditions. The cruise also sails
past the confluence of the

clear black waters of the
Chena River and the silty,
glacial Tanana River.

⑥ 🖋️ 🎨

Fairbanks Ice Museum

📍500 2nd Ave 🚌 ⏱️May-
Sep: 9am-9pm daily
🌐icemuseum.com

Held in Fairbanks in early
March, the World Ice Art
Championships draw top
ice sculptors from around
the world, who turn massive
7,800-lb (3,500-kg) blocks of
ice into works of art. Open
during the summer in the
historic Lacey Street Theater,
the Fairbanks Ice Museum
displays beautifully carved
ice sculptures at a chilly -7° C
(20° F). Children can enjoy the
ice slides and mazes.

DRINK

HooDoo Brewing Company

This small brewery has
a tasting room and is a
local favorite for special
events. The tasting
room opens into the
actual brewery itself,
so visitors can see the
process in action

📍1951 Fox Avenue
🌐hoodoobrew.com

Black Spruce Brewing

A relative newcomer
to the Interior Alaska
brewing scene, Black
Spruce has become a
force to be reckoned
with, offering ales,
pilsners, and some
toothy stouts. Tours
of the facility are
complimentary and
are held every
Saturday at 2 pm.

📍3290 Peger Road
🌐blacksprucebeer.com

Fairbanks Distilling Company

Housed in the old
Fairbanks City Hall, the
distillery combines city
history with small-
batch spirits made with
Yukon Gold potatoes.
Try the 68-Below Vodka
for a truly unique,
Alaska-infused taste.
Tours are available by
appointment, and offer
an interesting look at
the distilling process.

📍410 Cushman Street
🌐fairbanks
distilling.com

← A Riverboat Discovery
cruise sailing past a
riverside restaurant

BEYOND FAIRBANKS

⑦
North Pole

📍 15 miles (24 km) SE of Fairbanks 🚌 Green Line from Fairbanks ℹ️ 125 Snowman Lane; www.northpolealaska.com

This town is nowhere near the North Pole, or even in the Arctic Circle, but here, the name is everything. Homesteaded in 1944, it was eventually sold to a developer who hoped to attract toy manufacturers by naming the new town North Pole. While manufacturers never materialized, the name inspired a Christmas spirit, seen in such street names as Mistletoe Lane and Reindeer Alley. The charming **Santa Claus House**, next to the Richardson Highway, attracts youngsters with its enormous Christmas store, live reindeer, and the chance to speak with Santa. The Christmas season is ushered in with a tree-lighting ceremony.

Santa Claus House

📍 101 St Nicholas Dr
🕐 Mid May–mid-Sep: 9am–8pm daily; mid-Sep–mid-May: 10am–6pm daily
🌐 santaclaushouse.com

⑧
Chena Hot Springs

📍 Chena Hot Springs Rd, 57 miles (91 km) E of Fairbanks 🚌 Chena Hot Springs 🕐 7am–midnight daily 🌐 chenahotsprings.com

The most developed thermal spa in the state, Chena Hot Springs has functioned since 1905. It offers a complete resort experience with hot springs, pools, spa therapies, and many other activities such as canoeing and fishing.

Nordic skiing, sleigh rides, snowmobiling, dog sledding, and, of course, aurora viewing make the spa more popular in the winter. An addition is the unique **Aurora Ice Museum**, the word's largest year-round ice environment. It boasts an ice bar and elaborate ice carvings, such as igloos, a giant chess set, and a pair of jousting knights. The average room temperatures are 28° F (-2° C).

Aurora Ice Museum

🕐 Tours: 11am, 1pm, 3pm, 5pm, & 7pm

THE AURORA BOREALIS

The Fairbanks area is one of the best places in the world to see the aurora borealis, or northern lights. The effect is visible as faint green, light yellow, or rose curtains, pillars, pinwheels, wisps, and haloes of undulating, vibrating light. While summer visitors will miss out owing to the 24-hour daylight, there is a good chance of catching the celestial show on clear nights between late September and early April.

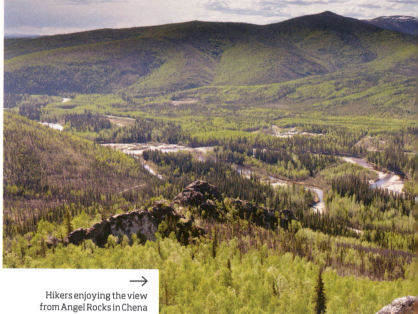

→

Hikers enjoying the view from Angel Rocks in Chena River State Recreation Area

⑨

Chena River State Recreation Area

🅐 Mile 26, Chena Hot Spring Rd 🛈 www.dnr.alaska. gov/parks/units/chena

A wonderful park in Fairbanks' backyard, the Chena River State Recreation Area follows the clear Chena River as it winds between low, forested hills topped by rocky tors sprouting from alpine tundra. The river is ideal for Arctic grayling fishing as well as for easy kayaking. The surrounding hills have hiking trails, from short walks to multiday routes. One popular walk goes uphill through birch and spruce to Angel Rocks, large outcrops with superb views. The excellent two-day Granite Tors Trail leads up into the hills to a free shelter overlooking the Plain of Monuments, a wide expanse dotted with towering volcanic rocks. It loops back down through forest and over boardwalks across a berry-studded muskeg bog. The three-day 29-mile (46-km) Chena Dome Trail climbs

above the timberline onto alpine tundra, with views across the wilderness. In the winter, there is plenty of scope for Nordic skiing and aurora viewing.

⑩

Elliott Highway

🅐 Starts 11 miles (18 km) NW of Fairbanks, off the Steese Highway

Connecting Fairbanks with Manley Hot Springs, the winding, undulating Elliott Highway is a breathtaking 152-mile (245-km) wilderness route through some of Interior Alaska's finest scenery. The landscape it passes through is especially lovely in early September, with the fall colors of the birch and aspen forests.

At the village of Livengood, the Dalton Highway (*p222*) turns north toward Prudhoe Bay while the Elliott Highway continues westward. At Mile 87, the road begins to climb to the trailhead for **Tolovana Hot Springs**, 11 miles (18 km) off the highway to the southeast (pre-booking is essential

for the springs and lodge). At Mile 98, the view opens up to take in the lake-studded Minto Flats, and a few miles later, a long side road turns south to the Athabascan village of Minto.

The Elliott Highway ends at the pretty village of **Manley Hot Springs**, which is home to the Gold Rush-era Manley Roadhouse. The village's growth dates from 1902, when the site became a supply center for the nearby Tofty and Eureka Mining Districts. The spa resort here closed after going bankrupt, and today,

> 💬 INSIDER TIP
> ## Steese Highway Tour
>
> Starting in the town of Fox, 11 miles (18 km) north of Fairbanks, the Steese Highway offers a delightfully scenic road trip. It winds through several river valleys and crosses a scenic alpine stretch, before descending into the flatlands around the Yukon River.

the way. First stop is by a section of the Trans-Alaska Pipeline, which carries around 15 percent of the nation's oil production. For a fun photo, stand under the pipe and have your picture taken "holding up" the structure.

The train then moves on to Dredge No. 8 – a huge mechanical gold pan which extracted over 7.5 million oz (210,000 kg) of gold between 1928 and 1959. Miners demonstrate the use of a sluice box and also give a brief history of mining in Alaska. Prospectors then demonstrate panning and washing gravel to extract the gold, and the guides encourage visitors to try it themselves using "pay dirt." Any gold found is weighed to determine its current value, and can then be kept by the lucky finder. The exit is, inevitably, through the gift shop, where your gold pannings can be encased in a locket if you wish, while everyone enjoys complimentary coffee and cookies.

This attraction is run by the Binkleys, a fifth-generation Alaskan steamboating family

DREDGING FOR GOLD

Large mining companies frequently employed mechanical dredges, which resembled massive houseboats equipped with machinery. To get at the gold-bearing quartz, water cannons blasted away soil and gravel permafrost layers. Upon reaching the bedrock, a dredge was brought in, usually to a streambed, to gouge out the rock using steel buckets on a conveyor belt. The rock was then sifted until it reached a riffle board, where mercury was introduced to bind with the gold.

who also operate the popular Riverboat Discovery trip on a picturesque sternwheeler *(p176)*; the two tours can be combined together as a full-day excursion.

the hot springs consist of three tubs in a spring-fed greenhouse, run by a local family.

Tolovana Hot Springs
🏠 100 miles (160 km) W of Fairbanks 🌐 tolovana hotsprings.com

Manley Hot Springs
🌐 152 miles (245 km) W of Fox 📞 672-3171

⑪ 🚫 🚫 🖥

Gold Dredge No. 8
🏠 1803 Old Steese Hwy N
🕐 Mid-May–mid-Sep: tours daily at 10:30am & 1:45pm (advance booking required)
🌐 golddredge8.com

A brief taste of the Fairbanks Gold Rush of 1902 can be experienced at Gold Dredge No. 8, which gives visitors a two-hour tour that faithfully explains gold-mining methods used in the early days. The tour begins with a ride on a replica of the Tanana Valley Railroad, with commentary and, if long-time conductor Earl is on board, old-time country songs along

↑ A guide demonstrating how to pan for treasure at Gold Dredge No. 8

Charming Nagley's Store, Talkeetna's only grocery and general store ↑

4

TALKEETNA

🅰 E4 🚗 114 miles (183 km) N of Anchorage 🚆🚌🚐 Anchorage-Fairbanks
ℹ Parks Hwy & Talkeetna Spur Rd; www.talkeetnachamber.org

With the mighty peak of Denali looming on the horizon, the town of Talkeetna is a great base for outdoor enthusiasts. This is no quiet pioneer town, and in the summer months it bustles with visitors wishing to explore the alpine area.

Talkeetna, meaning "meeting of the rivers" in Athabascan, began in 1896 as a trading post and grew into a riverboat port supplying the 1910 Susitna Valley Gold Rush. There was a second wave of development after 1915, when the Alaska Engineering Commission set up its headquarters here during the construction of the Alaska Railroad. Although the town was bypassed by the Parks Highway in the early 1970s, it still attracts a lot of traffic: busloads of tourists admire its old-fashioned air, young backpackers wonder how to settle in permanently, and climbers prepare to scale Denali.

One of Talkeetna's primary draws is flightseeing trips; several companies (including K2 Aviation and Talkeetna Air Taxi) depart the town many times daily in the summer, with ski-plane landings on Ruth Glacier within Denali National Park. Also popular are cycle tours with North Shore Cyclery and river trips with Mahay's Riverboat Service. Prospective climbers of Denali and

---

📷 PICTURE PERFECT
Majestic Mountain

Capture Denali in your camera's viewfinder, or simply stand in awe at North America's highest peak from the banks of the Susitna River, just a short walk along Main Street in downtown Talkeetna. The best time to go is in the morning or evening.

EAT

Denali Brew Pub

With daily specials and excellent beers, this spot is always crowded in the summer.

🏠 13605 E Main Street
Ⓦ denalibrewpub.com

$ $ $

Talkeetna Roadhouse

This must-visit restaurant and hotel serves two meals: "breakfast" and "not breakfast," in addition to mouthwatering baked goods.

🏠 13550 E Main Street
Ⓦ talkeetna roadhouse.com

$ $ $

Mountain High Pizza Pie

Hand-tossed pizza with fresh homemade dough, as well as sandwiches, flatbreads, and salads.

🏠 22165 C Street
Ⓦ pizzapie talkeetna.com

$ $ $

other peaks of the Alaska Range should head for the Walter Harper Talkeetna Ranger Station, at 22241 B Street. Inside, there is a reference library of books and maps. Rangers also conduct free orientation programs for climbing expeditions.

Exploring Talkeetna

For an insight into the history of mountaineering in the area it's well worth visiting the Talkeetna History Society Museum, located next to the old airstrip. The main displays are housed in the red 1937 schoolhouse, packed with pioneer artifacts, photographs, and articles on old Talkeetna. Also here are several relocated historic buildings, such as the 1933 Railroad Depot, complete with ticket office. The museum also provides a flyer for a self-guided walking tour of the town, or you can download the app for a more interactive experience.

The town's main hub is Fairview Inn, built by Ben Nauman in 1923 as the overnight stop on the Alaska Railroad between Seward and Fairbanks. It's a buzzing place for an evening out and is also a great spot for meeting locals and climbers. Across the street is the charming Nagley's Store, the town's only grocery and general store. Dating from 1921, it boasts that it was "established before most of you were born."

Talkeetna's cemetery would be of little interest to visitors if it were not for the memorial commemorating climbers who have died on Denali. It is a sobering reminder that the mountain and its weather can be harsh opponents. Among the headstones is that of Talkeetna glacier pilot Don Sheldon, whose exploits are immortalized in the book *Wager with the Wind*. Talkeetna's other hero, Ray Genet, is missing here as he was lost on Mount Everest in 1979 at the age of 48 and his body never found.

↑ Hiking through the rugged landscape of the Talkeetna Mountains

5 🍴 🍽 🛍

WRANGELL-ST. ELIAS NATIONAL PARK

🗺 F4 📍 Off the Richardson Highway 🚏 McCarthy 🚌 To McCarthy ⏱ Late May–early Sep: 9am–5pm daily ℹ Wrangell-St. Elias National Park Visitor Center, Mile 106.5 Richardson Highway; ranger stations at Chitina and Slana; www.nps.gov/wrst

At 20,000 sq miles (52,500 sq km), Wrangell-St. Elias is the largest national park in the United States – six times the size of Yellowstone. A vast wilderness of rugged mountains, fast-flowing rivers, and expansive glaciers, it is also one of the most remote parks in the country, with only a few road-based access points.

Located in the sprawling area that is Alaska's southeastern mainland section, the Wrangell-St. Elias National Park is dominated by the volcanic Wrangell Mountains and glaciated St. Elias range. The park has nine of the 16 highest mountains in the US, as well as a wealth of wildlife, and was designated a UNESCO World Heritage Site in 1992. Reflecting the history of the copper-mining industry in this area, it is also the site of Kennecott Mines, a National Historic Landmark and park-within-a-park where visitors can explore the restored buildings and trails of a now-faded copper company town (p186). Popular activities in Wrangell-St. Elias include short- and long-distance hiking, whitewater rafting, and taking flightseeing tours over the vast mountain expanses. Wild and taking some effort to reach, Wrangell-St. Elias National Park and the Historic Landmark will appeal to adventurous travelers looking to truly explore Alaska's dazzling backcountry.

↑ Homely Kennicott Glacier Lodge, picturesquely overlooking the mountains

← Cycling along the scenic Nabesna Road, built to access the Nabesna gold mine

STAY

Kennicott Glacier Lodge
A family-owned lodge and fine bistro.

📍 15 Kennicott Millsite, Glennallen 🌐 kennicott lodge.com

$$$

Ma Johnson's Hotel
Unique rooms and a great bistro.

📍 101 Kennicott Ave, McCarthy 🌐 mccarthy lodge.com

$$$

EAT

La Potato
Delicious burritos.

📍 Main St, McCarthy 🌐 theroadsidepotatohead

$$$

Meatza Wagon
Meatball subs, fish tacos, and curried rice.

📍 Lot 9, Upper Mill Rd, Kennecott 🌐 meatza wagon.com

$$$

Did You Know?

Mount Wrangell is one of the three largest active volanoes in the world.

The beautiful fall colors of the aspens in Wrangell-St. Elias National Park ↑

EXPLORING WRANGELL-ST. ELIAS NATIONAL PARK

Wrangell-St. Elias is incredibly large, with only the Nabesna and McCarthy Roads offering vehicle access into the park, and even then only to a tiny fraction of its vast acreage. Most people, therefore, visit via flightseeing tours in small bush planes or on hiking adventures from either McCarthy or the town of Chitina along the Edgerton Highway. If driving, many hikes of varying distances can be found along the roadway toward McCarthy. No private vehicles are allowed in either McCarthy or Kennecott, so visitors must rely on shuttle vans, bicycles, or their own two feet to explore these areas. A large network of trails connects the Kennecott townsite to Root Glacier, Bonanza Mine, and Jumbo Mine, and there are also a number of multiday excursions along the Nugget Creek or Dixie Pass trails.

*The **Wrangell-St. Elias National Park Visitor Center** provides information and has a short nature trail leading to spectacular mountain views.*

*The **McCarthy Road** (p200) crosses the Copper River. The river crossing is surrounded by hills that are sometimes obscured by clouds of billowing dust.*

East of Chitina, the

Mount Wrangell, a 14,160-ft (4,300-m) volcano that last erupted in 1900, was known to the Ahtna Athabascans as K'elt'aeni, "The One That Controls."

1 Slana
TOK CUTOFF
1 Chistochina
Copper River

Capital Mountain
7,731 ft (2,356 m) △

Gakona
Gulkana

Sanford River

Mount Sanford
16,237 ft (4,949 m) △

Copper Glacier

Glennallen

Mount Drum
12,010 ft (3,661 m) △

Wrangell

Wrangell-St. Elias National Park Visitor Center

RICHARDSON HIGHWAY

Copper Center

Dadine River

Mount Wrangell
14,163 ft (4,317 m) △

4

Long Glacier

Kenny Lake

Copper River

Kotsina River

Dixie Pass

10
EDGERTON HWY

NUGGET CREEK TRAIL

Chitina

Kuskulana Bridge

Chitina River

Nelson Mountain
5,457 ft (1,663 m) △

The Copper River, which flows along the western border of the park

←

Built in 1933 to access the Nabesna Mine, the 42-mile (67-km) **Nabesna Road** leads through muskeg and hills to the eponymous village. At Mile 36, a tough 5-mile (8-km) loop hike explores the area around the inactive Skookum Volcano.

↑ Ma Johnson's Hotel, a living museum in McCarthy

In the early 20th century, **Kennecott** (p186) was the site of rich copper mines. In the summer, rangers conduct tours of the abandoned buildings.

The old mining town of **McCarthy** (p201) was a supply and support center for the workers at Kennecott. It is now accessed via a short walk or shuttle ride from the Kennicott River footbridge.

Map labels:

NABESNA ROAD
Mentasta
Kendesnii Campground
Copper Lake
Skookum Volcano
Nabesna
Nabesna Mountains
Jacksina Creek
Mount Gordon 9,040 ft (2,755 m)
Mount Jarvis 13,421 ft (4,091 m)
Nabesna Glacier
Chisana
Chisana Glacier
Mountains
Solo Mountain 5,875 ft (1,791 m)
Mount Blackburn 16,390 ft (4,996 m)
Regal Mountain 13,845 ft (4,220 m)
Castle Mountain 8,620 ft (2,627 m)
Regal Glacier
Kuskulana Glacier
Root Glacier
Bonanza Mine
Kennicott Glacier
Kennecott
McCarthy Road Information Station
McCarthy
MCCARTHY ROAD
Chitistone River
Chitina River

0 kilometers 25
0 miles 25
N ↑

💬 **INSIDER TIP**
Float Trips

A great way to explore Wrangell-St. Elias is by water on a float trip. The seven-day excursion from McCarthy to Cordova is one of the most popular, but there are plenty of shorter rafting and kayaking trips, and even a stand-up paddleboard adventure. Check the park's website for details.

6 🏔 🍴

KENNECOTT MINES

🅰F4 🅰5 miles (8 km) NE of McCarthy 🔁Scheduled or charter flight to McCarthy, then 5 miles (8 km) on foot or by shuttle bus 🚌Glennallen to McCarthy 🛈Visitor Center at the old General Store; www.nps.gov/wrst

Overlooking the spectacular Kennicott Glacier, the abandoned Kennecott copper mines – now fully preserved as a National Historic Landmark – provide visitors with a fascinating insight into the rigors of life of an early 20th-century mining camp.

In 1900, while exploring the mountain east of the glacier, prospectors Clarence Warner and "Tarantula Jack" Smith discovered some of the richest deposits of copper ever found. Mining engineer Stephen Birch convinced wealthy East Coast families to finance the completion of the Copper River and Northwestern Railway to transport ore to Cordova. Over the years, nearly $200 million in copper was mined, but declining copper deposits and the high cost of railroad maintenance led to the closure of the mine in 1938.

The machine shop, one of the most prominent buildings at Kennecott, held the metal-working and maintenance operations of the mine.

Workers' cottages, dotted around the site and perched on the hillsides, are now used as private homes.

Electrical shop

Storage shed

Now partially restored, the Power House, overlooking Kennicott Glacier, provided enough steam and electricity for the entire operation.

KENNECOTT'S BEARS

Most visitors to Alaska assume bears are found in more remote places than an old townsite filled with eager visitors in the summer, but the black bears of Kennecott are quite visible at all times of the day here. Preferring the pathways and trails that humans use, the bears are often mistaken for small black dogs, surprising visitors when they come upon one. It is prudent to make noise, travel in groups, and carry bear spray whenever hiking outside the greater townsite area.

↑ The old mine buildings at Kennecott, including the Crusher/Concentration Mill

The General Manager's Office, Kennecott's oldest standing structure, had a large drafting room and was the heart of the mine's operations.

Low-grade ore was processed in the Crusher/Concentration Mill. Remnants of the tramways that brought ore from the Bonanza and Jumbo mines to the mill are still visible.

At the Ammonia Leaching Plant, copper carbonates were extracted from treated ore that had first passed through the Crusher/Concentration Mill.

↑ An illustrated plan of Kennecott Mines National Historic Landmark

💬 INSIDER TIP
Fall Colors

Consider visiting during Labor Day, the first full weekend of September and the last weekend that the park and lodge are open. The birch trees will have turned a brilliant gold by then, creating a stunning fall color palette.

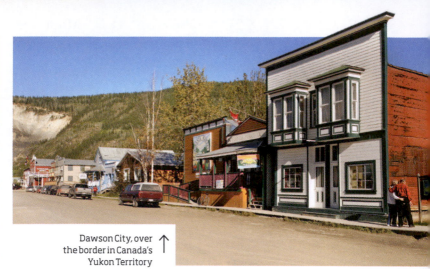

Dawson City, over the border in Canada's Yukon Territory →

⑦

DAWSON CITY

🗺 F3 🏠 328 miles (525 km) N of Whitehorse ✈ From Whitehorse, Canada, & Fairbanks 🚌 From Fairbanks & Whitehorse 🚐 ℹ Front & King St; www.dawsoncity.ca

Over the international border in the Yukon Territory of Canada, Dawson City – a Parks Canada National Historic Site – is a worthwhile side trip (just remember your passport). Once an Athabascan fishing camp, the area boomed in 1896 when gold was discovered in Rabbit Creek. Gold mining continues here, although the town's most reliable source of income is tourism.

showman and notorious gunslinger "Arizona Charlie" Meadows, the Palace Grand Theatre was at Dawson's cultural heart during the Gold Rush era. Everything from Wild West shows to opera was staged in its opulent auditorium. After gold was discovered in Nome (*p238*), Dawson began to decline, and in 1901, the theater was sold. Saved by the Klondike Visitors Association and reconstructed in the 1960s by the Canadian government, it is now open for daily tours in summer and stages the odd cultural event.

① 🏂 🎿 🛍

Tr'ondëk Hwëch'in Dänojà Zho Cultural Center

🏠 1131 Front St 🕐 Jun–Aug: 10am–5pm Mon–Sat 🌐 danojazho.ca

This center provides an insight into the cultural history and traditions of the Tr'ondëk Hwëch'in, the original inhabitants of the region. Designed to reflect Indigenous architecture, the center's award-winning building displays archeological artifacts, reproductions of traditional tools, historical photographs, and costumes. The center also hosts dance performances.

② 🏂 🎿

Palace Grand Theatre

🏠 King St between 2nd & 3rd 📞 (867) 993-7210 🕐 Late May–early Sep: 9am–5pm daily

Built from the remnants of two wrecked sternwheelers in 1899 by the Wild West

③ 🏂 🎿

Robert Service Cabin

🏠 8th Ave & Hanson St 📞 (867) 993-7210 🕐 May–Sep: 9am–5pm daily

One of Dawson City's most popular attractions is the humble two-room cabin once

---

SOURTOE COCKTAIL

Dawson City is perhaps most famous for the rather unappealing - yet wildly popular - SourToe Cocktail served at the Sourdough Saloon (*www.downtown hotel.ca/sourdough-saloon*). Now in its tenth "edition," the cocktail features a real, dehydrated human toe, preserved in salt, in honor of that lost by miner Louis Liken to frostbite in the 1920s.

owned by "the Bard of the Yukon," Robert Service (1874–1958). Nestled amid willows at the edge of town, the log cabin is typical of the era.

Service's seminal works, "The Cremation of Sam McGee," "The Shooting of Dan McGrew," and "The Spell of the Yukon" have long defined the Gold Rush era and the magic of the North. A guided tour takes place daily at 1pm.

④ 🧭 Ⓜ 🏛
Jack London Museum

📍 8th Ave & Firth St
🕐 Mid-May–mid-Sep: 11am–3pm daily 🌐 jacklondonmuseum.ca

The renowned author Jack London (1876–1916) first came to the Yukon in search of gold, but instead found a wealth of material for the tales of adventure he spun about frontier life. The cabin he lived in was located on the North Fork of Henderson Creek, 72 miles (120 km) south of Dawson City. Local trappers rediscovered his cabin in 1936, and it was dismantled and shipped to Dawson in 1965 by Jack London researcher Dick North. The original logs were used to make two replica cabins, one of which is in Oakland, London's California hometown. The other remains in Dawson and houses relics, photographs, and articles from the Gold Rush days. Every summer, Dick North interprets the site for visitors. Tours are at noon and 2:30pm.

⑤ 🧭 🍴 🖥 🏛
Diamond Tooth Gertie's

📍 4th Ave & Queen St
🕐 Hours vary, check website 🌐 dawsoncity.ca/diamond-tooth-gerties

Diamond Tooth Gertie's is the only legalized gambling hall in the Yukon Territory. Nightly shows by high-kicking dance hall girls attempt to re-create the bawdy atmosphere of the Gold Rush days.

⑥ 🧭 Ⓜ
The Goldfields

📍 10 miles (16 km) SE of Dawson City on Bonanza Creek Rd 🌐 klondikeexperience.com

Although numerous Gold Rush prospectors worked gravel for alluvial gold, the real environmental impact of mining came after 1910 with the introduction of dredges. For a close look at the effects of large-scale gold extraction, it is worth making a trip to Dredge No. 4. This enormous wooden-hulled dredge functioned from 1912 to 1966, when it was turned into a Parks Canada Historic Site. You can see the spot where George Carmack found ore in 1896, launching the Gold Rush that changed the area forever. Visits to the site are by tour, which can be arranged online.

EAT

Klondike Kate's
Hearty steaks, grilled elk and bison, and a full schnitzel menu.

📍 1102 Third Avenue
🌐 klondikekates.com

💲💲💲

Cheechakos Bakeshop
Home-baked goodies and sandwiches, as well as soups and salads.

📍 902 Front Street
☎ (867) 993 5303

💲💲💲

Alchemy Cafe
Great coffee, salads, sandwiches, and sushi.

📍 878 Third Ave #3
🌐 alchemycafe.ca

💲💲💲

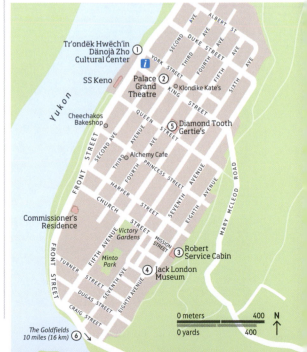

THE YUKON TERRITORY

Sharing a border with Alaska, the Yukon Territory is one of Canada's last frontiers. Inhabited by the First Nations since the end of the last Ice Age, this sparsely populated land is home to Canada's five highest mountains, a host of untamed rivers, and several legendary parks. Though much of this harsh mountainous territory lies barren, treeless, and frozen for most of the year, an abundance of wildlife flourishes: wolves, moose, bears, and caribou have all adapted to the subarctic climate. The harsh romance of the Gold Rush days still lingers over this starkly beautiful land, where you'll find plenty of opportunity to extend your Alaskan adventures.

THE YUKON RIVER

Rising in the high peaks of northwestern British Columbia in Canada and flowing 2,300 miles (3,680 km) across the Yukon Territory and Alaska to the Bering Sea, the Yukon River provides a vital transport route for the people who live along it. Only four bridges cross the river - at Tagish, Whitehorse, and Carmacks in Canada, and at Mile 56 of Alaska's Dalton Highway. In the winter, the frozen river is a venue for a part of the Yukon Quest International Sled Dog Race, while in the summer, it offers adventure activities that range from short paddles and cruises to expeditions from the river's headwaters to the Bering Sea.

↑ Two huskies playing in the snow on a winter's day in the Yukon

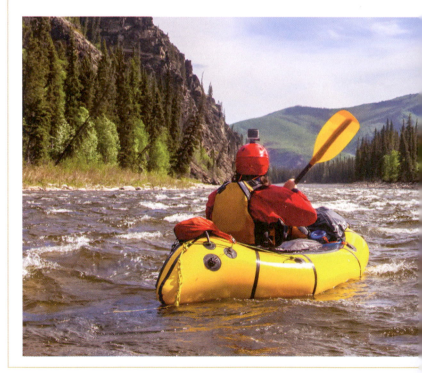

THE ALASKA HIGHWAY

For many drivers, a road trip along the Alaska Highway – formerly known as the Alcan, short for the Alaska-Canada Highway – is the adventure of a lifetime. Crossing some of the wildest territory in the world, this 1,390-mile (2,224-km) road offers breathtaking sights and experiences. Starting in Dawson Creek in Canada's British Columbia, it crosses remote ranges, running through taiga forests and past crystalline lakes into the Yukon Territory. At Haines Junction, drivers can take the Haines Cut-Off (p154) to Southeast Alaska, or continue northwest through the Yukon's strikingly lovely Kluane National Park. For the next 200 miles (320 km), it crosses scenic mountain country to the US–Canada border, and continues northwest past the Alaskan town of Tok for its final stretch to Fairbanks.

The highway has historically had a reputation for challenging road conditions, but these have improved over time. The entire two-lane highway is now paved or chip-sealed, and – due to rerouting and straightening – is also shorter than it was originally. Make sure to allow plenty of time for sightseeing en route.

↑ The scenic Alaska Highway, snaking through the Yukon Territory up to Alaska

↑ Rafters navigating the Yukon River, which is crossed (inset) at Whitehorse by one of only four bridges along its length

INSIDER TIP
Float Trips

The most popular routes for canoeists, kayakers, and rafters are the 8–10 day float from Whitehorse to Dawson, the 4-day float between Dawson and Eagle, and the 5-day trip from Eagle to Circle.

EXPERIENCE MORE

⑧ Big Lake

Ⓐ E4 **⌂** 60 miles (96 km) N of Anchorage **ℹ** 3261 Big Lake Rd; www.biglake chamber.org

Dubbed Alaska's "Year-Round Playground," Big Lake lives up to the moniker. In the summer, the lake echoes with the roars of motorboats, floatplanes, jet skis, and fireworks, while in the winter, it buzzes as snow-mobilers take to the trails.

While the community itself is small, most of the surrounding lakes are lined with the vacation cabins of city dwellers trying to get away to the outdoors. However, in contrast to Big Lake's constant hum of activity, many of these lakes, including the Papoose Twins and Horseshoe Lake, are quieter. Most have public boat launches that offer access to gentle sailing, kayaking, and canoeing, as well as being good for wildlife spotting.

Devastating forest fires in 1996 burned much of the area, but it now provides a first-hand look at the regeneration of the boreal forest.

⑨ Willow

Ⓐ E4 **⌂** 70 miles (113 km) N of Anchorage **🚌** **ⓦ** willowchamber.org

Founded in 1897 after gold was discovered in the Talkeetna Mountains, Willow flourished until the 1940s, when mining stopped and the town lapsed into obscurity. It rose to prominence again in 1976, when Alaskans selected it as their new state capital. Investments poured in, but the hype evaporated after a 1982 referendum in which Alaskans declined to fund the predicted costs of the move from Juneau. The town now serves as the restart location for the Iditarod (p238).

---

⑩ Nancy Lake State Recreation Area

Ⓐ E4 **⌂** Nancy Lake Pkwy **ℹ** Mile 1.3 Nancy Lake Pkwy; www.dnr.alaska.gov/parks/units/nancylk/nancylk.htm

The Susitna Valley landscape is dominated by the winding ridges and small hills – eskers and drumlins – left behind by retreating glaciers. Here, the low-lying bogs, lakes, and forested slopes of Nancy Lake State Recreation Area provide a serene environment for canoeing, fishing, and wildlife watching. The highlight is the two-day Lynx Lake Loop canoe trail; canoes can be rented at South Rolly Lake in summer. During the winter, the park's trails become excellent Nordic ski and snowmobile routes.

NO-SEE-UMS

The tiny biting midges known as no-see-ums are the smallest of the biting flies, and they appear in thick swarms that are impossible to ignore. Only a few Alaska midge species actually bite, but the variety found in the boreal forests of Interior Alaska raises large itchy welts and can make life intolerable from late June all through July. A DEET-based repellant is effective protection.

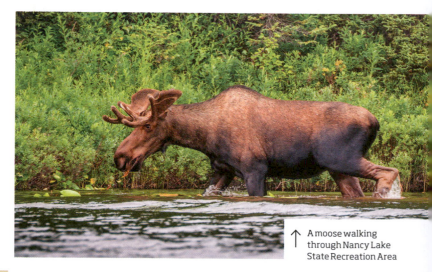

↑ A moose walking through Nancy Lake State Recreation Area

↑ Autumnal hues of the boreal forest at Riley Creek, Denali National Park

THE BOREAL FOREST

Most of Interior Alaska is cloaked in the vast circumpolar boreal forest that also covers much of subarctic Canada, northwestern Russia, Scandinavia, and Siberia. The term "boreal forest" includes dry lands in hilly or well-drained regions, such as the rolling country around Fairbanks, which are typically covered in white or black spruce and birch. These rich, lake-dotted lands produce a wealth of berries and are home to most of Alaska's lynx, bears, and forest-dwelling rodents such as beavers, porcupines, martens, and ermines.

NORTHERN HAWK OWLS
Northern hawk owls are atypical of most owls because they hunt during the day, preying on voles, mice, and occasionally small birds.

SPRUCE HENS
Spruce hens, marked by mottled feathers, usually nest in exposed bluffs or under spruce trees.

BLACK-CAPPED CHICKADEES
Black-capped chickadees – tiny song birds – do not migrate in the winter and are evident in Alaska all year round.

↑ A northern hawk owl scanning for prey

RED FOXES
Red foxes are recognized by their white-tipped tails and black "stockings." These omnivores are found across the Alaska Interior in hilly, forested country.

MARTENS
Martens, who feed mainly on voles, have non-retractable claws, used for climbing as well as holding prey.

RED SQUIRRELS
Red squirrels spend summer cutting and storing green spruce cones. They nest in trees, using ground burrows mostly as caches.

↑ A red fox, with its distinctive black leg markings

Backpacking the landscapes of Denali State Park, home to *(inset)* a large caribou population ↑

⑪ Denali State Park

🅐 E4 📍 135 miles (215 km) N of Anchorage 🚌 Anchorage-Fairbanks ℹ Alaska State Parks Office (Wasilla); www.dnr. alaska.gov/parks/units/ denali1.htm

The majority of travelers drive past Denali State Park en route to the better-known Denali National Park *(p168)*, effectively creating this park's quieter charm. Established in 1970, Denali State Park sprawls over 507 sq miles (1,313 sq km), which is about half the size of Rhode Island.

TOP 3 DENALI VIEWPOINTS

Curry Ridge/K'esugi Ridge Trail
Hike up from the K'esugi Ken campground for sweeping views.

Talkeetna/Susitna Rivers
Head down Talkeetna's Main Street to the rivers' confluence.

Denali Viewpoint South
Excellent views at Mile 134.7 of the highway.

The park offers uncrowded campgrounds, fabulous hiking trails, and views that equal those of its more renowned neighbor. K'esugi Ken is a recently opened area within the park. A paved road leads to a big campground, hiking trails (including K'esugi Ridge Trail), public-use cabins, picnic areas, and fantastic views of Mt. Denali. The K'esugi Ridge Trail is a challenging 13- to 35-mile- (21- to 56-km-) long hike, with superb mountain and glacier views from start to finish. It is accessed from Little Coal Creek Trailhead at Mile 163.9 of the Parks Highway, with exits back to the highway via the Troublesome Creek, Ermine Hill, or Cascade Trails. At the Cascade trailhead at Byers Lake, there is a campground, a visitor center (summer only), and a tasteful Veterans' Memorial.

The flora of the park is dominated by white spruce and paper birch, as well as moss campion and mountain avens – although many of the spruce trees have suffered in recent years from a massive bark beetle infestation. The park's varied landscape, with valley glaciers and alpine ridges, as well as meandering lowland streams and Arctic tundra, make it the favored habitat of a wide range of wildlife, including caribou, moose, bears, wolves, and lynx. Beavers and muskrats inhabit the park's wet areas, while both marmots and pikas (small rabbit-like mammals) can be seen on treeless hillsides and rocky outcrops.

Other notable sights just north of the park include the spectacular Hurricane Gulch at Mile 174 and the Igloo at Mile 188.5. Built in the 1970s, this enormous structure – intended to be a hotel but never actually opened – marks the midway point between Anchorage and Fairbanks.

⑫ Cantwell

🅐 E3 📍 210 miles (340 km) N of Anchorage 🚌 Anchorage-Fairbanks

This small village takes its name from the Cantwell River, the former name of the Nenana River. This scenic area was originally inhabited by itinerant Athabascan hunters, but the first person to settle there was trapper Oley Nicklie in the early 20th century. As more people settled there, Cantwell was designated a federally recognized tribal community. Today, a quarter of its residents are of Native descent. Cantwell, with a food shop and a lodge, is a convenient refueling stop. It is also the western terminus of the Denali Highway.

⑬ Denali Park

🅰 E3 📍 124 miles (200 km) S of Fairbanks
🚉/🚌 Anchorage–Fairbanks, then take shuttle buses to the park

This huge cluster of hotels, RV parks, lodges, restaurants, and outdoor activity operators is the main service center for the Denali National Park area (p168). Also referred to as either Nenana Canyon or Denali Village, this place was formerly just a roadside stretch of development, but a growing number of hotels, shops, and tourist-driven businesses have earned it the moniker "Glitter Gulch." By any name, however, it would still be one of Alaska's villages in the summer. Since the demolition of the Denali National Park Hotel, which provided well-heeled accommodations inside the park, visitors who want to appreciate Denali in comfort usually take hotel rooms here. Visitors can also plump for less expensive options in Healy (p197) to the north, or Carlo Creek, 13 miles (21 km) south on the Parks Highway.

⑭ Nenana River

🅰 E3 📍 S of Nenana Bridge in Denali Park

Rising on Nenana Mountain in the Alaska Range, the 150-mile- (240-km-) long Nenana River tumbles down to join the Parks Highway at Mile 215. From this point on, the river and highway flow side by side.

> **The steep-sided Nenana Canyon is perhaps the most popular whitewater rafting spot in the whole of Alaska.**

Spruce occasionally topple off the eroding banks, forming "sweepers" – logs that float in the water and are a real navigation hazard for rafts and canoes.

Beyond Healy (p197), the Nenana enters the flats north of the Alaska Range and flows more lethargically until it merges with the Tanana River at the village of Nenana. From the south side of the Nenana Bridge in Denali Park, thrilling whitewater rafting through the steep-sided Nenana Canyon is provided by three main outfitters: **Raft Denali**, the **Denali Outdoor Center**, and **Denali Raft Adventures**. This is perhaps the most popular whitewater rafting spot in the whole of Alaska, and difficulty levels range from easy Class I rapids to more challenging Class IV whitewater. The price of a half-day trip includes raingear, boots, and personal flotation devices, as well as transfers to and from hotels in the area.

Raft Denali
📍 Mile 238, Parks Hwy
🌐 raftdenali.com

Denali Outdoor Center
📍 Mile 238.5, Parks Hwy
🌐 denalioutdoorcenter.com

Denali Raft Adventures
📍 Mile 238, Parks Hwy
🌐 denaliraft.com

← Two inflatable rafts making their way through the scenic Nenana Canyon

15

Nenana

△E3 🚗 58 miles (93 km) S of Fairbanks 🚆 Anchorage–Fairbanks 🛈 A St & Parks Hwy; 832-5446

The little service center of Nenana lies at the confluence of the Nenana and Tanana rivers. At the turn of the 20th century, it was known as Tortella or Tortilli, apparently derivations of a long forgotten Athabascan word. The town began as a trading post for river travelers, and eventually came to be called Nenana, meaning "a good campground between the rivers." In the 1920s, it served as a railroad construction camp, and gained fame on July 15, 1923, when President Warren G. Harding drove in the spike that completed the railroad between Seward and Fairbanks.

The old railroad depot at the end of Main Street houses the Alaska Railroad Museum. A block away, the log-built St. Mark's Mission Church is worth a visit, as is the *Taku Chief*, a river tug that once pushed barges down the Tanana. Today, it stands outside the Nenana Visitor Center. The Alfred Starr Cultural Center has displays on Native culture.

Nenana is the site of the Nenana Ice Classic competition. Each year, people from all across the state place bets on when the ice will go out on the Tanana. Any surge in the river ice shifts a four-legged "tripod" on shore, which pulls a cord, which in turn trips the clock on the adjacent tower. All correct entries split half the take and the organizers get the other half.

> The town began as a trading post for river travelers, and eventually came to be called Nenana, meaning "a good campground between the rivers."

HIDDEN GEM
To Market

The Ester Village Farmers and Craft Market is located at the village's entrance along the Parks Highway. With gloriously fresh produce and handcrafted items for sale, this is where the community shops.

16

Ester

△E3 🚗 6 miles (10 km) W of Fairbanks 🚆 Anchorage–Fairbanks

Northeast of Nenana on the Parks Highway is the old mining and Gold Rush town of Ester. During its heyday in 1906, Ester had a population of 5,000. The Fairbanks Exploration Company built the Ester Gold Camp in the mid-1930s to service the area's

Nenana's old railway depot, which now houses the Alaska Railroad Museum ↑

dredging operations. The camp closed in the 1950s, but enjoyed a stint as a mining-themed tourist camp from 1958 to 2008. Today, Ester retains a small mining village ambience, but is entering a new phase as a growing suburb of Fairbanks. Most residents are employed in Fairbanks or at the University of Alaska Fairbanks (p174), although there are some small local businesses: a saloon, a library, fire station, post office, arts and crafts studios, three active gold mines and a summer farmers' market.

17

Healy

E3 113 miles (182 km) S of Fairbanks Anchorage-Fairbanks www.denali chamber.com

North of Denali, the village of Healy has long been the service center for the Usibelli coal fields 3 miles (5 km) to

the east. Discovered by Emil Usibelli in 1943, these fields contain the state's largest deposits of sub-bituminous coal. The mine now provides energy for Alaska's military bases, fuels Fairbanks' power plant, and exports coal. Healy is best known as an inexpensive place to stay and plan a visit to Denali National Park (p168). It is also well-known for the rough winter route from here to Kantishna (p170). Known as the Stampede Trail, the route is accessible by snowmobile in winter, but river crossings make it practically impassable in summer.

About 4 miles (6 km) north of Healy, the trail passes an old Fairbanks city bus. It was here that 24-year-old Chris McCandless died of injury and starvation in 1992. He intended to live off the land, away from civilization, and to experience the raw Alaska wilderness. His tragic story is documented in Jon Krakauer's book *Into the Wild* and the film of the same name. No attempts should be made to cross the river here; a number of people have died while trying to reach the bus.

Not just a place to retreat after a busy day exploring Denali National Park, Healy has plenty of activities that rival those within the park boundaries. Try an ATV tour or zipline adventure, or enjoy

↑ A camper truck on Healy's tree-dotted Stampede Trail

a covered wagon ride and evening dinner before a campfire. If driving to or from Fairbanks, Healy is a quieter option than lodging in the Nenana Canyon area near the national park entrance. The Denali Chamber of Commerce can help visitors with Healy lodging and activities.

DRINK

49th State Brewing
This wildly successful Healy brewpub serves burgers, sandwiches, and amazing craft beers. They also fill takeout jugs if you're on the road to another destination. The atmosphere is laid-back and outdoorsy, and you're likely to find kids tossing beanbags in a cornhole game and adults taking photos in the replica of Chris McCandless' bus from the movie *Into the Wild*.

E3 248 Parks Hwy, Healy 49state brewing.com

↑ Ice climber tackling
the stunning
Matanuska Glacier

> Drivers on the Glenn
> Highway cannot
> fail to notice the
> Matanuska Glacier,
> a broad blue river
> of ice descending
> 12,000 ft (3,600 m).

Much of the lakeshore lies
within the Lake Louise State
Recreation Area, which offers
camping, swimming, berry
picking, boating, and fishing
for trout and grayling in the
summer, and snowmobiling
and ice fishing in the winter.

20 Glennallen

🅰 E4 🚗 Mile 187 on
the Glenn Highway
🚌 Anchorage-Whitehorse
ℹ The Hub, 189 Glenn Hwy;
www.coppervalley
chamber.com

Deriving its name from two
early explorers in the Copper
River Valley, Major Edwin F.
Glenn and Lieutenant Henry T.
Allen, Glennallen is mainly a
food and fuel service center at
the junction of the Glenn and
Richardson highways. Despite
an unusually high mosquito
population, Glennallen has
a beautiful location, and its
approaches are dominated
by vistas of the mountains
Sanford, Drum, and Wrangell.
Rising from the flats, they
appear unimaginably lofty,
and become even more
dreamlike in the haze from
humidity or wildfires.

Don't pass through the
town of Glennallen without
stopping at the Bureau of
Land Management's office,
especially if you're on the way
to drive the all-dirt Denali
Highway. Offering maps and

18 Matanuska Glacier

🅰 E4 🏠 66500 S Glacier
Park Rd 🕐 May–mid-Oct
🌐 matanuskaglacier
adventures.us

Drivers on the Glenn Highway
cannot fail to notice the
Matanuska Glacier, a broad
blue river of ice, descending
12,000 ft (3,600 m) to its
2-mile- (3-km-) wide face. It
is thought that about 18,000
years ago, the glacier filled
the entire Matanuska Valley
and probably even flowed
into Knik Arm near Palmer.

Access to the glacier is via
the privately owned Glacier
Park, where hiking to the
glacier face is permitted.
MICA Guides leads ice treks
and climbing classes on the
glacier. Drivers can stop at
the Matanuska Glacier State
Recreation Site, which provides
a lofty vantage point and
interpretive panels. The Edge
Nature Trail loops from here to
another point with fine views.

MICA Guides
🌐 micaguides.com

19 Lake Louise State Recreation Area

🅰 E4 🚗 Mile 160 on the
Glenn Highway 🕐 May–
Sep ℹ 441-7575

Not often visited by non-
residents, the 26-sq-mile
(67-sq-km) Lake Louise lies
19 miles (30 km) north of the
Glenn Highway. It was named
in 1889 by Major Edwin F. Glenn
of the US Geological Survey,
who reported its existence.

→

Dramatic mountain
views of the Alaska
Range, near Paxson

interpretive information, it is a valuable place for obtaining advice on driving conditions. If heading toward Wrangell-St. Elias National Park (p182), stop by the beautiful park visitor center along the Richardson Highway for short walking trails, tourist information, park maps, and indoor and outdoor exhibits.

21 Copper Center

⚑ F4 ⌖ 100 miles (161 km) N of Valdez ⛟ Glennallen-McCarthy ℹ www.oldtown coppercenter.com

Dotted with historic buildings, this small town makes a worthwhile side trip off the Richardson Highway. In an old bunkhouse, the **George I. Ashby Memorial Museum** is filled with artifacts such as birch baskets, an enormous mouse trap, and a kerosene tin cradle. It also has information on the Copper River and Northwestern Railway (CR&NW). The annex next door displays old tools and an antique snowmobile. A block away, in the Copper Rail Depot Pub, a 1:24 scale replica of the CR&NW railway winds around the beer garden. The town is also the location of the region's first church, the 1942 log Chapel on the Hill.

George I. Ashby Memorial Museum
⊕ ⌂ Copper Center Loop Rd
⏰ Jun–mid-Sep: 11am–5pm daily

22 Paxson

⚑ E4 ⌖ 176 miles (283 km) SE of Fairbanks ⛟ Fairbanks -Valdez

The tiny village of Paxson consists of little more than a road junction – the nearest gas station is at Tangle Lakes. However, for five days in early April, attendance at the Arctic Man Classic snowmobile contest makes it the fourth largest city in the state.

The area is dotted with vacation cabins along the shores of Paxson and Summit lakes, and Paxson Lake has one of the best-maintained campgrounds in Alaska. The lake itself serves as a launching point for kayaking and rafting trips on the Gulkana River, with Class II to Class III rapids.

North of Paxson, the area around Summit Lake offers great fishing and long views across open tundra to glaciers on the southern slopes of the mighty Alaska Range.

23 Delta Junction

🗺 E3 📍 98 miles (158 km) SE of Fairbanks ✈ Fairbanks-Valdez ℹ Richardson Hwy; www.deltachamber.org

In 1910, Delta Junction was little more than a roadhouse on the wagon road from Valdez to Fairbanks, but in the early 1920s, it grew as a construction camp for the Richardson Highway. After the Alaska Highway connected with the Richardson Highway here in the early 1940s, the town developed into a major service center. Several private and governmental projects were set up here, including a Trans-Alaska Pipeline pump station and reindeer, yak, and elk farms. There were also bison farms, following the relocation of a herd from the Lower 48 states in the 1920s.

Although Delta Junction remains a small rural outpost, it has a couple of interesting museums. Pioneer life can be explored at the 1905 **Sullivan Roadhouse Museum**. Once located in the wilderness 14 miles (22 km) west of the modern town, it was moved here in 1996. Just outside town, the **Big Delta State Historical Park** includes the historic Rika's Roadhouse, with sweeping river views.

Sullivan Roadhouse Museum

♿ 📍 266 Richardson Hwy ☎ 895-5068 🕐 May–Sep: 10am–5pm daily

Big Delta State Historical Park

♿ 🅿 📍 Mile 275, Richardson Hwy 🕐 Mid-May–early Sep: 8am–8pm daily 🌐 dnr. alaska.gov/parks/units/deltajct/bigdelta.htm

---

24 Edgerton Highway/ McCarthy Road

🗺 F4 📍 Off the Richardson Hwy at Mile 82.6 🚌 Backcountry Connection shuttle bus

The Edgerton Highway/McCarthy Road is among the most picturesque drives in North America. It begins calmly, gradually descending from the Richardson Highway into the Copper River Valley, with long views of the river's characteristic eroded bluffs. Entering Wrangell-St. Elias National Park (p182) at Chitina, the often rutted and dusty road follows the Copper River and Northwestern Railway (CR&NW) as it twists along above the Chitina River. Dramatically crossing the Kuskulana River, the road parallels the glaciated Wrangell Mountains to McCarthy, deep inside the park. Although extensive road renovations have improved the condition of the highway, most rental car agencies will still not allow their vehicles to be driven on this road, so be sure to check in advance.

Huddling in a narrow valley, the community of **Chitina** was founded in 1908 as a halt on the CR&NW railway and a supply center for the copper mines at Kennecott. Of the few remaining original buildings, the former tinsmith's shop is the best restored and now houses an art gallery.

About 10 miles (16 miles) short of Chitina, the road passes camping and picnic spots at the Liberty Falls

← Quirky decorations outside the Sullivan Roadhouse Museum in Delta Junction

↑ The Kuskulana Bridge, carrying the Edgerton Highway/McCarthy Road

State Recreation Site. Entering a tight canyon, it passes three lovely blackwater lakes before it reaches Chitina. Heading east from town, the road crosses the 1,378-ft- (413-m-) long Copper River Bridge, where subsistence fish wheels are visible. The river current turns the wheels, trapping salmon in the rotating baskets.

Two dramatic reminders of the days when ore trains clattered along the CR&NW route are the large railroad trestles between Chitina and McCarthy. The incredible **Kuskulana Bridge** at Mile 17, built in 1910, is a three-span former trestle above the roiling Kuskulana River. At Mile 29, the road crosses the Gilahina River just downstream from the towering wooden **Gilahina Trestle**.

Homesteaded in 1906, **McCarthy** was a lively rest and supply town for workers at the Kennecott Mine *(p186)* in the early 20th century. During World War I, the rise in copper prices boosted McCarthy's economy. The town declined in 1938 when the mines and railroad closed down, but its fortunes revived in the 1980s with the creation of Wrangell-St. Elias National Park.

Scenic little McCarthy retains much of its original flavor thanks to the restored buildings, some of which are still in use. The free **McCarthy-Kennicott Historical Museum**, housed in the old Railway Depot, features historical photographs and artifacts from the two towns. Kennecott can be accessed by a shuttle bus or on foot along the Old Wagon Road out of McCarthy.

Chitina
🏠 66 miles (106 km) SE of Glennallen 🚐 🚌 Glennallen-McCarthy 🛈 Chitina Ranger Station; 823-2205

THE TRANS-ALASKA PIPELINE

When oil was discovered at Prudhoe Bay in 1968, no one knew how to transport it to market. It was eventually decided to create an 800-mile (1,280-km) pipeline from the North Slope oil fields to the ice-free port of Valdez, where a shipping facility was to be built to handle the crude. Construction of the pipeline began on April 29, 1974, and was completed three years later at a total cost of $8 billion. Now run by a consortium, the pipeline transports an impressive 525,000 barrels of oil per day.

EAT

Buffalo Center Drive-In
Traditional drive-in food to sustain even the most weary traveler, plus excellent ice cream, floats, and sundaes.

🅰E3 🏠Mile 265.5 Richardson Hwy, Delta Junction 📞895-4055

$$$$$⑤

Clearwater Lodge
This iconic spot has been operating since 1956, and offers fabulous views over the Clearwater River.

🅰E3 🏠7826 Remington Rd, Delta Junction clear waterlodgeak.com

$$$$$⑤

Rika's Roadhouse and Landing

Head here for a slice of pie and to browse the charming gift shop full of Alaska-themed products.

🅰E3 🏠274 Richardson Hwy, Delta Junction 📞895-4201

$$$$$⑤

Kuskulana Bridge and Gilahina Trestle
🚌 Glennallen-McCarthy

McCarthy
🏠 60 miles (96 km) W of Chitina 🚌 Glennallen-Kennicott River bridge, then on foot or by shuttle bus

McCarthy-Kennicott Historical Museum
🏠 Kennicott Road ⏰ Late May-early Sep: 11am-7pm daily 🌐 mccarthy kennicott historical museum.com

25

Tok Cut-Off

🅰 F4 🏠 Gakona Junct to Tok 🚌 Anchorage–Whitehorse

For drivers heading from Anchorage to the Alaska Highway, the scenic 125-mile (200-km) Tok Cut-Off links Glennallen with the village of Tok. The southern half of the route looks eastward to Mount Drum, Mount Sanford, Mount Jarvis, and Mount Blackburn in the Wrangell Mountains. At Mile 60 is the junction with the Nabesna Road, which leads east, past the town of Slana and several hiking trailheads into the northern reaches of Wrangell-St. Elias National Park (p182).

The Native village of Mentasta Lake, the northernmost outpost of the Ahtna Athabascans, lies in the heart of the Mentasta Mountains, which form the easternmost extent of the Alaska Range. About 16 miles (26 km) short of Tok, the Eagle Trail State Recreation Site includes a large campground and a steep 2-mile (3-km) trail to spectacular views over the surrounding hills and valleys.

Did You Know?

"Tok" is an abbreviation of "Tokyo" – the name of the original camp for construction workers on the highway.

26

Tok

🅰 F3 🏠 206 miles (331 km) SE of Fairbanks 🚌 From Fairbanks or Anchorage to Whitehorse 🅸 Tok Main St Visitors Center, Mile 1314, Alaska Hwy; www.tokalaskainfo.com

Situated in the upper Tanana River Valley, at the junction of the Tok Cut-Off and the Alaska Highway, Tok is the first major Alaska town west of the Canadian border. While there have been Athabascan settlements in the region for centuries, the modern town came up as a housing site for workers during the construction of the Alaska and Glenn highways in the 1940s. Tok's economy was later enhanced by a fuel line from Haines to Fairbanks in 1954 and the opening of a loran station, built in 1976 as an aid to long-range navigation.

Tok is now a service center with a range of accommodations, RV parks, eateries, and gas stations. It also has three information centers: the Tok Main Street Visitors Center, the Alaska Public Lands Information Center next door, and a Tetlin National Wildlife Refuge ranger station about 5 miles (8 km) southwest of town. Fortymile Country (p204), a renowned gold-mining region with historical and active claims, stretches north over undulating landscape along the Taylor Highway to the Yukon River.

27

Tok River State Recreation Site

🅰 F3 🏠 5 miles (8 km) E of Tok at Mile 1309, Alaska Hwy 🚌 Anchorage–Whitehorse 🕐 Mid-May–mid-Sep: 24 hrs daily 🔗 alaskastateparks.org

Located beside a sandy beach on the eastern bank of the Tok River, the Tok River State Recreation Site is a popular venue with both locals and highway travelers. Families spend sunny afternoons fishing and picnicking at this lovely site, which also offers good boating opportunities. Although the area was burned in the Tok wildfire in 1990 and in the devastating fires of 2004, the campground itself was spared and remains a pleasantly green place to stop and take a break.

In addition to 43 campgrounds, ten of which have room for RVs up to 60 ft (18 m) long, there is a picnic shelter with drinking water and facilities, a boat launch, a short nature loop, and interpretive sign boards that describe the human and natural history of this part of Interior Alaska. A campfire area is provided on the beach.

28

Northway

🏕 F4   🚩 59 miles (95 km) E of Tok   ✈ Charter plane only 🚌 Anchorage-Fairbanks

This small village was named in 1942 to honor the local Athabascan chief, Walter Northway, who passed away in 1993 at the age of 117. The modern settlement consists of three separate sectors. Northway Junction lies right on the Alaska Highway, with a café, lodge, and gas station. There is an airstrip on the Northway Road, 6 miles (10 km) south of the Alaska Highway, and another 2 miles (3 km) to the south is the Athabascan Native village of Northway, where visitors can purchase a range of authentic souvenirs, including basketry, Native moosehide and fur clothing, and shoes decorated with fine beadwork.

During the 1940s, the village served as an airstrip on the Northwest Staging Route, a chain of air bases and radio ranging stations that were built every 100 miles (160 km) from Edmonton in Alberta, Canada, to Fairbanks, Alaska, to provide defense during World War II.

Today, Northway remains the main US port of entry for private aviators arriving from the Lower 48 states, with some 700 planes clearing customs here each year. It is also the first US village for travelers arriving via the Alaska Highway.

EAT

Fast Eddy's Restaurant

This popular spot does brisk business. Their hearty comfort food is guaranteed to fuel you up for a day of driving.

🏕 F3   🚩 Mile 1313, Alaska Hwy, Tok   🌐 fasteddys restaurant.com

💲💲💲

SHOP

3 Bears Tok Outpost

This Alaska-specific chain prides itself on serving rural, road-based areas. There's a little bit of everything in stock, from food to recreational equipment.

🏕 F3   🚩 Mile 1313.3 Alaska Hwy, Tok   🌐 threebearsalaska.com

← The beautiful Tok River, overlooked by an imposing mountain range

↑ The small town of Chicken, Alaska, and *(inset)* "Eggee," a large sculpture at Chicken Gold Camp

29 Ⓜ
Chicken

🅰 F3 **🅰 71 miles (114 km) N of Tok** **🚌 Tour bus from Tok to Eagle**

Chicken reputedly got its unusual name when early gold miners were unable to spell the chosen name, Ptarmigan, which is a bird that somewhat resembles a chicken. Today, the chicken theme is rather pronounced, with chicken T-shirts for sale, stuffed chickens, a cutout of a chicken-pulled dog sled, and even a set of Chicken Poop outhouses.

Modern Chicken, south of the Taylor Highway, is divided into three main communities: Chicken Center, Beautiful Downtown Chicken, and Chicken Gold Camp. The Pedro Creek Dredge, which operated on Chicken Creek in the 1960s, lies in the grounds of Chicken Gold Camp and can be viewed on a guided tour. The historic town lies north of the highway. The Goldpanner in Chicken Center arranges guided tours of the area, which include panning opportunities and taking in the schoolhouse made famous in Anne Purdy's 1976 book, *Tisha*.

💬 INSIDER TIP
Funky Chicken

The tiny town of Chicken plays host to an annual music event known as "Chickenstock" *(www.chickenalaska. com)*. Drawing enthusiastic concertgoers from around the world, the festival is the community's biggest draw, and sells out every year well in advance of the June dates.

30
Fortymile Country

🅰 F3 **🅰 Mile 75 to Mile 112, Taylor Highway** **ℹ BLM Field Office; 474-2200 or (800) 437-7021**

Passing through some of Alaska's richest gold-bearing country, the Fortymile National Wild & Scenic River descends from the highlands around the southern end of the Taylor Highway, down through forested canyons, and past the Canadian border to the mighty Yukon River. It was given this name by Gold Rush prospectors because it joins the Yukon River about 40 miles (64 km) below Fort Reliance, an old Canadian trading post.

Gold mining in the region began as early as 1881, when gold was discovered on the North Fork of the Fortymile River. It proved to be one of the richest veins in Alaska, with its ore assaying $20,000 per ton (900 kg). Relics from the past lie all along the graveled highway, and there are also a large number of

active gold claims that are off limits to visitors. Bureau of Land Management (BLM) recreation sites and waysides are similarly closed to recreational panning.

The region has plenty of recreational activities on offer; outdoor adventurers can choose from several canoe, raft, or kayak trips on the Fortymile. The South Fork Bridge Wayside at Mile 75 of the Taylor Highway is the starting point for a popular two-day whitewater trip (with rapids up to Class III) that winds past historic 1880s Gold Rush sites to the Fortymile Wayside take-out at Mile 112. For those looking to make a longer trip, it is possible to take a week or more and continue all the way to the Yukon River (canoeists will have several portages) and then downstream to Eagle. Note that it is necessary to carry your passport for the border crossing into Canada.

→

A moose wading across a river within the Tetlin National Wildlife Refuge

31 Tetlin National Wildlife Refuge

F3 ☐ E of Tok on the Alaska Highway 🚌 Anchorage-Whitehorse ⏰ Mid-May-mid-Sep: 8am-4:30pm daily ℹ Mile 1229, Alaska Highway; www.tetlin.fws.gov

Snowcapped peaks, glacial rivers, open tundra, lakes, and seemingly endless forests and muskeg flats make up the glorious scenery of the 1,140-sq mile (2,955-sq km) Tetlin National Wildlife Refuge. Along with the Kenai National Wildlife Refuge *(p106)*, it is one of the few Alaska refuges that are accessible by road. Situated under a bird migration corridor, the refuge attracts over 185 species of waterfowl, songbirds, and raptors. At least 115 of these, including the once-threatened trumpeter swan, breed and nest here, and the annual migrations of sandhill cranes through the Tetlin corridor are spectacular events. In addition, some 25 hardy bird species remain in the refuge through the frigid winters of the Alaska Interior.

The northern boundary of the refuge runs along the Alaska Highway, with seven interpretive turnouts and two free campgrounds. At Mile 1229 of the Alaska Highway, just west of the Canadian border, there is an informative visitor center that presents a wealth of natural history, wildlife, and cultural exhibits, as well as a spectacular view from its elevated deck.

> **Snowcapped peaks, glacial rivers, open tundra, lakes, and seemingly endless forests and muskeg make up the glorious scenery of the Tetlin National Wildlife Refuge.**

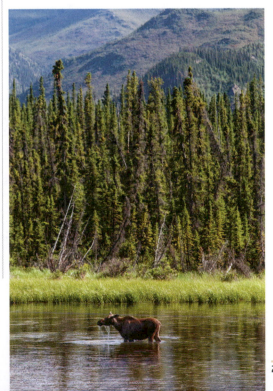

32

Eagle

🏔F3 🚗166 miles (267 km) NE of Tok 🚢Dawson-Eagle cruise ℹ️1st Ave West End; 547-2325

The town of Eagle sits beside the Yukon River *(p190)* at the end of the Taylor Highway. Started as the Belle Isle Trading Post, just 12 miles (19 km) west of the Canadian border, the town was founded in 1897 by unsuccessful Klondike Gold Rush prospectors. They named it Eagle after the birds nesting on the bluff.

As the Gold Rush boomed, the founders staked 400 town lots and sold them to settlers for a $5 recording fee. By 1898, the settlement had rapidly grown into the military, judicial, and commercial heart of the region. New settlers set up gambling halls, saloons, restaurants, and businesses. Fort Egbert was established by the US Army in 1899, and the

↑ An antique cannon at Fort Egbert historic site in Eagle

following year, the legendary Judge Wickersham *(p137)* chose Eagle as the site of the Interior's first federal courthouse. In 1905, Norwegian explorer Roald Amundsen mushed a dog team from the Beaufort Sea to Eagle to announce that his ship, the *Gjoa*, had successfully negotiated the Northwest Passage.

In 2009, a devastating flood destroyed the entire riverfront, but the town has been rebuilt and today offers much to explore. Five of **Fort Egbert**'s 46 original buildings were restored by the Bureau of Land Management (BLM) between 1974 and 1979, and they are now open to the public as a National Historic Landmark. The structures include the Mule Barn, built in 1900 to house the army's horses and mules. It now holds tools used in early mining, woodcutting, trapping, agriculture, and transportation. The distinctive Waterwagon Shed was used in the winter to prevent the fort's water supply from freezing. Sliding doors admitted the horse-drawn wagons and sleds that

delivered water. Today the building houses exhibits on transportation, including a selection of vintage vehicles. The Scandinavian-style Non-Commissioned Officers Quarters, built in 1901, is set up as a military residence, complete with period furnishings. There is also an 1899 Quartermaster Storehouse and a 1903 Storehouse, which features an interpretive display on the restoration.

Many of Eagle's other fine historic buildings are still in place, having fortunately escaped the 2009 flood that damaged much of Eagle's commercial center. In the summer, the **Eagle Historical Society Museum Tour** guides visitors along a three-hour walking route that takes in the town's most prominent sights. These include the 1901 Wickersham Courthouse, which still contains Judge James Wickersham's original courtroom and also houses a museum of town history, and the old Customs House, part of Fort Egbert, which contains a period residence. The tour also covers the 1904 Improved Order of Redmen Lodge (now

---

◔ GREAT VIEW

American Summit

Be sure to stop and admire the landscape from the top of the Taylor Highway at American Summit. The highway connects Eagle with the Alaska Highway and the Top of the World Highway.

→

Negotiating whitewater in the Yukon-Charley Rivers National Preserve

the home of the Historical Society), and the town icon, the 1903 Wellhouse.

The stroll west of town to the BLM campground makes for a pleasant excursion, while the summit of Eagle Bluff, to the north, offers great views. The 8–10 day float down the Yukon from Dawson City (p188) is a popular paddling trip for canoe enthusiasts.

Fort Egbert

Ⓐ 4th St Extension
Ⓞ Late May- early Sep: 9am–5pm daily

Eagle Historical Society Museum Tour

Ⓐ Wickersham Courthouse Ⓒ 547-2325 Ⓞ Late May–early Sep: 9am daily

③③ Ⓟ

Yukon-Charley Rivers National Preserve

Ⓐ F3 Ⓐ 12 miles (20 km) N of Eagle Ⓐ Dawson-Eagle cruise Ⓘ 1st Ave West End, Eagle; www.nps.gov/yuch

Administered by the US National Park Service, the Yukon-Charley Rivers National Preserve spreads over a vast 3,906 sq miles (10,117 sq km), protecting 115 miles (185 km) of the Yukon River and the entire Charley River basin. This New Jersey-sized preserve, with only 30 year-round residents, is one of the wildest places in the US.

During the Klondike Gold Rush, the rivers in the area served as the main highways for prospectors trying to reach their claims along smaller gold-bearing streams. Today, most visitors to the area are canoeists, kayakers, and rafters who stay in public use cabins scattered along the wilderness floodplain of the Yukon River. Most trips begin in Dawson City (p188), in Canada's Yukon Territory, or in Eagle, and float down the Yukon to Eagle or Circle respectively. To raft the more challenging Charley River requires good whitewater skills and a chartered bush flight to the Finger-Charley or Golvins airstrips within the park, with a take-out at Circle. Maps of the area are available at the preserve's visitor center in Eagle, while canoes can be hired in either Dawson City or Eagle.

STAY

Falcon Inn Bed & Breakfast and Cabins

After a busy day exploring this remote section of Alaska, rest your head at the pleasantly quiet Falcon Inn. There are beautiful views of the Yukon River Valley and aurora borealis August through April. Note that credit cards are not accepted.

Ⓐ F3 Ⓐ 220 Front St, Eagle Ⓦ falconinn lodgelogcabins.com

⑤⑤⑤

SOUTHWEST ALASKA

From the Koniag Alutiiq of forested Kodiak Island to the Aleuts who settled the windswept islands of the Aleutian Chain, the people of Southwest Alaska have historically been dependent upon the Bering Sea and the rivers that drain into it. Early Aleutian Island inhabitants are thought to have arrived from Russia at least 10,000 years ago via a land bridge now covered by the Bering Sea. While the land was not very productive, the sea provided nearly everything early Native people required. Seals were highly valuable for their oil, fur, and meat, and their hides and intestines provided a waterproof material from which umiaks (canoes) and parkas could be made. Riverine Native groups thrived on Kodiak Island and along the Yukon and Kuskokwim rivers of the southwestern mainland, with forest or marshland in which to hunt, fish, and trap.

As elsewhere in the state, Southwest Alaska was overrun by fur traders from Russia in the late 18th century. From 1743 until the Alaska Purchase of 1867, Russian traders in the island regions exploited the local Aleut population, often forcing men to hunt for them by holding their wives and children hostage. In spite of this, the region began to adopt the Russian Orthodox faith, largely due to the conversion efforts of missionary priest Father Ivan Veniaminov, later canonized as St. Innocent of Alaska.

Following Russia's sale of Alaska to the US in 1867, sealing and whaling became the main regional industries, and were later joined by gold prospecting in the early 20th century. All three were steadily replaced by fishing, which continues to be a mainstay of the local economy today.

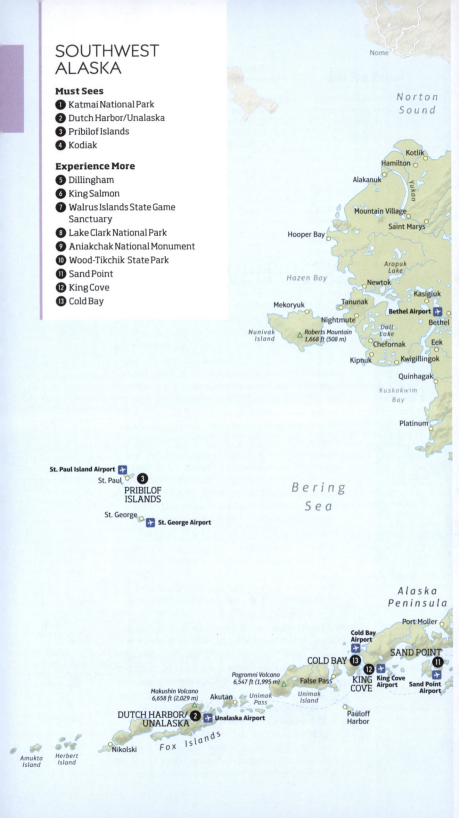

SOUTHWEST ALASKA

Must Sees
1. Katmai National Park
2. Dutch Harbor/Unalaska
3. Pribilof Islands
4. Kodiak

Experience More
5. Dillingham
6. King Salmon
7. Walrus Islands State Game Sanctuary
8. Lake Clark National Park
9. Aniakchak National Monument
10. Wood-Tikchik State Park
11. Sand Point
12. King Cove
13. Cold Bay

Norton Sound

Nome

Kotlik
Hamilton
Alakanuk

Yukon

Mountain Village
Saint Marys

Hooper Bay

Aropuk Lake

Hazen Bay

Newtok

Kasigluk

Mekoryuk
Tanunak
Bethel Airport
Nightmute
Dall Lake
Bethel
Nunivak Island
△ Roberts Mountain 1,668 ft (508 m)
Chefornak
Eek
Kipnuk
Kwigillingok
Quinhagak
Kuskokwim Bay
Platinum

St. Paul Island Airport
St. Paul
3
PRIBILOF ISLANDS
St. George
St. George Airport

Bering Sea

Alaska Peninsula

Port Moller

Cold Bay Airport
COLD BAY 13
SAND POINT
12
11
Pogromni Volcano 6,547 ft (1,995 m) △
False Pass
KING COVE
King Cove Airport
Sand Point Airport
Makushin Volcano 6,658 ft (2,029 m) △
Akutan
Unimak Pass
Unimak Island
Pauloff Harbor
DUTCH HARBOR/ UNALASKA 2
Unalaska Airport
Nikolski
Fox Islands
Amukta Island
Herbert Island

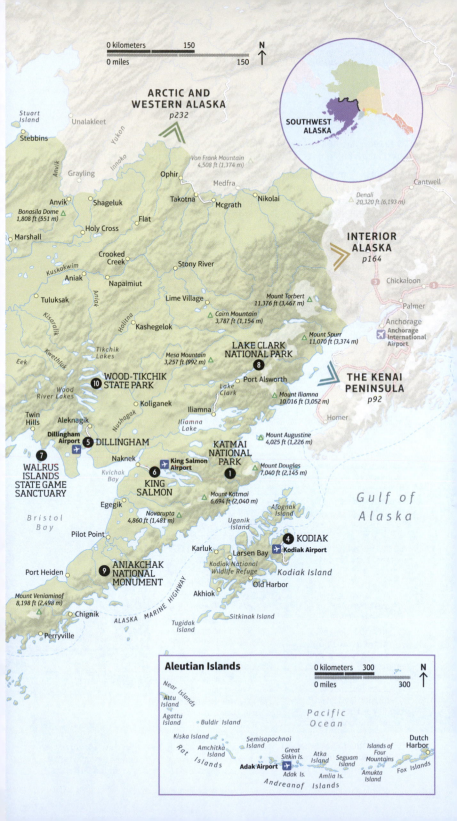

SOUTHWEST ALASKA

ARCTIC AND WESTERN ALASKA
p232

INTERIOR ALASKA
p164

THE KENAI PENINSULA
p92

N

0 kilometers 150
0 miles 150

Stuart Island
Stebbins
Unalakleet
Yukon
Innoko
Anvik
Grayling
Ophir
Von Frank Mountain 4,508 ft (1,374 m)
Medfra
Takotna
Mcgrath
Nikolai
Cantwell
Denali 20,320 ft (6,193 m)
Anvik
Shageluk
Bonasila Dome 1,808 ft (551 m)
Holy Cross
Flat
Marshall
Crooked Creek
Stony River
Kuskokwim
Aniak
Napaimiut
Lime Village
Chickaloon
Tuluksak
Aniak
Kashegelok
Cairn Mountain 3,787 ft (1,154 m)
Mount Torbert 11,376 ft (3,467 m)
Palmer
Kisaralik
Kwethluk
Tikchik Lakes
Mesa Mountain 3,257 ft (992 m)
Mount Spurr 11,070 ft (3,374 m)
Anchorage
Anchorage International Airport
Eek
LAKE CLARK NATIONAL PARK
Port Alsworth
10 WOOD-TICHIK STATE PARK
Wood River Lakes
Koliganek
Lake Clark
Mount Iliamna 10,016 ft (3,052 m)
Homer
Twin Hills
Aleknagik
Nushagak
Iliamna
Iliamna Lake
Dillingham Airport
5 DILLINGHAM
Mount Augustine 4,025 ft (1,226 m)
7 WALRUS ISLANDS STATE GAME SANCTUARY
Naknek
King Salmon Airport
KATMAI NATIONAL PARK
1
Mount Douglas 7,040 ft (2,145 m)
Kvichak Bay
6
KING SALMON
Gulf of Alaska
Egegik
Novarupta 4,860 ft (1,481 m)
Mount Katmai 6,694 ft (2,040 m)
Afognak Island
Bristol Bay
Pilot Point
Uganik Island
Karluk
Larsen Bay
4 KODIAK
Kodiak Airport
Port Heiden
9 ANIAKCHAK NATIONAL MONUMENT
Kodiak National Wildlife Refuge
Kodiak Island
Old Harbor
Mount Veniaminof 8,198 ft (2,498 m)
Chignik
Akhiok
ALASKA MARINE HIGHWAY
Sitkinak Island
Perryville
Tugidak Island

Aleutian Islands

0 kilometers 300
0 miles 300

N

Near Islands
Attu Island
Agattu Island
Buldir Island
Pacific Ocean
Kiska Island
Semisopochnoi Island
Islands of Four Mountains
Dutch Harbor
Rat Islands
Amchitka Island
Great Sitkin Is.
Atka Island
Seguam Island
Amukta Island
Fox Islands
Adak Airport
Adak Is.
Amlia Is.
Andreanof Islands

KATMAI NATIONAL PARK

ⒶD5 **290 miles (466 km) SW of Anchorage** **From Homer or charter floatplane to Brooks Camp & Kulik Lodge** **King Salmon Airport; www.nps.gov/katm**

One of Alaska's most isolated national parks, Katmai encompasses 6,400 sq miles (17,000 sq km) of scenic valleys, volcanic landscapes, and wild seacoasts. The area is also a haven for some of Alaska's most majestic wildlife species, including large numbers of brown bears.

Katmai was proclaimed a National Monument in 1918 in order to preserve the unique geological features that were formed after the 1912 eruption of Novarupta (p215). It became a National Park in 1980, when the Alaska National Interest Lands Conservation Act was passed (p61). The Brooks and McNeil rivers draw a great many visitors, who come to view the numerous brown bears feeding at the red salmon runs into Bristol Bay. Katmai provides an important habitat for brown bears and salmon, as well as moose, red fox, caribou, wolves, and lynx. Its lakes and marshes serve as nesting sites for waterfowl, including swans, ducks, grebes, loons, and Arctic terns. Bear-viewing is centered mainly around Brooks Camp, from where Brooks Lodge runs daily bus tours to the Valley of 10,000 Smokes. Visitors can also enjoy great hiking and kayaking in the park.

McNeil River, one of the best places for watching brown bears fishing for salmon ↑

↑ The popular Brooks Lodge, offering accommodations, meals, and daily bus tours

↑ The Valley of 10,000 Smokes, carpeted in a profusion of pink wildflowers

STAY

Brooks Lodge
Located on the shores of beautiful Naknek Lake, Brooks Lodge is the gateway to Brooks Falls, which is famous for its views of brown bears fishing for salmon. Meals are included, and there is also a bar.

⌂ Brooks River, King Salmon
Ⓦ katmailand.com

$ $ $

2,220
—
coastal brown bears live in Katmai National Park.

EXPLORING KATMAI NATIONAL PARK

Bear viewing is by far the most popular activity in Katmai National Park, and the vast majority of visitors do this at the well-equipped Brooks Camp. But there are plenty of other areas that are also worth exploring, such as American Creek, with its scenic waterfalls and abundant fishing holes, or Hallo Bay, where bears not only fish for salmon, but spend hours digging for clams deep in the sand. Naknek Lake makes an excellent place to launch a canoe, kayak, or packraft, and is easily accessible from King Salmon (*p226*), where there are several outfitters who can organize tours and rentals. For adventurous travelers, the backcountry hiking and camping opportunities are endless, with the whole park wide open for exploration.

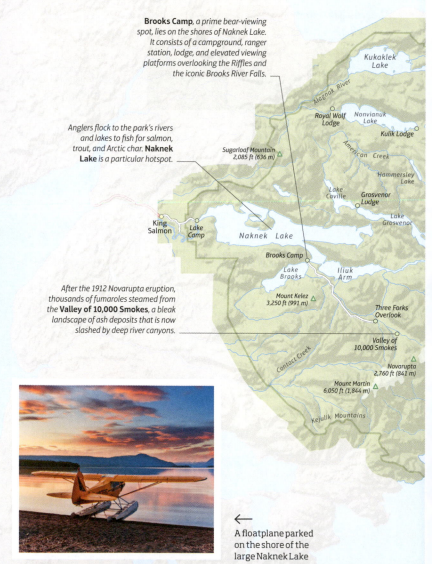

Brooks Camp, *a prime bear-viewing spot, lies on the shores of Naknek Lake. It consists of a campground, ranger station, lodge, and elevated viewing platforms overlooking the Riffles and the iconic Brooks River Falls.*

Anglers flock to the park's rivers and lakes to fish for salmon, trout, and Arctic char. **Naknek Lake** *is a particular hotspot.*

After the 1912 Novarupta eruption, thousands of fumaroles steamed from the **Valley of 10,000 Smokes***, a bleak landscape of ash deposits that is now slashed by deep river canyons.*

Kukaklek Lake

Alagnak River

Royal Wolf Lodge

Nonvianuk Lake

Kulik Lodge

American Creek

Sugarloaf Mountain 2,085 ft (636 m)

Hammersley Lake

Lake Coville

Grosvenor Lodge

Lake Grosvenor

King Salmon

Lake Camp

Naknek Lake

Brooks Camp

Lake Brooks

Iliuk Arm

Mount Kelez 3,250 ft (991 m)

Three Forks Overlook

Valley of 10,000 Smokes

Contact Creek

Novarupta 2,760 ft (841 m)

Mount Martin 6,050 ft (1,844 m)

Kejulik Mountains

← A floatplane parked on the shore of the large Naknek Lake

→

Hiking through the park, with views of Mount Katmai

*The **McNeil River State Game Sanctuary** provides reliable summer bear viewing. Often, a big group of brown bears congregates at the falls to feast on salmon, offering good opportunities for photographs. Access is by lottery permit only.*

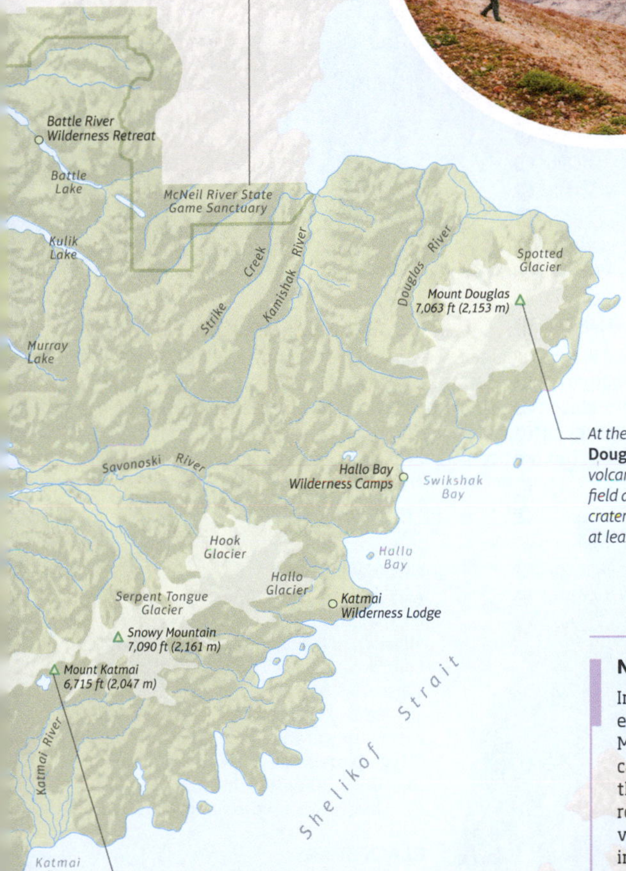

Battle River Wilderness Retreat

Battle Lake

McNeil River State Game Sanctuary

Kulik Lake

Strike Creek

Kanishak River

Douglas River

Spotted Glacier

Mount Douglas 7,063 ft (2,153 m)

Murray Lake

Savonoski River

*At the summit of **Mount Douglas**, a 7,000-ft (2,100-m) volcano, is an active fumarole field and a warm, highly acidic crater lake. The park contains at least 14 active volcanoes.*

Hallo Bay Wilderness Camps

Swikshak Bay

Hook Glacier

Hallo Bay

Serpent Tongue Glacier

Hallo Glacier

Snowy Mountain 7,090 ft (2,161 m)

Katmai Wilderness Lodge

Mount Katmai 6,715 ft (2,047 m)

Shelikof Strait

Katmai River

Katmai Bay

*The 1912 explosion of Novarupta emptied **Mount Katmai**'s magma chamber, causing its summit to collapse and leaving a caldera with a crater lake.*

NOVARUPTA

In June 1912, severe earthquakes around Mount Katmai led to a cataclysmic eruption that covered the surrounding tundra with volcanic debris. It was initially thought that Mount Katmai had erupted, but Novarupta proved to be the source. The eruption lasted for six hours and covered nearby Kodiak Island in ash and pumice. The landscapes that were left behind are unique.

0 kilometers 25

0 miles 25

N ↑

THE BEARS OF ALASKA

Most visitors to Alaska want to see bears, and nearly everyone does. With the exception of the Aleutian Islands, the state is prime bear habitat and home to three species of bears: black, brown, and polar. Active in summer, many bears become dormant in winter, retreating to dens and living on fat reserves; it is often at this time that cubs are born. Bears can sometimes be aggressive, particularly when protecting cubs or competing with each other during the breeding season.

↑ A black bear resting in open grassland

BROWN BEARS

Alaska brown bears *(Ursus arctos)* are split into two types: the smaller grizzlies of the Interior and the huge Kodiak bears *(p224)* of Southwest Alaska. The latter are not a true subspecies, however, and the size variations are due only to differences in diet. The grizzlies eat more vegetation, whereas Kodiaks eat lots of high-protein fish. Brown bears are resident from the Southeast to the Arctic, and are most frequently seen in summer and fall.

BLACK BEARS

Black bears *(Ursus americanus)* are the smallest Alaska bears, measuring an average of 5 ft (1.5 m) in length. These predominantly vegetarian creatures are found everywhere in Alaska except the Arctic tundra and the Aleutian Islands. They are recognizable by their black or cinnamon coat and pointed muzzle, and can be seen in the wild from spring through to fall.

↑ A female brown bear with her cubs in Katmai National Park

POLAR BEARS

Polar bears (Ursus maritimus), which inhabit the Arctic Ocean coastline, subsist mainly on marine mammals. Swimming across open water, they spend most of their lives roaming the ice floes in search of seals, but come ashore in the fall to breed (p237). Among the best places to see them are Utqiagvik (p236) and Kaktovik. In addition to their creamy coat, they are also distinguishable from Alaska's other bear species by their longer neck.

↑ Polar bear cubs on a snowy beach next to the Beaufort Sea

BEAR SAFETY

Staying safe in bear country involves a trifecta of preparation, awareness, and protection. Remember the following points at all times.

Be Aware of Your Surroundings Take note of any environmental factors (brushy areas, rushing water) that may impede sounds, and look out for evidence of bears (scat, tracks, flattened vegetation). Pay attention to all posted warning signs.

Take a Guide Do not hike or walk in polar bear country without a trained guide.

Make Noise Sing, rattle stones in a can, or talk loudly to let bears know you are entering their territory.

Travel in Groups Hike or walk with other people. Instruct children to stay within an arms' reach at all times.

Carry Bear Spray Studies show that capsaicin-based aerosol spray is most effective in deterring bears. Make sure to read all directions for safe use.

Do Not Run If you see a bear closer than 550 yd (500 m) away, keep your eyes on it and back away slowly. Do not ever run.

Stay Together If a bear approaches you, group all individuals together, raise your arms, and talk to the bear in a firm, calm voice. Ready your bear spray, and if the bear continues to approach, spray it in a sweeping motion toward the bear's nose. Once the bear walks away, leave the area and report the encounter to the nearest park or forest service.

2

DUTCH HARBOR/ UNALASKA

🔺A6 🏠850 miles (1,370 km) SW of Kodiak
✈From Anchorage ⛴From Homer & Kodiak
ℹ5 Broadway Ave, Unalaska; www.unalaska.org

For thousands of years, Dutch Harbor and its sister town Unalaska have offered shelter from stormy seas. The Aleuts, or the Unangan, have lived here for centuries, fishing and hunting sea mammals from hide boats. After buying Alaska from Russia, the US used the islands as a seal hunting base. The king crab boom and the growth of the fishing industry have made this ice-free port the largest fishing port in the US.

① 🖼

Church of the Holy Ascension

🏠Broadway Rd 📞581-6404

The focal point of Unalaska, the cruciform Church of the Holy Ascension stands on a small spit at the western end of the village. In 1808, it was the site of Alaska's first Russian Orthodox church. The present building, dating from 1896, had suffered so much damage from Aleutian storms that by 1990 it needed repairs. The renovated church was rededicated in 1996, in time for its centenary. Its interior is filled with a rich collection of icons from abandoned villages around Unalaska Islands, as well as an ornate candelabra, and paintings.

↑ The Russian Orthodox church, in its atmospheric setting at the sea's edge

② 🖼 🛍

Museum of the Aleutians

🏠314 Salmon Way
🕐11am–4pm Tue–Sat
🌐aleutians.org

Opened in 1999 on the site of an old World War II warehouse, this museum is one of the finest attractions in the area. The modern building has an extensive collection that includes old photographs, drawings, and relics from the Russian era, as well as objects salvaged from the World War II defense of the islands and from a 1920s herring fishery.

Also on display are Aleut artifacts uncovered in several archeological digs around Unalaska and other Aleutian Islands, including many of the 100,000 items found in the adjacent Margaret Bay village site. Once a flourishing fish camp, this village is thought to have thrived about 2,000 years ago. Volunteers and students are welcome to apply to participate in the museum-sponsored digs around the Aleutian Islands.

THE TRUSTY TUSTY

Built in 1964, the 296-ft- (89-m-) long MV *Tustumena*, a ferry affectionately known as the "Trusty Tusty," plies some of the roughest waters on earth. Once a month from April to September, this sturdy vessel - the oldest ship in the Alaska Marine Highway fleet - does the stormy four-day run from Homer to Dutch Harbor/Unalaska. This spectacular trip attracts adventurous visitors hoping to see one of the most remote parts of the world.

③ Aleutian World War II National Historical Park

🏠 Dutch Harbor Airport
🕐 Visitor center: 8am–5pm Mon–Fri 🌐 nps.gov/aleu

The Aleutian World War II National Historical Park showcases the little-known war history of the state, focusing on the culture and role of the Aleuts and their islands in the defense of the US. The visitor center, located at the airport in Dutch Harbor, houses a 1940s-era radio room and exhibits on the mass evacuation of the Aleuts.

④ Mount Ballyhoo

During World War II, Mount Ballyhoo was the site of Fort Schwatka, one of Dutch Harbor's four coastal defense posts. Part of the Aleutian Islands World War II Historic Area, the fort is the highest battery in the United States at 897 ft (269 m) above sea level, and the views are spectacular. Wander the now derelict buildings and bunkers with the help of the National Park Service maps, and hike along trails used by American troops as the Japanese crept closer to US land in 1942.

⑤ Summer Bay

Heading east from Unalaska, a gravel road along the scenic coastline of Iliuliuk Bay turns north to reach the beautiful inlet known as Summer Bay. Behind coastal sand dunes, the pristine freshwater lake of Summer Bay reflects the surrounding green hills and magical Aleutian light. At the head of the lake, the road winds uphill across the tundra to Ugadaga Pass. From here, a relatively easy hiking trail leads down to Ugadaga Bay on the east coast of Unalaska Island. In fine weather, this makes an excellent day hike.

EAT & DRINK

Harbor View Bar and Grill

Serving solid pub food with a view of the harbor and all its goings on, this bar and grill is a hangout for fishermen and seafood industry managers alike.

🏠 76–94 Gilman Way
📞 907 581-7389

$$$

SHOP

Museum of the Aleutians

Look for excellent books about the Aleutian Islands, jewelry, paintings, and other artworks at the gift shop attached to this absorbing museum.

🏠 314 Salmon Way
🌐 aleutians.org

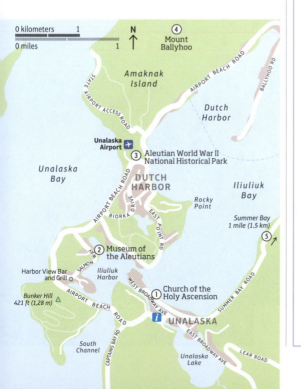

0 kilometers / 0 miles

N

Mount Ballyhoo ④

Amaknak Island

Dutch Harbor

Unalaska Airport

③ Aleutian World War II National Historical Park

Unalaska Bay

DUTCH HARBOR

Rocky Point

Iliuliuk Bay

Summer Bay 1 mile (1.5 km)

⑤

② Museum of the Aleutians

Harbor View Bar and Grill

Iliuliuk Harbor

Bunker Hill 421 ft (1,28 m)

① Church of the Holy Ascension

ℹ UNALASKA

South Channel

Unalaska Lake

A colony of kittiwakes nesting on the dramatic cliffs of St. George Island ↑

3

PRIBILOF ISLANDS

A5 ◻️200 miles (320 km) SW of Cape Newenham ➡️📧 *i* St. Paul:
Tanadgusix Corporation, PO Box 88, St. Paul, www.tanadgusix.com;
St. George: St. George Tanaq Corporation, 4141 B St #301, Anchorage,
www.discoverak.com

The Pribilof Islands, made up of five islands in the middle of the Bering
Sea, have been dubbed "the Northern Galapagos" owing to their dense
concentrations of breeding pinnipeds and nesting birds.

In 1786, Gerassim Pribilof claimed the Pribilof
Islands for Russia and set up Russian trade
interests based on the large fur seal colonies
he found there. Following the Alaska Purchase
in 1867, the islands became part of the United
States. While the larger islands of St. Paul and
St. George have small Aleut communities,
Otter Island, Walrus Island, and Sea Lion Rock
are inhabited only by wildlife. Bird-watching
groups dominate island tourism, but an
increasing number of visitors also come
to appreciate the local Aleut culture, the
profusion of summer wildflowers, and the
stark beauty of the islands.

St. Paul Island

St. Paul Island covers an area of just over
40 sq miles (104 sq km). The island's only
village, also called St. Paul, has the state's
largest Aleut community. Life revolves around
the St. Peter and Paul Russian Orthodox Church.
For visitors, highlights include trips to the
spectacular bird cliffs and northern fur seal
rookeries. There are also plenty of opportunities to hike through the wild interior to see
reindeer herds, volcanic formations, numerous
small lakes, and a changing tableau of vibrant

> **For visitors, highlights include
> trips to the spectacular bird cliffs
> and northern fur seal rookeries.**

wildflowers. While it is possible to visit the
island independently, tours are also available
via St. Paul Island Tours (www.stpaultour.com).

St. George Island

Lying 47 miles (75 km) south of St. Paul,
St. George Island is less visited but is considered to be even more spectacular. It has six
fur seal rookeries, harboring up to 250,000
animals, and the most prolific bird cliffs in
the Pribilofs. About 90 percent of the islanders
are Aleut or belong to other Indigenous groups.
As on St. Paul, the church dominates local life –
here, it's centered on the beautiful Russian
Orthodox church of St. George the Martyr.
Visits are organized by the St. George Tanaq
Corporation, headquartered in Anchorage.

→
Two horned puffin,
a common sight on
St. George Island

←
St. Paul, with its
distinctive onion-domed
Russian Orthodox church

WILDLIFE OF THE PRIBILOF ISLANDS

The biodiversity of the Pribilof Islands is largely due to the bounty of the Bering Sea, which is rich in fish, shellfish, seaweed, and plankton, as well as to the island's range of habitats, which include sand dunes, tundra, beaches, lagoons, and towering cliffs. Half of the world's population of northern fur seals breeds on St. Paul and St. George, while Steller sea lions breed on Walrus Island and harbor seals on Otter Island. In the summer, the spectacular cliffs that gird the islands hum with millions of nesting birds.

MAMMALS

While Harbor seals are easily spotted and Steller sea lions are seen occasionally, the main draw for visitors is a glimpse of the world's largest northern fur seal colony. Northern fur seals are "eared" seals, with a waxy coating in their ears and nostrils that prevents water from entering during dives. Their large bare flippers regulate body temperature by shedding heat while on land. Hunting of the animals is now restricted to Alaska Natives, who take around 2,000 a year.

Terrestrial mammals on the islands include Arctic foxes, who arrived via sea ice that once reached this far south from the Arctic. The foxes den in grassy bluffs, foraging for sea bird eggs and chicks. They have both blue and white phases, when their coats change color, but the blue phase is most common in the Pribilofs. Also found

↑ Arctic fox cubs, with their coats in the more common blue phase

↑ A breeding colony of northern fur seals on St. Paul Island

on St. Paul Island is a herd of reindeer, introduced in 1911. These domesticated caribou are shorter and stockier than their wild counterparts.

BIRDS

The towering cliffs of these treeless islands annually attract over two million birds of at least 200 species, including Asian migrants that are blown off course by strong westerly winds. Commonly seen species include the horned puffin, an awkward flier that can dive up to 20 ft (6 m) and swim underwater while retrieving the small fish that form its main diet, and the crested auklet, which sports a distinctive plume of dark feathers during the breeding season. The Pribilofs are also one of the few breeding grounds of the red-legged kittiwake, which is similar to the black-legged kittiwake but has red legs and darker wing undersides.

↑ Red-legged kittiwakes by St. George Island

← Crested auklets, displaying their breeding plumage

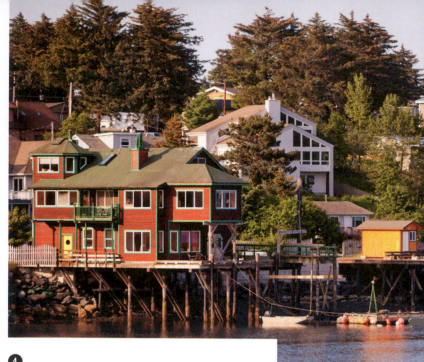

4

KODIAK

Ⓐ D5 🚗 150 miles (241 km) SW of Homer ✈ From Anchorage 🚢 From Homer 🛈 100 Marine Way (Marine Hwy Terminal building); www.kodiak.org

This historic island was settled by Alutiiq hunters and fishermen more than 7,000 years ago. Dubbed Alaska's Emerald Isle, today Kodiak is best known for its bear spotting and fishing opportunities.

Kodiak's name comes from the Alutiiq word Qiq'rtaq, which simply means "island" and was corrupted by the Russians to Kodiak. The first Russian explorer, Stephan Glotov, landed here in 1763, and about a decade later, Alexander Baranov set up a trading post, designating it the capital of Russian America. Used as a base for hunting and whaling in the 19th century, Kodiak suffered two major natural disasters in the 20th century: the 1912 explosion of Novarupta (p211) and the 1964 earthquake (p29).

The town of Kodiak, the island's main settlement, holds a number of interesting sights, including the Holy Resurrection Russian Orthodox Cathedral, which contains an original 1790s Russian icon and the reliquary of the 18th-century Russian monk St. Herman, canonized here in 1970. The neighboring chapel houses a collection of 17th-century manuscripts and a hand-carved chandelier. Each August, some 300 boats join a pilgrimage to nearby Spruce Island, the saint's retreat.

The nearby Kodiak History Museum occupies the white weatherboard Erskine House, built in 1808 as a warehouse for otter pelts. Although minor changes have been made, this is the oldest existing building on the US West Coast. The museum

---

KODIAK BEARS

The world's largest land carnivores, Kodiak bears (Ursos arctos middendorffi) are a subspecies of brown bear, found only in the Kodiak archipelago. The bears stay at sea level during spring, feeding on grasses, but as summer progresses, they move uphill to eat alpine shoots. In mid-July, they begin congregating around streams to partake in a feast of spawning salmon.

← Downtown Kodiak and *(inset)* the colorful iconostasis inside the Russian Orthodox Cathedral

EAT

Java Flats

This little coffee and sandwich shop is a gem for fresh food and fantastic scenery. Stop there on your way to explore other parts of Kodiak Island and grab a boxed lunch.

🏠 **11206 Rezanof Dr W**
🌐 **javaflats.com**

$ $ $

Kodiak Island Smokehouse

Take out some smoked salmon, halibut, or black cod. They also make salmon gravlax and smoked salmon sausage.

🏠 **1819 Mill Bay Rd**
🌐 **kodiakisland smokehouse.com**

$ $ $

DRINK

Kodiak Island Brewing Company

Stop by this hip taproom located in downtown Kodiak. The creative beers infused with spruce tips each spring are particularly worth a try.

🏠 **117 Lower Mill Bay Rd** 🌐 **kodiak brewery.com**

---

features such oddities as a three-seat baidarka (kayak) and a Russian sealskin banknote. It also holds Alutiiq and Aleut artifacts such as woven grass baskets, seal-gut bags, and bone carvings. Alutiiq culture is explored more fully at the Alutiiq Museum; its displays include a replica of an 1883 ground-squirrel parka and a fabulous *awirnaq* (spruce-root hat). The renowned Alutiiq Dancers occasionally perform here.

Out on Miller Point is the Fort Abercrombie State Historical Park, crisscrossed by numerous short hiking trails. A military post, later dismantled, was set up here in 1941. Remnants of the garrison can still be seen around the lovely wooded site. The Kodiak Military History Museum, with a wealth of military artifacts, is housed in the Ready Ammunition Bunker.

Kodiak National Wildlife Refuge

The Kodiak National Wildlife Refuge covers the southwestern end of Kodiak Island, as well as Uganik and Ban islands. This wild area of rugged mountains, lakes, bogs, and meadows, including hundreds of miles of convoluted shoreline, is home to about 3,500 Kodiak brown bears, as well as 50 million wild salmon, 250 bird species, and 1.5 million seabirds. The refuge has no roads or trails, so access is limited to floatplane, bush flights, or watercraft from Kodiak town. The most popular activity is taking a half- or one-day flightseeing trip to prime bear-viewing areas such as Frazer Lake and Karluk Lake.

EXPERIENCE MORE

5

Dillingham

⚑C5 ⏱481 miles (774 km) SW of Anchorage ✈ 🛈141 Main St; www.dillingham ak.us

Founded in 1822 by Russian fur traders as a fort called Alexandrovski Redoubt, the city of Dillingham is the largest community in the Bristol Bay region as a result of its renowned commercial fishing industry. In 1884, after the US took possession of Alaska, huge runs of salmon in the Wood and Nushagak rivers made Dillingham a logical fish processing and canning site. Today, up to 10,000 tons (9 million kg) of fish is pro-cessed every year from the Bristol Bay salmon fishery.

The chief attraction here is the **Sam Fox Museum**, named for Yup'ik carver Sam Fox and featuring a large collection of his works, as well as skin and fur pieces and basketry. The city is also a staging point for visits to Togiak National Wildlife Refuge, Walrus Islands State Game Sanctuary, and Wood-Tikchik State Park *(p229)*.

Sam Fox Museum

 ⏯ 🅙306 D St W 📞842-4831 🕐10am-5:30pm Mon-Fri, 10am-2pm Sat

6

King Salmon

⚑D5 ⏱285 miles (459 km) SW of Anchorage ✈ 🛈 Airport terminal; 246-3325

The rugged little village of King Salmon occupies a lovely setting amid wide open spaces. The town overlooks the banks of the Naknek River, 15 miles (24 km) upstream from the fishing port of Naknek on Bristol Bay. Much of the current population of King Salmon is descended from people who were forced to relocate after the 1912 eruption of the Novarupta volcano in what is now Katmai National Park *(p212)*.

As the gateway to Katmai National Park, King Salmon features an airstrip and lodg-ing for those without reserva-tions at Brooks Camp inside the national park. Located right next to the King Salmon airport, the King Salmon Visitor Center is worth a stop. It has great natural history displays, as well as information about the Alaska Peninsula.

7

Walrus Islands State Game Sanctuary

⚑C5 ⏱100 miles (160 km) W of Dillingham ✈To Dillingham, then by charter boat 🕐May–mid-Aug: 24 hrs daily 🛈www.adfg. alaska.gov

Located in the northwestern reaches of Bristol Bay, the Walrus Islands State Game Sanctuary is an archipelago of seven rocky islands. The most popular destination is Round Island, where lounging walruses cover the beaches.

After the northern pack ice recedes in the spring, male walruses – as many as 14,000 a day – haul out onto the rocky, exposed beaches between feeding excursions at sea. In the summer, the surrounding seas abound with harbor seals, as well as gray, orca, and hump-back whales. The beaches of Round Island and the neigh-boring islands also attract several hundred breeding Steller sea lions, and the cliffs above bustle with nearly 400,000 nesting sea birds.

Access to Round Island is by permit only; these are secured via the Alaska Department of Fish and Game. Visitors need to be self-sufficient with gear that will accommodate a range of climatic conditions.

THE TUSKY PINNIPED

The Pacific walrus *(Odobenus rosmarus divergens)*, found in the western Gulf of Alaska, Bristol Bay, the Bering Sea, and the Chukchi Sea, is a large brown pinniped covered with coarse hair. It has a shaggy "old man" moustache and two ivory tusks, which are actually enlarged canine teeth. Walruses use their tusks to anchor themselves to the sea bed while digging for mollusks. Male walruses can grow up to 12 ft (4 m) in length and weigh 3,700 lbs (1,480 kg).

TOP 5 FOODS OF BRISTOL BAY

Salmon
The red fish is a staple here, whether smoked, baked, or grilled.

Beach Greens
Foraged from grassy beaches, these are then steamed like asparagus.

Moose
One moose can feed a family of five for a month, and nothing is wasted.

Seagull Eggs
These protein-packed eggs can be gathered each spring.

Berries
From blueberries to tart cranberries, these are vital to winter diets.

Walruses sprawling across the rocks in the Walrus Islands State Game Sanctuary ↑

8

Lake Clark National Park

🅰D4 🅾200 miles (320 km) SW of Anchorage ➡To Iliamna, then charter plane to Port Alsworth ℹwww.nps.gov/lacl

When the Alaska National Interest Lands Conservation Act was passed in 1980 (p61) Lake Clark National Park came into being to protect the 50-mile- (80-km-) long Lake Clark and its surrounding ecosystems. This impressive 6,250-sq-mile (16,187-sq-km)

💬 INSIDER TIP
Gear Up

It takes considerable effort to get to Lake Clark National Park by small plane, and one of the biggest considerations is managing all the necessary equipment. Tulchina Adventures rents camping and outdoor gear, and watercraft (www.tulchina adventures.com).

↑ A brown grizzly bear roaming through a meadow in Lake Clark National Park

area includes the shores of Cook Inlet, which is prime bear territory, and the glaciated heights of the Chigmit Mountains and the Aleutian Range. The twin volcanoes Mount Iliamna and Mount Redoubt are also within its boundaries. The park boasts an array of wildlife, most prominently brown bears and migrating herds of caribou. Activities include canoeing, kayaking, fishing, and hiking, but the only marked hiking trail leads from Port Alsworth to Tanalian Falls. A worthwhile destination is the cabin of Dick Proenneke on Twin Lakes, which features in the film *Alone in the Wilderness*.

Port Alsworth, the park's headquarters, has several small lodges, but the park has no other services, so non-lodge visitors will need to carry camping and cooking gear. Access to remote parts of the park is by chartered bush flight only.

RICHARD PROENNEKE, WILDERNESS STEWARD

Perhaps one of the quietest, yet strongest influences in Lake Clark National Park was Richard "Dick" Proenneke, an amateur naturalist, filmmaker, and craftsman. Having first visited the Twin Lakes area of the park in 1962, Proenneke returned in 1968, aged 51, to build his own hand-hewn log cabin. While staying in the park he wrote daily in journals, which have since become icons of wilderness homesteading. Dick Proenneke donated the cabin to the National Park Service after his final visit there in 2000, offering it as a way for visitors to better understand the value of Alaska and the park, and as a means to get to know oneself.

out. The resulting whitewater Aniakchak River created the canyon known as the Gates and flowed 27 miles (43 km) to the Gulf of Alaska. Fed by brilliant red iron springs, Surprise Lake provides float-plane access to the park and is the put-in point for whitewater rafting trips. The park has excellent hiking opportunities, but hikers and rafters must be self-sufficient and prepared for long weather-related delays.

⑩

Wood-Tikchik State Park

🅰️ C5 🕐 25 miles (40 km) N of Dillingham ➡️ To Dillingham, then by floatplane or bus ℹ️ Ranger Station, Dillingham; www.dnr. alaska.gov/parks/units/ woodtik.htm

America's largest state park, the 2,345-sq-mile (6,070-sq-km) Wood-Tikchik State Park is also one of the country's most remote. It comprises a vast landscape of two inter-connected lake systems, those of the Wood River in the south and the Tikchik River in the north. The park is situated in a biological transition zone between coniferous forest and tundra, with willow and alder thickets as well as spruce and birch forests. Its eastern side consists of low, boggy wetlands that are studded

with lakes and streams, while to the west rise the wild and untracked peaks of the Wood River Mountains.

The remoteness of the park makes it especially good wild-life habitat. Brown bears, caribou, and moose are all abundant, as are porcupines, wolverines, marmots, land otters, beavers, and foxes. Throughout the park, well-appointed fly-in lodges serve as staging points for canoeing and fishing trips. Anglers will find all five Alaska salmon species, especially sockeyes (reds), along with trout, Arctic char, Arctic grayling, and northern pike.

The most common way for independent groups to access the state park is to fly in to one of the lakes on the Wood River system, and then canoe downstream to Aleknagik on Lake Aleknagik, accessible from Dillingham (p226) via a gravel road. On the Tikchik River system, most people opt to fly in to one of the lakes and then float down-stream along the Nuyakuk and Nushagak rivers to be picked up at the airstrips at Ekwok or New Stuyahok.

Visitors who are considering an expedition here but not planning to stay in one of the fly-in lodges should keep in mind that very few resources are available, and well-honed survival skills are essential for trips into the park's remote wilderness.

⑨

Aniakchak National Monument

🅰️ C6 🕐 200 miles (320 km) SW of Kodiak ➡️ To King Salmon, then charter floatplane to Surprise Lake ℹ️ King Salmon airport terminal; www.nps.gov/ania

With the unofficial distinction of being the least-visited unit in the US National Park System, Aniakchak National Monument is tucked away in a remote corner of the Alaska Peninsula. The park's most striking feature is the 2,000-ft- (600-m-) deep, 6-mile- (10-km-) wide Aniakchak Caldera, an ash-filled bowl formed 3,500 years ago when Aniakchak Volcano collapsed into its own empty magma chamber. Over the millennia, minor erup-tions, including one in 1931, have added small cinder cones and lava flows to the crater. Located within the caldera, Surprise Lake is the remnant of a larger lake that once existed here. After a weakness devel-oped in the caldera's south-eastern wall, the lake drained

↑ Boating along the glassy Nuyakuk River within Wood-Tikchik State Park

⑪

Sand Point

🅰 C6　🏛 440 miles (710 km)
SW of Kodiak　🚹📧
🌐 sandpointak.com

Situated on the northwest coast of Popof Island, the town of Sand Point was settled in the late 19th century by the Russians. Like nearby King Cove, it has Aleut and Scandinavian heritage, and these two groups still constitute the majority of its population. As with the rest of the region, the area's economy has always been based on the fishing industry. In 1898, a trading post and cod fishing station were set up by a San Francisco seafood company, and by the 1930s, fish processing had become the dominant activity. Today, Sand Point is home to one of the largest fishing fleets in the Aleutian region.

Visitors can view the large flocks of bald eagles that gather near the shore, ride the popular 14-mile (23-km) bike trail, and visit the 1933 Russian Orthodox Church, which is listed on the National Register of Historic Places.

To visit Sand Point, travelers will most likely take the Marine Highway ferry from Kodiak (p224). The first stop on the journey is the tiny, beautifully situated village of Chignik, which is flanked by snow-capped peaks. Farther south is Perryville, founded by villagers from Katmai who moved after their homes were devastated in the 1912 eruption of Novarupta. The ferry arrives at Sand Point nine hours after leaving Chignik. Note that the ferry arrival and departure times may limit sightseeing opportunities here.

The small harbor of Sand Point, home (inset) to a large bald eagle population that gathers just off the shore ↓

> **The first stop on the ferry journey to Sand Point is the tiny, beautifully situated village of Chignik, which is flanked by snow-capped peaks.**

⑫

King Cove

🅰 B6　🏛 551 miles (887 km)
SW of Kodiak　🚹📧
🌐 cityofkingcove.com

Founded in 1911, King Cove developed around a salmon cannery belonging to the Pacific American Fisheries. The first settlers in the village were Scandinavian, Aleut, and Anglo fishermen who either hauled in the fish or worked in the processing plant. The plant operated until 1976, when it was damaged by fire and replaced by the Peter Pan Seafood Cannery.

Today, half the residents are of Native descent, while the rest are descended primarily from the early Scandinavian settlers. They continue to fish

A lone red fox by the edge of the lagoon in Izembek National Wildlife Refuge

commercially or work for the cannery, which has grown into one of Alaska's most successful commercial operations. Locals also engage in subsistence fishing and hunting for geese, caribou, and ptarmigan.

Most visitors arrive on the Alaska Marine Highway's "Trusty Tusty" *(p219)*, a twice-monthly ferry between Homer and Dutch Harbor/Unalaska, which stops at King Cove long enough for a visit to the Russian Orthodox Church. The church's bells and interior icons were brought here in the 1980s by residents who moved from the abandoned town of Belkofski, 12 miles (19 km) to the southeast. As in Sand Point, your time here is likely to be limited by the ferry's schedule.

Visitors should be wary of the unusually large numbers of bears that visit the town, chasing dogs, tipping over trash cans, and trying to break into buildings.

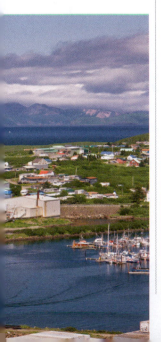

⑬ Cold Bay

🅰 **B6** 🅰 **579 miles (930 km) SW of Kodiak** ✈ 🚢 Ⓦ **coldbayak.org**

The small town of Cold Bay, within view of the dramatic 9,370-ft (2,850-m) Shishaldin Volcano, officially came into existence in August 1941 as a covert US military base to ward off Japanese attacks. Its construction was classified and its military contractor, General William Buckner, assumed a civilian name and claimed to have built a salmon cannery.

Even after Fort Randall was constructed here in 1942, the Japanese failed to realize its military significance. In 1945, the US and Russia forged an alliance and made Fort Randall a training site for over 12,000 Russian troops. During the Vietnam War in the 1960s, Cold Bay sprang back to life as a freight hauling base and the headquarters of the famed Flying Tigers squadron. Today, its massive airport provides an emergency landing site for trans-Pacific travel.

The main attraction is the beautiful 650-sq-mile (1,700-sq-km) **Izembek National Wildlife Refuge**, partly accessible via gravel roads from Cold Bay. The refuge protects the habitat of bears, caribou, seals, sea lions, and whales. At the 150-sq-mile (390-sq-km) brackish Izembek Lagoon, vast beds of eelgrass provide food for migrating birds. These include 98 percent of the world's population of Pacific black brant, a small dark goose. Visitors can watch the wildlife from the Grant Point viewing hide at the lagoon.

Izembek National Wildlife Refuge

🛈 Izembek St, Cold Bay; www.fws.gov/refuge/izembek

WORLD WAR II IN COLD BAY

In the early days of World War II, when Japanese forces threatened the Aleutians and Western Alaska, places like Cold Bay became strategic base locations for military operations. Fort Randall was an Army airfield as well as a small US Navy installation for coastal defense, and provided support to other Aleutian bases. As the war drifted toward the Western Aleutians, installations such as Cold Bay became useless and were abandoned. Today, local kids comb the former base dump for vintage bottles, coins, and other artifacts that they can sell to Alaska ferry passengers stopping in Cold Bay.

ARCTIC AND WESTERN ALASKA

Geologically precious due to ancient organic matter that gradually decomposed below the permafrost into fossil fuels, the Arctic Basin is a major source of oil and natural gas. The story of human occupation of this dark, cold, and harsh region is thought to have begun 30,000 years ago, with the arrival of humans from what is now Asia. The Inuit people of Western Alaska and the Arctic are believed to be descended from the Thule people, who arrived around AD 900–1100 during the "climatic optimum," a warming trend that also brought abundant marine mammals and birds to the area. This was followed by a cooling trend, which left the Thule isolated for hundreds of years amid vast expanses of icy land.

European explorers began arriving in the Alaska Arctic during the 18th century. Many were painfully ill-prepared for the conditions, however, and numerous expeditions failed after becoming trapped in fast-moving sea ice, with crew members often perishing from the extreme cold and lack of provisions. By the 19th century, it was becoming clear that a wealth of mineral resources was lurking beneath the wild landscape. Gold rushes – as well as minor discoveries of nickel, ore, and copper – led to further exploration, but it was oil and gas that sealed the Arctic's role as a major player in natural resource development. The Prudhoe Bay Oil Field was discovered in 1968 and the construction of the 800-mile (1,300-km) Trans-Alaska Pipeline was completed in 1977. Much of the region remains relatively untouched, but climate change now threatens both its wildlife and the centuries-old ways of the Inuit, Yup'ik, and Aleut Native groups.

ARCTIC AND WESTERN ALASKA

Must Sees
1. Utqiagvik
2. Nome
3. Dalton Highway

Experience More
4. Gates of the Arctic National Park
5. Arctic National Wildlife Refuge
6. Prudhoe Bay
7. Kotzebue
8. Kobuk Valley National Park
9. Cape Krusenstern National Monument
10. Noatak National Preserve
11. Bering Land Bridge National Preserve
12. Gambell

Arctic

Peard Bay

Wainwright

Chukchi Sea

Point Lay

Utukok

Kukpowruk

Kokolik

Wevok

B r o o k s

Point Hope

Kukpuk

DeLong Mountains

Kivalina

Noatak

10 NOATAK NATIONAL PRESERVE

Baird Mountains

Noatak

Enurmino

CAPE KRUSENSTERN NATIONAL MONUMENT 9

KOBUK VALLEY NATIONAL PARK 8

Ambler

Kobuk

RUSSIA

Uelen

Kotzebue Sound

KOTZEBUE 7

Kiana

Selawik

Lavrentiya

Shishmaref

Ralph Wien Memorial Airport

Arctic Circle

Little Diomede Island

11

BERING LAND BRIDGE NATIONAL PRESERVE

Kiwalik

Buckland

Tagagawik

Cape Prince of Wales

Kougarok

Bering Strait

Teller

Kuzitrin

Koyuk

Koyukuk

Provideniya

Cape Rodney

Council

Koyuk

Galena

Nome Airport ✈

2

NOME

Solomon

Elim

Nulato Hills

Norton Bay

Shaktoolik

Kaltag

GAMBELL

12

Savoonga

St. Lawrence Island

Norton Sound

Unalakleet

Yukon

Kaiyuh

Ophir

Stebbins

Bering Sea

Kotlik

Yukon

Grayling

Flat

SOUTHWEST ALASKA
p208

Mountain Village

Hooper Bay

Marshall

O c e a n

B e a u f o r t
S e a

**ARCTIC AND
WESTERN ALASKA**

CANADA

1 UTQIAGVIK
✈ **Wiley Post-Will Rogers
Memorial Airport**

Meade

Atqasak

Ikpikpuk

*Teshekpuk
Lake*

*Harrison
Bay*

PRUDHOE
BAY
6

Deadhorse   ✈ **Deadhorse
Airport**

*Camden
Bay*

Martin Point

Kaktovik

*Demarcation
Point*

Awuna

Colville

Chandler

Itkillik

Sagavanirktok

DALTON HIGHWAY

Mount Chamberlin
8,989 ft (2,740 m) △

Mount Michelson
8,826 ft (2,690 m) △

Kongakut

**ARCTIC NATIONAL
WILDLIFE REFUGE
5**

Sheenjek

R a n g e

11

Philip Smith Mountains

**4 GATES OF THE ARCTIC
NATIONAL PARK**

Atigun Pass

Sukakpak Mountain
4,460 ft (1,360 m) △

Spike Mountain
3,725 ft (1,135 m) △

Mount Igikpak
8,482 ft (2,585 m) △

Endicott Mountains

Wiseman

Chandalar

Coleen

Porcupine

Kobuk

John

Coldfoot

Venetie

Christian

Bettles

Hodzana

Fort Yukon

Arctic Circle

Allakaket

Koyukuk

11

Hogatza

Yukon

Yukon   Flats

Circle

Hughes

**3
DALTON
HIGHWAY**

Yukon Crossing

Huslia

Livengood

Coal Creek

Eagle Village

*Wolf Mountain
4,960 ft (1,512 m)* △

Tanana

Minto

Kokrines

2

Fairbanks

Manley Hot Springs

Ruby

✈ **Fairbanks
International Airport**

*Mount Harper
6,542 ft (1,994 m)* △

Chicken

M o u n t a i n s

2

Delta Junction

Poorman

Lake
Minchumina

**INTERIOR
ALASKA**
p164

*Mount Hayes
13,832 ft (4,216 m)* △

Tok

*Von Frank Mountain
4,508 ft (1,374 m)* △

Medfra

*Denali
20,320 ft (6,193 m)*

Summit

Denali

Paxson

4

Nabesna

McGrath

8

2

Talkeetna

3

0 kilometers   150

0 miles   150

N
↑

Willow Lake

Downtown Utqiagvik, bathed in the warm glow of the setting sun

1

UTQIAGVIK

D1 580 miles (928 km) N of Fairbanks Momegana & Ahkovak St; www.north-slope.org

The northernmost town in the US and seat of the vast North Slope Borough, Utqiagvik sits on the tundra beside the Chukchi Sea. For years the town was called Barrow, for British statesman Sir John Barrow. After a vote in 2016, the name was changed back to Utqiagvik, a term the Inupiat people had used for hundreds of years. Many of the local inhabitants here continue to live by subsistence fishing and hunting.

①

Ukkuqsi Archeological Site

Stevenson St

Along the coast at the western end of town, a series of sod ruins and remnants of archeological digs sit on the bluffs overlooking a lonely stretch of beach. While contact between Europeans and Indigenous peoples began around 1825, trade was not common until the 1870s. For that reason, the types of items unearthed – ivory points, weapons, tools, and artwork – were still in use until relatively recently. This grassy bluff is a pleasant place to stroll and enjoy the views over the Arctic Ocean.

②

Will Rogers and Wiley Post Monument

Junction of Akhovak & Momegana Sts

This memorial honors the renowned pilot Wiley Post and his friend, Cherokee humorist Will Rogers. Post, famous for setting 1920s distance records in his Lockheed Vega, decided to survey an air route from California to Russia in 1935. Funded by interested airlines, he constructed a low-wing monoplane. In July 1935, Post and Rogers left Seattle for Alaska. Near Utqiagvik they encountered bad weather and made an emergency landing. However, soon after they took off again, the engine failed and the plane plunged into a lagoon, killing both men. Visitors can also hire ATVs or hike to view the monument at the Rogers-Post Site, which lies 15 miles (24 km) to the south.

③

Inupiat Heritage Center

5421 North Star St
8:30am-5pm Mon-Fri
Federal holidays nps.gov/inup

Affiliated with the US National Park Service, Utqiagvik's Inupiat Heritage Center was set up in recognition of the Inuit contribution to whaling. For hundreds of years, the Inupiat set out in umiaks (hide-covered canoes) to hunt bowhead whales for their baleen and blubber. In the 19th and 20th centuries, the Inupiat crewed on whaling ships and also provided shelter for shipwrecked sailors.

In addition to the whaling connection, the Inupiat Heritage Center celebrates Inupiat culture, holding crafts workshops and displaying diverse objects used in local life, such as a whale baleen sled, and ivory tools. A performance area hosts singing, drumming, and dance displays.

④

Whalebone Arch

🅰 **Brower St**

This lonely spot at Browerville on the Arctic Ocean coast is the historic site from where generations of Inuit whalers have set out across the icy seas in hopes of killing a whale to feed the community through the winter. An arch made from the massive jawbone of a bowhead whale commemorates this long-standing Indigenous tradition.

Next to the arch is the former trading post (closed to the public) of the first European settler, Charles Dewitt Brower, who arrived in Utqiagvik in 1884. Married twice to Inupiat women, he acted as postmaster, census taker, military recruiter, and unofficial surgeon. Brower's grave, marked by whalebones, is beside the nearby lagoon.

---

⑤

Point Barrow

🅰 **12 miles (19 km) N of Utqiagvik**

A windswept, desolate place, Point Barrow is situated 12 miles (19 km) north of Utqiagvik, and separates the Chukchi Sea to the west from the Beaufort Sea in the east. Reachable via a gravel road, this spit of rocky land is roughly the same latitude as North Cape in Norway (71 degrees north), but with harsher winter conditions and a large population of polar bears that come here each spring to den. After seeing the warmest summer on record, Point Barrow ice was at its lowest levels ever recorded in 2019, and howling storms have resulted in erosion as winds shift shoreward. Bowhead whale populations, a vital part of the Inupiat peoples' traditional subsistence hunting practices, have also declined.

↑ The striking Whalebone Arch at Browerville

POLAR BEARS

The largest of all four-footed carnivores, polar bears (*Ursus maritimus*) grow to enormous proportions, standing up to 5 ft (1.5 m) at the shoulder and weighing up to 1,200 lbs (545 kg). Polar bears range for miles searching out seal and walrus – their main sources of food – by diving among the sea ice and riding floes until their prey is found. Alaska's 3,000-odd bears are navigating climate change by hunting not only on ice, but on land as well. This is becoming a problem in some Arctic cities; bear patrols are a regular part of local law enforcement shifts and residents are cautioned against leaving any food on porches or in cars.

2

NOME

B3 | **650 miles (1,050 km) W of Fairbanks** | ✈
301 Front St; www.visitnomealaska.com

Attractively situated on the shores of Norton Sound, this mixed Inupiat and Anglo community is the commercial and transportation hub of northwest Alaska. A former Gold Rush town, Nome is also famous for its superb bird-watching and for being the finish line of the Iditarod. Visitors in January can see the whimsical Nome National Forest, created each year when residents plant their old Christmas trees in the sea ice.

①

The Burled Arch

Front St | **iditarod.com**

Each March, the Red "Fox" Olson Trail Monument – better known as the Burled Arch – becomes the ultimate destination of all Iditarod mushers. The original arch, with the inscription "End of the Iditarod Dog Race," was erected for the first Iditarod in 1973. It succumbed to dry rot after 26 years and was replaced with a large burled spruce log, which rests outside the Town Hall in the summer. During the race, a kerosene lantern hangs from the arch until the last competitor crosses the finish line and retrieves it, winning the Red Lantern Award. This recalls the early days of transportation in Alaska, when mushers would look for the lanterns outside roadhouses along their route.

---

②

Carrie M. McLain Museum

100 W 7th Avenue
Noon-7pm Mon-Thu, noon-6pm Fri & Sat
nomealaska.org/museum

Named after its founder, writer Carrie M. McLain, this renovated city-run museum reveals Nome's colorful history with original displays on its Gold Rush days. Other exhibits focus on modern Nome, as well as on historic aviation, the arts and culture

---

IDITAROD

Held each March, the Iditarod is a 1,000-mile (1,600 km) sled dog race from Anchorage to Nome. "The Last Great Race" is said to have been inspired by the 1925 Great Serum Run, in which dog teams transported life-saving diptheria serum to the epidemic-stricken Nome when bad weather forced airplanes to stay grounded. The first competitive race was held in 1973 with 22 teams; today's race registers at least 60, all vying for the impressive prize money. Questions about the ethics of the race have been raised by animal rights activists, but supporters argue that the dogs are carefully monitored by veterinarians and love doing what they were bred to do.

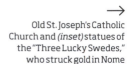

→ Old St. Joseph's Catholic Church and *(inset)* statues of the "Three Lucky Swedes," who struck gold in Nome

> **On its steeple, a cross lit by electric lights served as a beacon to guide mushers and miners into town.**

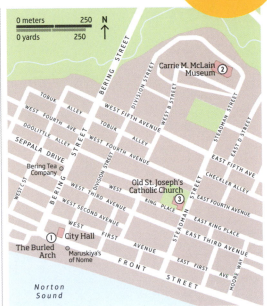

of the Bering Strait Inuit, the famous Iditarod, and the original Nome Kennel Club and its All Alaska Sweepstakes sled dog race.

③

Old St. Joseph's Catholic Church

🅐 279 King Place, Anvil City Sq ☎ 443-7856

The 1901 St. Joseph's Catholic Church, Nome's oldest building, was constructed on the waterfront as a counterpoint to the rollicking Gold Rush atmosphere of the time. On its steeple, a cross lit by electric lights served as a beacon to guide mushers and miners into town. The building eventually fell into decay and a new one was built. In 1996, the old church was moved to its present site, restored, and given a new steeple. The church is now a community hall and is only open for special events.

In front of the church are statues of Jafet Lindberg, John Brynteson, and Erik Lindblom, "the Three Lucky Swedes" who discovered gold in nearby Anvil Creek, thereby initiating Nome's short-lived Gold Rush in the late 1890s.

SHOP

Maruskiya's of Nome
This small, family-owned business is one of the finest places in all Alaska to purchase Alaska Native art, jewelry, and dolls. Handcrafted with care, the works are brought in from around the Northwest Alaska area.

🅐 247 Front Street
🆆 maruskiyas.com

Bering Tea Company
This coffee shop has designated wall space for local artisans and shelves full of their pottery wares. One of Nome's most popular places to find free wi-fi, a warm drink, and friendly staff.

🅐 310 Bering Street
☎ 387-0352

BEYOND NOME

④
Council Road

🚗 **72 miles (115 km) from Nome to Council**

The causeway-like Council Road follows the coastline east of Nome past camp-grounds of speculative wild-cat prospectors, who brave the freezing waters of Norton Sound to mine the beach sands with gas-powered dredges. Passing superb bird-watching sites at the marshes of Safety Sound, it arrives at the photogenic Last Train to Nowhere, three locomotives and several decrepit railcars of the 1881 Council City and Solomon River Railroad that stand rusting on the tundra at Mile 33. The railroad was envisioned as a link between Nome and the Lower 48, but was halted in 1907 owing to lack of funds. At this point, the road turns inland, through the tiny village of Solomon, now virtually abandoned. After crossing scenic Skookum Pass, the road ends at the Niukluk River. There is a ford here into the Gold Rush village of Council, but it is best accessed with the help of local boat owners.

→

Last Train to Nowhere on Council Road, which is also *(inset)* a top spot for bird-watching

---

TOP 3

BIRDS TO SPOT AROUND NOME

Arctic Terns
Arctic terns migrate 25,000 miles (40,000 km) each year between their breeding grounds in the Arctic and their wintering grounds in Antarctica.

Snowy Owls
Snowy owls are perhaps the most spectacular summer birds on the Arctic coast. Diving from the sky with outstretched talons, these birds can drive away even an advancing caribou.

Red-Throated Loon
Much rarer than the iconic common loon, the red-throated loon is one of Alaska's five loon species. Their haunting calls are a signature sound of the North American wilderness.

0 kilometers 40
0 miles 40
N ↑

Kougarok

Kougarok Bridge

Kuzitrin

Teller

Bendeleben Mountains

Pilgrim Hot Springs

Imuruk Basin

Kigluaik Mountains

Niukluk

⑥ Teller Road

Salmon Lake

Council

⑤ Kougarok Road

Council Road ④

Skookum Pass

Nome Airport ✈

Solomon

Last Train to Nowhere

See Nome map on p239

Safety Sound

Norton Sound

⑤
Kougarok Road

🏠 **89 miles (143 km) from Nome to Kougarok Bridge**

Also known as the Taylor Road, the wonderfully scenic Kougarok Road runs from Nome through the Kigluaik Mountains, paralleling the Wild Goose Pipeline, which was built in 1909 to transport water to Nome but never used. North of the mountains, a graveled spur road leads to an oasis of cottonwood trees at **Pilgrim Hot Springs**, a former Catholic orphanage within range of a geothermal spring that belies its frigid northwestern location. The site has a simple wooden hot tank, which visitors can use after getting a permit from the Nome Visitor Center. The springs area is a lovely site, with well-preserved buildings and plants that flourish in the warm microclimate. It is best visited with a guide out of respect for its Native ownership, and to obtain accurate historical information.

Beyond the springs, the road passes through wetlands and tundra to its end point at Kougarok Bridge. From here, a rough track leads to Taylor.

Pilgrim Hot Springs

🏠 Turn-off at Mile 62
📞 443-5252

⑥
Teller Road

🏠 **66 miles (110 km) from Nome to Teller**

Leaving Nome, this beautiful, lonely road follows clearwater streams, grasslands, and steep climbs on its way to Teller. Passing through the Kigluaik Mountains, it reaches rolling tundra, where there is a good chance of seeing wild musk oxen and domestic reindeer. Teller, at the westernmost tip of this westernmost road in North America, lies on a gray gravel spit at Port Clarence on the Bering Sea. It is known as the site where Norwegian explorer Roald Amundsen landed after his legendary 70-hour airship flight over the North Pole in 1926.

> **Did You Know?**
>
> Nome's curious name is likely a misreading of the note "?Name" on a 19th-century naval chart.

> 🔍 **HIDDEN GEM**
> **Going for Gold**
>
> Near Anvil Creek, the AKAU Gold Resort (*www.akaugold.com*) – a former homestead that is now a rustic gold-mining resort – supports first-time gold miners and seasoned pros alike. Housing 20 guests at a time, the resort also offers fishing, hiking, and ATV tours of former mine sites and other historic landmarks.

3

DALTON HIGHWAY

🅰 E2 🏠 Highway starts at Livengood on the Elliot Highway, 73 miles (117 km) N of Fairbanks

The Dalton Highway is the only road in Alaska that crosses into the icy Arctic Circle. It runs for 414 miles (666 km) through remote wilderness, offering an unforgettable road trip for the adventurous.

The highway was originally built in the 1970s to supply equipment to the Prudhoe Bay oil fields and provide a service corridor for the Trans-Alaska Pipeline. The pipeline, in fact, runs parallel with the road all the way. Also known as the Haul Road, the highway was initially accessible only to supply trucks, but in the 1990s, the full route was opened to private drivers. While astoundingly scenic, much of the highway is a bone-jarring gravel route that should not be undertaken lightly. Services are only available in a handful of places but supplies are not, and drivers should travel with essentials such as food, water, a first aid kit, spare tires, and fuel.

↑ Driving through the Brooks Range on the little-traveled Dalton Highway

The Dalton Highway, sweeping through breathtaking scenery ↑

Highlights

Finger Mountain

Distant views from the Finger Mountain wayside stop take in the majestic Caribou Mountain and a lovely tor-studded landscape.

Arctic Interagency Visitor Center, Coldfoot

▽ An essential stop, the center has exhibits and interpretive programs on the Arctic. Also worth a look is Coldfoot's temperature sign, which describes the day in 1989 when the temperature dropped to -63° C (-82° F), the coldest ever recorded in North America.

E. L. Patton Yukon Bridge

▲ This 2,295-ft- (688-m-) long bridge carries both the Dalton Highway and the Trans-Alaska Pipeline. Built in 1975, this is the only US bridge across the Yukon River (p190).

Arctic Circle Wayside

The highway crosses the Arctic Circle at Mile 115, where there is a wayside stop with a picnic area, a basic campground, and a viewing deck, as well as information boards on life in the Arctic Circle.

INSIDER TIP
Gas Stops

There are only four gas stations on the Dalton Highway – at Yukon Crossing, Five-Mile Camp, Coldfoot, and Deadhorse. Be sure to bear this in mind when considering whether or not to refuel.

Wiseman

▽ Wiseman was founded in 1907 as a camp to service the gold strike at nearby Nolan. Today, the site is home to a historic church and an open-air museum.

Sukakpak Mountain

This dramatic and distinctive 4,460-ft (1,360-m) peak was a limestone deposit before heat and pressure metamorphosed it into marble.

Franklin Bluffs

▽ The iron-rich soil on the east bank of the Sagavanirktok River gives Franklin Bluffs – home to wildlife such as caribou – their striking hues.

Atigun Pass

The highway crosses the Brooks Range at the 4,800-ft- (1,440-m-) high Atigun Pass, the highest point on Alaska's road system. Its steep grades demand extreme caution.

Trans-Alaska Pipeline

△ Near the northern end of the highway, the gleaming pipeline winds along the western edge of the Arctic National Wildlife Refuge.

EXPERIENCE MORE

4

Gates of the Arctic National Park

🏔D2 ⏱200 miles (320 km) NW of Fairbanks ✈🚌 ℹ Bettles Visitor Center, Arctic Interagency Visitor Center (Coldfoot), Anaktuvuk Pass Ranger Station; www.nps. gov/gaar

The second-largest national park in the US after Wrangell-St. Elias (p182), Gates of the Arctic National Park covers an area of 12,500 sq miles (32,000 sq km). The park was given its name in the 1930s, when US wilderness advo-cate Bob Marshall described Frigid Crags and the Boreal Mountains as the "gates" to the Arctic North Slope. The heart of the park is the Brooks Range, the northernmost part of the Rocky Mountains. The abundant wildlife here includes black and brown bears, caribou, moose, and migratory birds, and the vegetation away from the glaciated peaks ranges from boreal forest of spruce, birch, and aspen to alder thickets, taiga, and muskeg.

Most visitors fly in for hiking or rafting on National Wild and Scenic Rivers such as the Kobuk, John, and Noatak. Commercial trips are available, but lone travelers usually take an air taxi to Bettles, and then a bush plane to a drop-off point. Lodges at Bettles offer accommodations and meals.

5

Arctic National Wildlife Refuge

🏔E2 ⏱200 miles (320 km) N of Fairbanks ✈🚌 ℹ101 12th Ave, Fairbanks; www. arctic.fws.gov

The 30,000-sq-mile (78,000-sq-km) Arctic National Wildlife Refuge (ANWR, pronounced AN-wahr) was established in 1960 to protect the region's abundant wildlife, flocks of migratory birds, and range of ecosystems. However, studies of the ANWR coastal plain east of Prudhoe Bay have determined that the northwestern corner of the refuge also holds vast amounts of natural gas and oil. Political forces have long

tussled over ANWR, with pro-development organizations lobbying to allow oil drilling on the coastal plain, while environmental groups oppose opening the wildlife refuge to oil exploitation.

Scenically stunning, ANWR is bisected by the Brooks Range and crossed by the Sheenjek, Kongukut, Hulahula, and other "wild rivers" that are popular for rafting trips. Wildlife enthusiasts may have the chance to spot all three of Alaska's bear species, as well as musk oxen, wolves, caribou, and over 140 species of birds. ANWR has no trails or facil-ities, and visitors need to be self-sufficient.

6

Prudhoe Bay

🏔E1 ⏱487 miles (784 km) N of Fairbanks ✈🚌 ℹ Prudhoe Bay Hotel, 100 Airport Way; 659-2449

The North Slope oil fields, often collectively called Prudhoe Bay, make up the largest oil-producing field in North America. Although surveys took place in the 1950s, the first major discov-ery was made only in 1968. The Alyeska Pipeline Service Company was formed a year later to construct a pipeline (p201) across the state to the ice-free port of Valdez. Today, the vast oil fields use the latest technology to minimize their impact on the delicate tundra.

Deadhorse is the oil fields' service center. Prudhoe Bay and the Arctic Ocean coast, which lie beyond a checkpoint, can only be accessed on tours run by the Prudhoe Bay Hotel.

←

Hiking over a mountain ridge in the Gates of the Arctic National Park

↑ An Alaska wolf crossing the tundra of the Arctic National Wildlife Refuge

THE ARCTIC TUNDRA

Lying north of the Brooks Range, Alaska's North Slope covers 88,000 sq miles (227,920 sq km) of largely flat, open Arctic tundra. This circumpolar environment is characterized by low temperatures and thin topsoil that supports only ground-hugging vegetation such as mosses, sedges, lichens, liverworts, berries, dwarf birch, and tiny wildflowers. Tundra areas typically have little precipitation, a growing season of less than 60 days, and average temperatures of 12° C (54° F) during the summer and around -34° C (-30° F) in winter.

Underlying the thin tundra surface is permafrost. This permanently frozen ground cannot absorb surface water, resulting in millions of small shallow ponds and bogs. Crater lakes are sometimes found in pingos – domed ice-cored mounds of earth. The expanding ice can cause the summit of the pingo to crack, which exposes the ice core and allows part of it to melt, forming the crater lake. On top of the tundra, a carpet of vibrant miniature wildflowers appears during the short flowering season in summer. Common species include woolly lousewort, harebell, and monkshood.

TOP 3 ANIMALS TO SPOT

Arctic Ground Squirrel
The Arctic ground squirrel digs burrows in the ground and hibernates through the long, cold winter.

Musk Oxen
Musk oxen live year-round on the open tundra, protected from the extreme cold by a soft insulating layer of hair known as *qiviut*.

Caribou
Caribou have broad hooves that give support in soft tundra and snow, and function as paddles when the animal swims.

↑ Dainty wildflowers providing a summer splash of color to the tundra

↑ Skiffs lining the shores of the lagoon in Kotzebue on an early fall morning

❼

Kotzebue

🅰C2 📍550 miles (880 km) NW of Anchorage ✈ ℹ258A 3rd Ave; www.cityofkotzebue.com

Located on the shores of the Chukchi Sea, Kotzebue, with a 75 percent Native population, is the commercial, economic, and political center of the Northwest Arctic Borough. A gateway to the Kobuk Valley National Park, the site lies 26 miles (43 km) north of the Arctic Circle on a 3-mile- (5-km-) long sandspit at the end of the Baldwin Peninsula. Kikiktagruk, its Inupiat name, simply means "the peninsula," and its modern name honors Otto von Kotzebue, a Russian naval office who explored Kotzebue Sound in 1816.

The economy of modern Kotzebue depends largely on the Red Dog Mine, a lead and zinc mine 100 miles (160 km) north of town, which employs hundreds of workers and provides a good income for the Northwest Arctic Native Association (NANA). Kotzebue also has Alaska's only power grid that is supplemented by wind-generated electricity.

Kotzebue is not a major tourist destination, but visitors to the area will get an idea of what life is like in this harsh place, where the winters are long and summers are brief and intense. On the shore south of town are local fish camps, where fish, seal, and walrus meat are smoked and dried. The cemetery is also worth a visit for its beautifully decorated graves. East of Kotzebue is rolling tundra to explore – be sure to pack head nets and mosquito repellent, as well as plenty of water.

The National Park Service's **Northwest Arctic Heritage Center** has a wealth of exhibits on Kobuk Valley National Park, Cape Krusenstern National Monument, Noatak National Preserve, and Bering Land Bridge. These offer visitors a taste of some of the least-visited units in the US National Park Service (the parks themselves are very remote and require bush flights and total self-sufficiency for the duration of the trip). The heritage center also gives an interesting introduction to Inupiat culture; educational programs are offered, along with occasional Native dance performances and blanket toss demonstrations.

Northwest Arctic Heritage Center

🕐 🅰171 3rd St 🕐Jun-Aug: 9am-6:30pm Mon-Fri, 10am-6:30pm Sat; Sep-May: 9am-5pm Mon-Fri 🌐nps.gov/kova

❽

Kobuk Valley National Park

🅰C2 📍125 miles (200 km) E of Kotzebue ✈Charter plane from Kotzebue 🚢Charter boat from Ambler ℹ171 3rd Ave, Kotzebue; www.nps.gov/kova

Kobuk Valley National Park is a sanctuary for the area's range of Arctic wildlife. Its most visited attraction is the Great Kobuk Sand Dunes, which lie along Kavel Creek. Covering over 25 sq miles (65 sq km), the dunes were created when glacier-ground rock built up in an area where vegetation could not take hold.

Did You Know?
—
On the winter solstice, the sun is over the horizon for just two hours in Kotzebue.

→

Noatak National Preserve, where the headwaters of the *(inset)* Noatak River are found

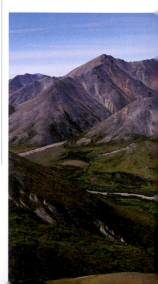

THE BLANKET TOSS

The blanket toss, in its most traditional form, is performed using a large walrus hide blanket held by a dozen or more people. The jumper stands in the middle of the blanket and begins making increasingly higher jumps, as on a trampoline. Once a bit of altitude and momentum are gained, those holding the fringes provide a serious boost, and the jumper is propelled high into the air. Historically, the toss was used to allow lookouts to gain a bit of elevation over the largely flat coastline and determine whether whales, seals, walrus, or polar bears were in sight. Today, it is used mostly in celebration of a successful whaling season, hence the Inupiat name of Utqiagvik's main festival, Nalukataq, which means "blanket toss."

The park is popular with river runners, who fly to Walker Lake and raft, canoe, or kayak down the Kobuk River over three weeks to the village of Kiana. Those who prefer a tamer adventure fly to Ambler and float the relatively calm 85-mile (136-km), six-day section to Kiana.

⑨
Cape Krusenstern National Monument

🅰 C2 🕿 50 miles (80 km) NW of Kotzebue ✈ Charter bush plane from Kotzebue
ℹ 171 3rd Ave, Kotzebue; www.nps.gov/cakr

The broad coastal plain of the haunting Cape Krusenstern National Monument is made up of 114 parallel limestone bluffs and ridges that create the Chukchi Sea coastline. It is one of the most remote such sites in the US, curving gracefully around the shore. In the autumn, this changing landscape of alternating lagoons and beaches attracts migrating waterfowl with its swarms of protein-rich insects. There is also rewarding bird-watching, hiking, and wildlife viewing.

The monument's only facility is a lonely summer ranger station at Anigaaq, near the beach ridges. There are no roads, trails, cabins, or campgrounds, and visits must be carefully planned.

The area is still in use by the Inupiat people, particularly for seal hunting along the outer beaches.

⑩
Noatak National Preserve

🅰 C2 🕿 200 miles (320 km) NE of Kotzebue ✈ Charter bush plane from Kotzebue
ℹ 171 3rd Ave, Kotzebue; www.nps.gov/noat

The wonderfully wild Noatak National Preserve, between the DeLong and Baird mountain ranges, encompasses some of the loneliest landscapes in the country and protects an array of plants and wildlife. The Noatak River, with its headwaters in the Brooks Range inside Gates of the Arctic National Park (p244), is the preserve's main highway. River runners regard the wild descent of the Noatak as one of Alaska's best river trips. The trips, which can take up to three weeks, involve a bush flight into the Noatak headwaters from either Kotzebue or Bettles, with a pickup in Noatak village.

The steaming Serpentine Hot Springs in the Bering Land Bridge National Preserve ↑

11

Bering Land Bridge National Preserve

🅰B2 📍100 miles (160 km) N of Nome ✈Charter bush plane, then hike ℹSitnasuak Building, 214 Front St, Nome; www.nps. gov/bela

Designated a National Monument in 1978, Bering Land Bridge received National Preserve status when the Alaska National Interest Lands Conservation Act was passed in 1980 (p61). Encompassing 4,200 sq miles (10,900 sq km), the preserve commemorates the 55-mile- (88-km-) long and 1,000-mile- (1,600-km-) wide land bridge that once connected North America and Asia (p56). It is believed that during the last major Ice Age, this bridge allowed the passage of both prehistoric wildlife and early human settlers from Asia into North America. Around 15,000 years ago, the melting of the ice caused a rise in sea level, and the land bridge disappeared beneath the waves of the newly formed Bering Strait.

The broad Arctic landscape of the preserve includes wide expanses of tundra, as well as scenic granite tors that bear testament to the area's distant volcanic past. The six public-use cabins scattered around the preserve, and the 20-bed bunkhouse and hot tub at the preserve's main attraction, Serpentine Hot Springs, may be used free of charge and require no reservations, although users may have to share the space. The preserve's visitor center in Nome has exhibits showcasing its cultural and natural history.

Access to the preserve is almost exclusively by bush plane in the summer and snowmobile in the winter, although a few people do hike the 40 miles (64 km) to Serpentine Hot Springs from Kougarok Bridge.

12

Gambell

🅰A3 📍230 miles (370 km) E of Nome ✈From Nome

The small Siberian Yup'ik village of Gambell sits on beach gravel at the northwestern corner of St. Lawrence Island, which is 70 miles (112 km) long and includes the even more isolated village of Savoonga. Lying near the Siberian coast, the island is one of Alaska's most remote outposts.

When the Alaska Native Claims Settlement Act was passed in 1971 (p60), Gambell and Savoonga decided not to participate, and thus gained title to about 1,780 sq miles (4,600 sq km) of land. The villagers are therefore able to charge an "outsider tax" from non-residents wishing to access this area; permits are also required.

Getting around the island requires an ATV, and visitors can usually get rides from the villagers for a small fee. Most visitors to the island come to view birds not seen elsewhere in North America, including several incidental Eurasian species such as Lapland longspurs. Summer visitors can also spot flocks of eider ducks, murres, kittiwakes, puffins, and auklets either nesting or heading north.

In addition to the birdlife, the island's main attractions include the unique "bone-yards" (archaeological sites) south of the village and at the base of Sivaquaq Mountain. Some locals dig through these ancient sites for fossilized walrus ivory, but visitors should not purchase any of these looted artifacts.

> **The broad Arctic landscape of the Bering Land Bridge National Preserve includes wide expanses of tundra, as well as scenic granite tors.**

WILDFLOWERS AND BERRIES

Beginning in the spring and through the short northern summer, a series of wildflowers splash color across the Alaska landscape. Plants of the same species may bloom as much as six weeks apart, depending on their location. From mid- to late summer, edible berries also emerge throughout the state, many developing from the flowers of the early summer.

Tiny northern anemones and delicate pasqueflowers appear first during the short flowering season, often just after the snow melts. At the height of summer, bright fireweed, lemon yellow Arctic poppies, skunk cabbage, and other flowers carpet the landscape - one of the finest displays is in the Pribilof Islands *(p220)*, where the summer-long sequence of wildflowers is renowned. Wild strawberries grow in southern and central Alaska in late June, followed by cloudberries, blueberries, and then rose hips and lowbush cranberries in late summer. After the salmon runs, this rich harvest provides sugar for the bears, fattening them before they take to their winter dens.

← Purple pasqueflowers, one of the first blooms to appear in spring

TOP 3 WILDFLOWERS TO SPOT

Chocolate Lily
Also called skunk lily due to its smell, this is found in woodlands and open meadows.

Alpine Forget-Me-Not
Alaska's state flower blossoms between May and August.

Villous Cinquefoil
Grows in cracks in boulders and cliff faces and is one of the first wildflowers to bloom.

↑ Brown bears foraging for food amid a carpet of wildflowers

FIREWEED

Every summer, large swathes of the landscape turn purple as fireweed blooms. The young stems and leaves are rich in vitamins A and C, and Athabascans have long eaten them either boiled or raw, and used cut stems to draw infection from boils. When the blooms go to seed and turn to cotton fluff, Alaskans say that the winter is only six weeks away.

NEED TO KNOW

Driving along the Alaska Highway

BEFORE YOU GO

Forward planning is essential to any successful trip. Be prepared for all eventualities by considering the following points before you travel.

AT A GLANCE

CURRENCY
US Dollar (USD)

AVERAGE DAILY SPEND

SAVE **$100**

SPEND **$200**

SPLURGE **$300+**

BOTTLED WATER **$2.50**

COFFEE **$2–6**

BEER **$6**

DINNER FOR TWO **$120**

CLIMATE

 The longest days occur between May and July, and the shortest between November and January.

 Southcentral temperatures average 18°C (65°F) in summer, and regularly drop below 0°C (32°F) in winter.

 May and June are usually the rainiest months. Interior Alaska is typically drier than other regions.

ELECTRICITY SUPPLY

Standard voltage is 110 volts and 60 Hz. Power sockets are usually type A or B with two or three flat pins.

Passports and Visas

All travelers to Alaska and the US should have a passport that is valid for six months beyond the intended period of stay. Citizens of Australia, New Zealand, and the EU do not need a visa, but must apply for an **ESTA** (Electronic System for Travel Authorization) permit at least 72 hours ahead of the trip. All other visitors need a tourist visa, and will be photographed and have their fingerprints taken. Entry regulations may change, so always check ahead of travel with the US Department of State for the most up-to-date visa and travel information.

ESTA
w esta.cbp.dhs.gov/esta

Travel Safety Advice

Visitors can get up-to-date travel safety information from the **US Department of State**, the **UK Foreign and Commonwealth Office**, and the **Australian Department of Foreign Affairs and Trade**.

Australia
w smartraveller.gov.au
UK
w gov.uk/foreign-travel-advice
US
w travel.state.gov

Customs Information

Passengers may carry the following into the US without incurring tax:

Tobacco products One carton of cigarettes, 50 cigars (not Cuban) or 2 kilograms (4.4 lbs) of smoking tobacco.

Alcohol A liter (2 pints) of alcohol as beer, wine, or liquor (if aged 21 years or older).

Cash If you are carrying $10,000 or more in cash (or other monetary instruments) you must declare it to the customs authorities.

All travelers need to complete a **Customs and Border Protection Agency** form when crossing the US border.

Customs and Border Protection Agency
w cbp.gov/travel

Insurance

It is wise to take out comprehensive travel and medical insurance covering theft, cancellations and delays, loss of belongings, medical issues, and repatriation costs. All medical and dental treatment is private, costs can be very high, and the US health services do not have reciprocal arrangements with other countries.

Vaccinations

No vaccinations are required for entry into the US. However, it is a good idea to get a tetanus booster if you will be hiking or camping.

Money

Major credit and debit cards are accepted by most businesses. While contactless payments are becoming widely accepted, they are not yet common. In rural areas where Wi-Fi connections or cell services are weak, pre-payment may be requested upon booking, or you may be asked to pay with cash at the time of purchase. It is always prudent to carry at least $100. Cash machines can be found at banks, airline terminals, and in many tour-based businesses.

Booking Accommodations

Alaska offers a huge variety of accommodations, but space fills up fast – sometimes as far as a year in advance – so planning is essential. **Travel Alaska** has information about different accommodation options across Alaska.
Travel Alaska
w travelalaska.com

Travelers With Specific Needs

Travelers are guaranteed accomodations for most physical disabilities as outlined in the Americans With Disabilities Act, which means ramps, lifts, and assistance onto transportation is provided. However, the Alaskan backcountry can prove challenging for those with limited mobility, due to the remote locations and the rugged nature of the terrain. That said, front-country areas surrounding visitor centers often have amenities such as wheelchair-friendly trails and viewing decks. US citizens or permanent residents with permanent disabilities can apply for an **America the Beautiful Access Pass**, which grants free access to all US public lands. **Access Alaska** in Anchorage provides loaner equipment, while the **Society for Accessible Travel and Hospitality** can provide help finding equipment to make snowy weather easier to navigate. For those with emotional or behavioral disorders like autism, Alaska is slowly but surely providing more quiet spaces to accommodate sensitivities to noise, light, or commotion.
Access Alaska
w accessalaska.org
America the Beautiful Access Pass
w store.usgs.gov/access-pass
Society for Accessible Travel and Hospitality
w sath.org

Language

As in the rest of the United States, English is the primary language spoken in Alaska.

Closures

Sunday Post offices and most banks and smaller businesses are closed.
Federal and State Holidays Alaska observes most federal holidays, plus the state holidays of Seward's Day (last Monday in March) and Alaska Day (October 18 or the closest Monday). State offices, post offices, banks, and some schools may be closed. Check ahead with individual venues for specific closures.
Winter Many seasonal attractions are closed between Labor Day and Memorial Day.

FEDERAL HOLIDAYS	
Jan 1	New Year's Day
3rd Mon, Jan	Martin Luther King Day
3rd Mon, Feb	President's Day
Last Mon, May	Memorial Day
Jul 4	Independence Day
1st Mon, Sep	Labor Day
Nov 11	Veterans Day
4th Thu, Nov	Thanksgiving
Dec 25	Christmas

GETTING
AROUND

Whether you're hopping between towns or heading out into the wilderness, discover how best to reach your destination and travel like a pro.

AT A GLANCE

PUBLIC TRANSPORT COSTS

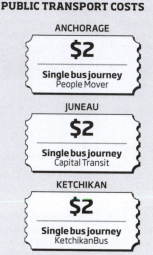

ANCHORAGE

$2

Single bus journey
People Mover

JUNEAU

$2

Single bus journey
Capital Transit

KETCHIKAN

$2

Single bus journey
KetchikanBus

TOP TIP
Ask at local visitor information centers about free summer shuttle services.

SPEED LIMIT

SPECIFIED HIGHWAYS

65 mph
(105 km/h)

OTHER HIGHWAYS

55 mph
(89 km/h)

GRAVEL ROADS

30 mph
(48 km/h)

RESIDENTIAL AREAS

25 mph
(40 km/h)

Arriving by Air

Most travelers arrive in Alaska via **Ted Stevens Anchorage International Airport** (ANC), then branch off to other destinations. **Alaska Airlines** is the chief carrier, although increasing numbers of carriers are scheduling flights to and from Anchorage. **Fairbanks International Airport** (FAI) is the next busiest, followed by **Juneau International Airport** (JNU) and **Ketchikan International Airport** (KTN), largely catering to one-way cruise ship passengers. Most flights to and from Alaska originate in Seattle (SEA), but a growing number of airlines have also begun flying direct from Portland (PDX), Denver (DEN), and Vancouver in British Columbia (YVR).

Alaska Airlines
W alaskaair.com
Fairbanks International Airport
W fai.alaska.gov
Juneau International Airport
W beta.juneau.org/airport
Ketchikan International Airport
W borough.ketchikan.ak.us/130/airport
Ted Stevens Anchorage International Airport
W dot.state.ak.us/anc/

Internal Flights

Several domestic airlines offer convenient, if sometimes expensive, services. Alaska also has a host of charter airlines that can take passengers to just about any airport or airstrip in the state, as well as bush airlines that land fly-in hunters, anglers, river runners, or hikers on remote lakes, rivers, glaciers, or gravel bars. Rates vary according to the type of plane, number of passengers, and flight duration. For bush flights, a prearranged pickup is usually scheduled, but bad weather can cause delays so travelers need to be flexible. Bear in mind that you are on your own until the pickup, so always carry extra supplies in case of problems with the return flight.

Rail Travel

The **Alaska Railroad** runs a series of routes between Seward, Anchorage, and Fairbanks, stopping at several smaller communities

Airport	Distance to City	Transport	Journey Time	Fare
Anchorage	5 miles (8 km)	Taxi	20 mins	$20
	5 miles (8 km)	People Mover bus	25 mins	$2
Fairbanks	5 miles (8 km)	Taxi	20 mins	$13
	5 miles (8 km)	MACS bus	60 mins	$1.50
Juneau	12 miles (19 km)	Taxi	30 mins	$22
Ketchikan	3 miles (5 km)	Ferry	60 mins	$6 (pedestrians)/$7 (cars)

along the way, including Denali National Park. Although primarily used as a sightseeing trip for cruise passengers on land tours, the railroad can be a delightful means of transportation for those not in a hurry. Scheduled services include the Coastal Classic between Anchorage and Seward, the Denali Star between Anchorage and Fairbanks, and the Glacier Discovery between Anchorage and Whittier; all three operate from mid-May to mid-September only.

Alaska Railroad also operates two flag stop services. Passengers can flag down the train anywhere along the route, and it will stop to let them board. The Hurricane Turn operates year-round to Hurricane, departing from Talkeetna in summer and Anchorage in winter, while the Aurora Winter Train runs weekly between Anchorage and Fairbanks from mid-September to mid-May.

Additionally, the **White Pass & Yukon Route Railway** runs between Skagway in Alaska and Whitehorse in Canada's Yukon Territory.

Note that seats can get booked up quickly in summer – especially in Alaska Railroad's luxurious dome cars with extra large windows – so it pays to reserve as far in advance as possible. The Alaska Railroad also offers a variety of special seasonal package tours; details of these can be found online.

Alaska Railroad
w alaskarailroad.com
White Pass & Yukon Route Railway
w wpyr.com

Long-Distance Bus Travel

Much of Alaska's bus market revolves around cruise tour passengers, but there are also some interstate shuttles with regular services, though many of these operate only between May and September. The biggest company is **Park Connection Motorcoach**, running between Seward and Denali Park, with stops in Whittier, Anchorage, and Talkeetna. **Seward Bus Lines** connects Anchorage with Seward, while the **Homer Stage Line** runs between Anchorage, Homer, and Seward. **Alaska/Yukon Trails** has a year-round service between Anchorage and Fairbanks, as well as summer services to Dawson City and Whitehorse in Canada. **Interior Alaska Bus Lines** operates services between Fairbanks, Anchorage, and Tok. **Kennicott Shuttle** buses run between Glennallen and McCarthy in Wrangell-St. Elias National Park. Several tour companies also operate vans or small buses between Seward and Fairbanks, and sometimes beyond; check with **Travel Alaska** for full listings.

To reach Alaska by bus from the Lower 48 states, it is best to take **Greyhound Canada** to Whitehorse, and connect to the Alaska/Yukon Trails service to Fairbanks.

Alaska/Yukon Trails
w alaskashuttle.com
Greyhound Canada
w greyhound.ca
Homer Stage Line
w stagelineinhomer.com
Interior Alaska Bus Lines
w interioralaskabusline.com
Kennicott Shuttle
w kennicottshuttle.com
Park Connection Motorcoach
w alaskacoach.com
Seward Bus Lines
w sewardbuslines.net
Travel Alaska
w travelalaska.com

Ferry Services

The state-run **Alaska Marine Highway** – whose ferries are affectionately known as the "Blue Canoes" – is an unhurried, authentic way to explore coastal Alaska along the only water-based National Scenic Byway. It has three main routes: Southeast, Southcentral, and Southwest. The Southeast route is the longest, following the spectacular Inside Passage up the west coast of North America from Bellingham in Washington state northward through Southeast Alaska's islands and channels to Haines and Skagway. The Southcentral route connects Whittier to Cordova, Valdez, and Chenega Bay, and also to Kodiak, Port Lions, Homer, and Seldovia. The Southwest route, operational from April to September, connects Homer to Seldovia, Kodiak, and Port Lions, and down the Alaska Peninsula and the Aleutians to Chignik, Sand Point, King Cove, Cold Bay, and Dutch Harbor. However, drastic cuts to ferry funding have left the status of many of these services in flux, so always check the Alaska Marine Highway website for the latest updates before traveling.

Inter-Island Ferry links Ketchikan to Prince of Wales Island. Ferry services to Canada can be picked up across the border at Prince Rupert, from where **British Columbia Ferries** sails to Port Hardy on Vancouver Island.

To take a vehicle on a Marine Highway ferry, especially between Bellingham and Haines in the peak season (April to September), book as far in advance as possible. Tariffs depend on the size of the vehicle. Boats under 100 lb (45 kg), bicycles, and kayaks incur an extra charge, while larger boats will be charged as vehicles. Except in some of the smaller ports, drivers will usually be required to check in two hours before sailing. RV propane tanks and firearms must be reported to the purser upon boarding so that they can be sealed by the crew.

Alaska Marine Highway
W ferryalaska.com
British Columbia Ferries
W bcferries.com
Inter-Island Ferry
W interislandferry.com

Public Transport

Only Anchorage, Juneau, the Mat-Su, Fairbanks, and Ketchikan have regular public bus services, but Utqiagvik, Kodiak, Sitka, and Skagway have limited services. The **Alaska Department of Transportation** has a useful list of transport providers. Anchorage's **People Mover** covers most parts of the city from the Downtown Transit Center, and goes as far north as Eagle River. Within the Mat-Su Borough, **Valley Transit** operates buses around Wasilla and Palmer, as well as into Anchorage. **Capital Transit** in Juneau links downtown with the Mendenhall Valley and Douglas Island; **MACS** covers the Fairbanks area; and **KetchikanBus** in Ketchikan connects downtown with the North Tongass Highway and Saxman village.

Alaska Department of Transportation
W dot.alaska.gov/stwdplng/transit/rcs_providers.shtml
Capital Transit
W juneaucapitaltransit.org
KetchikanBus
W kgbak.us/145/Transit
MACS
W fnsb.us/transportation
People Mover
W peoplemover.org
Valley Transit
W valleytransitak.org

Taxis

Taxis are available in nearly every community. This is true even in rural areas, where many people do not own cars due to the high cost of maintenance and fuel. Rates vary widely between urban and rural areas, with the latter generally around double the former due to the cost of fuel. Carry cash for payments.

Driving

There is nothing quite like exploring Alaska by car. Even though there are no freeways and only a handful of formal highways, driving is often the simplest, most affordable way to get around, offering the most opportunities to get to know the state. However, note that Alaskan summers (May–September) are famously known as "construction season" and drivers can be subjected to long delays. Always ensure your vehicle is full of gas, and you have plenty of food and water. Those traveling on remote routes should carry extra gas as filling stations can be few and far between. The longest stretch without fuel is the 244-mile (390-km) leg between Coldfoot and Deadhorse on the Dalton Highway (p242).

Renting a Car
Anyone over the age of 20 can rent a vehicle, but some agencies impose a surcharge on drivers under 25. It is essential to have a valid driver's license, a clean record, and a major credit card to pay the rental deposit, as few agencies accept cash. Overseas visitors will need an International Driving License if their home license is not in Roman script. State and local taxes and Collision Damage Waiver (CDW) insurance, covering the car for any visible damage, can increase the final total by 20 to 30 percent. Most rental agencies do not allow their cars to be taken on unpaved

roads, including the Taylor, Denali, Elliott, Steese, Dalton, and Top of the World Highways and the McCarthy Road. Doing so will invalidate insurance and maintenance agreements, so accidents or breakdowns could end up being very costly. **Alaska Auto Rental** and **Alaska 4X4 Rentals** allow gravel road travel, but both require advance booking, especially in the summer peak season.

Alaska Auto Rental
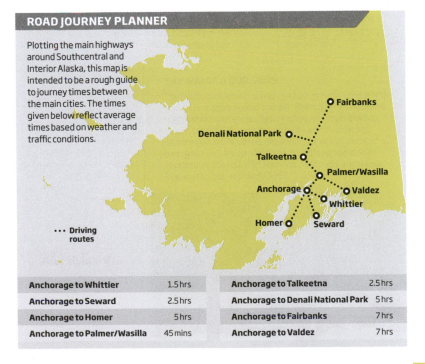 alaskaautorental.com

Alaska 4X4 Rentals
w alaska4x4rentals.com

Renting an RV

Renting a Recreational Vehicle (RV) can be an excellent way of getting around. Rates are lowest before mid-May and after mid-September, and start around $185 per day in midsummer with various mileage plans. National agencies such as **Cruise America** and local ones such as **Great Alaskan Holidays** and **ABC Motorhome Rentals** offer a wide range of RVs. Private parks usually provide dump stations, as do some US Forest Service and State Parks; private sites also offer water and electricity hookups. Few agencies allow RVs to be driven on gravel roads; Alaska 4X4 Rentals is the exception.

ABC Motorhome Rentals
w abcmotorhome.com

Cruise America
w cruiseamerica.com

Great Alaskan Holidays
w greatalaskanholidays.com

Rules of the Road

Speed limits range from 50 mph (80 km/h) on frost-heaved roads to 65 mph (105 km/h) on specified highways. Gravel road limits are 30–50 mph (48–80 km/h). Town limits vary, going down to 20 mph (30 km/h) in school zones. Police and State Troopers vigilantly enforce limits in and around Anchorage, Fairbanks, and Juneau; fines are doubled in road construction zones and "safety corridors" (Sterling–Soldotna, Anchorage–Girdwood, Knik–Wasilla, Wasilla–Big Lake). The blood alcohol content limit is 0.08 percent and drunk driving has heavy penalties.

Cycling

The numbers of commuter and recreational cyclists have steadily grown in Alaska. Most ride mountain bikes suited to the multisurface trails in and around towns. Bike rentals are widely available and include **Downtown Bicycle Rental**, **Trek Bicycle Store**, and **Pablo's Bicycle Rentals**.

Downtown Bicycle Rental
w alaska-bike-rentals.com

Pablo's Bicycle Rentals
w pablobicyclerentals.com

Trek Bicycle Store
w trekstorealaska.com

ROAD JOURNEY PLANNER

Plotting the main highways around Southcentral and Interior Alaska, this map is intended to be a rough guide to journey times between the main cities. The times given below reflect average times based on weather and traffic conditions.

Fairbanks

Denali National Park

Talkeetna

Palmer/Wasilla

Anchorage

Valdez

Whittier

Homer

Seward

••• Driving routes

Anchorage to Whittier	1.5 hrs		Anchorage to Talkeetna	2.5 hrs
Anchorage to Seward	2.5 hrs		Anchorage to Denali National Park	5 hrs
Anchorage to Homer	5 hrs		Anchorage to Fairbanks	7 hrs
Anchorage to Palmer/Wasilla	45 mins		Anchorage to Valdez	7 hrs

PRACTICAL
INFORMATION

A little local know-how goes a long way in Alaska. Here you will find all the esential advice and information you will need during your stay.

AT A GLANCE

EMERGENCY NUMBER

GENERAL EMERGENCY

911

TIME ZONE
AKST/AKDT. Alaska Daylight Time (AKDT) runs from the first Sunday in March to the first Sunday in November. Parts of the Aleutian Islands use Hawaii-Aleutian Standard/Daylight Time (HAST/HADT).

TAP WATER
Unless stated otherwise, tap water is safe to drink in all areas of Alaska.

TIPPING

Restaurant Server	10-20 percent
Bartender	$1 per drink
Barista	$1 per drink
Hotel Porter	$1 per bag
Tour Operator	10-20 percent per person, per day
Taxi/Rideshare	10-15 percent

Personal Security

Alaska's cities and towns are generally safe. However, it is wise to take sensible precautions against thefts and muggings in downtown Anchorage late at night and on secluded trails within the city. Avoid bringing valuables to trailheads, but if you must then lock them in the trunk of the car. If you have anything stolen, report it as soon as possible to local police; get a copy of the crime report to claim on insurance. Contact your embassy or consulate immediately in the event of a serious crime or accident or if your passport or other identification is stolen.

It is also important to note that many rural areas of Alaska have no cell service or Wi-Fi, so travelers need to take responsibility for their own safety and environmental awareness. If driving, carry a survival kit in your rental car or RV; if visiting a rural village, check in with the local Village Public Safety Officer upon your arrival. Consider a satellite phone if venturing along the Steese, Dalton, or Denali Highways. The Alaska Public Lands Information Centers can provide up-to-date road conditions and weather reports, and national parks and forests have their own law enforcement ranger force.

Wildlife Safety

As part of bear-safety protocols (p217), visitors should always be highly aware of their surroundings when hiking, biking, or camping. Keep trash in secure receptacles, and never keep food or smelly items (toothpaste, soaps, or other personal products) in a tent with you. Carry bear spray when hiking in any region of Alaska, and consider a short class on bear safety upon your arrival (enquire at local visitor information centers).

Moose should also be treated with respect, as more people are killed by moose than bear attacks. An adult moose weighs over 1,000 lbs (450 kg), and can strike out with all four feet and run up to 35 mph (55 km/h) when threatened. In the spring, females are extremely protective of their young. Never approach a moose at any time, and if confronted by one, hide behind a tree or run out of its immediate area.

Health

All of Alaska's cities and towns have a hospital or at least a community clinic. Prescriptions can be filled at pharmacies (drugstores) within these facilities and at other locations in larger cities. The US does not have a government health program, and private emergency medical or dental care, while excellent, can be very expensive. Buying medical travel insurance is highly recommended.

Smoking, Alcohol, and Drugs

Smoking and vaping are banned in all public spaces and in the enclosed areas of restaurants, hotels, and bars, although some places have outdoor seating with designated smoking areas. Alcohol may not be sold to or bought for anyone under the age of 21. Rules in rural Alaska vary (p43); check local alcohol laws ahead of your visit. Alaska's recreational cannabis regulations are still in flux, but dispensaries have been legal for a few years. No one under 21 is allowed on the premises, and consumption must be done in the privacy of one's home or lodging.

ID

Passports (or a Real ID for US residents) must be presented at airports, train depots, and ferry terminals. All alcohol purchases need a valid ID.

Local Customs

As a general rule, Alaskans are polite, friendly, and helpful, although they may be a bit outspoken at times. Dress is typically very casual, with fancy clothing reserved for only the most upmarket of events.

Visitors from across the world are welcomed, but it is important to respect local traditions, particularly within Alaska Native communities. Always ask permission before taking photographs, especially of ceremonies, dances, or homes. Bear in mind that Alaska Native speakers can be reflective and slow to respond.

One of the best ways to support Alaskans is to participate in activities operated by local businesses, and to purchase Alaska-made crafts, art, or souvenirs. Look for items with the words "Made in Alaska" and the symbol of a polar bear.

Visiting Places of Worship

Most places of worship in the state are open to the public, with the exception of Russian Orthodox churches. Speak quietly and do not use cameras, smartphones, or other devices without asking permission first.

Cell Phones and Wi-Fi

Cell phone services are highly unreliable outside Alaska's larger cities, and even in some parts of Anchorage. Always carry a paper map or guidebook and ask for directions before you set off. If traveling extensively in rural Alaska, consider renting a satellite phone to make calls when there is no cell service. In cities and towns, there are many Wi-Fi hotspots in public spaces such as stores, hotels, and airports.

Post

The US Postal Service is present in all Alaskan cities in some form. Post offices are generally open between 10am and 5pm and are closed on Sundays and state and federal holidays. Letters and small parcels (less than 13 oz/370 g) with correct postage may be placed in any blue mailbox or at a post office counter.

Taxes

Most Alaska cities do not assign a sales tax, but there are a few that do, so ask if you are not sure. Generally the tax is between 5 and 8 percent.

WEBSITES AND APPS

Travel Alaska
Visit the official state tourist board website at www.travelalaska.com.

Visit Anchorage
For useful information on visiting Anchorage, see www.anchorage.net.

AKontheGO
www.akonthego.com is a good travel resource for families.

The Alaska App
This app is a great planning tool and has downloadable audio guides.

Cruising in Alaska

For many travelers, an Alaska cruise is a once-in-a-lifetime experience, providing a luxurious way to see some of the wildest places on earth. Budget is often the most important factor in influencing the type of cruise, but it is also essential to decide which is more important – the ship or the itinerary.

When to Go

The Alaska cruise season typically operates from early May to early October, although some cruise lines are beginning to offer cost-saving deals on popular itineraries from as early as March. The best chance of sunny weather and warm temperatures is generally between June and August, which is when prices are at their peak. Summer also brings the added bonus of exceptionally long days around the June solstice.

Wetter weather and the possibility of storms are highest in the spring and fall, but prices are often lower in these seasons and they each have their own advantages. In spring, vegetation starts to bloom and animals can be spotted with their young, while late summer and early fall sees a wave of golden leaves sweep across the landscape. Often underrated, August and September are truly beautiful months in which to cruise, and also have fewer crowds.

Choosing an Itinerary

There are two main routes to choose from: the Inside Passage or the Gulf of Alaska. The more popular Inside Passage route offers the largest concentration of accessible towns, as well as majestic glaciers and impenetrable forests, with the chance to spot whales, bears, and eagles. Common stops include Glacier Bay, Haines, Hoonah, Juneau, Skagway, Sitka, Ketchikan, and Misty Fiords. Many people undertake the journey as a round trip, starting in either Seattle in the US or Vancouver in Canada.

Vast seascapes and endless mountain ranges are the attractions of a Gulf of Alaska cruise. The shoreline has fewer conventional ports of call, but benefits include the glaciers, deep fjords, and marine life of Hubbard Glacier and Prince William Sound. Many passengers also tack on a multiday trip north from Seward to Denali. A popular itinerary goes across the Gulf of Alaska between Seward or Whittier and Juneau, and includes points of interest both in the Gulf and in the Inside Passage.

Choosing a Ship

Cruise ship options in Alaska range from small vessels carrying only a handful of passengers to huge liners that can accommodate thousands. The vast majority of visitors to Alaska generally travel on large and midsized ships operated by major cruise lines. Common facilities include restaurants and buffets, health spas and salons, theaters, themed lounges, bars, dance clubs, swimming pools and hot tubs, and children's clubs. Onboard meals are normally included in the purchase price, with the exception of some larger ships that have individual restaurants; alcohol is usually extra. Onboard activities such as kids' clubs, swimming, and fitness areas are also generally included, but shore excursions come at an additional cost and can add up quickly. You can organize shore excursions at the time of booking or wait to decide once on the ship, but note that some popular activities such as helicopter tours, sled dog rides, or bear viewing fill up fast. Prices vary depending on the activity, and range from $50 to $500 per person per shore excursion.

Small ships may lack the glitzier cruise entertainments of bigger vessels, but they have the great advantage of being able to sail into secluded villages and hidden coves that large ships cannot approach. There's often a high standard of comfort and good food on these trips, and many also provide onboard experts in subjects such as marine biology and photography. The more exclusive nature of these trips does mean that prices are often higher, but they frequently include all meals and drinks, as well as all activities and shore excursions, with the exception of some add-on adventures. **Alaskan Dream Cruises**, **Lindblad Expeditions**, and **UnCruise Adventures** are among some recommended small-ship operators.

Alaskan Dream Cruises
W alaskandreamcruises.com
Lindblad Expeditions
W world.expeditions.com
UnCruise Adventures
W uncruiseadventures.com

CRUISE SUSTAINABLY

A cruise is one of the best ways to see Alaska, but it can come with a substantial environmental impact. The average cruise liner creates the same amount of pollution as 14,000 cars, and in 2019 more than 3 million lbs (1.4 million kg) of trash were produced by Alaska cruise ships alone. However, many companies, particularly the small-ship cruise lines, are working hard to establish sustainable practices for sailing within Alaska's pristine wilderness environment. Ask your cruise line about their sustainability policies before booking, and do your bit by bringing a reusable water bottle for use both on and off the ship.

INDEX

Page numbers in **bold** refer to main entries

ACKNOWLEDGMENTS

The publisher would like to thank the following for their kind permission to reproduce their photographs:

Key: a-above; b-below/bottom; c-centre; f-far; l-left; r-right; t-top

123RF.com: carmengabriela 29cla.

Alamy Stock Photo: AA World Travel Library 58br; AB Forces News Collection 41br, 54crb; Accent Alaska.com 11br, 34tr, 34-5b, 59tr, 60-1t, 61cb, 61bc, 174-5t, 196-7b, 205br, 217bl, 242cl, 247crb; Alpha Stock 58tl, 149tr; America 225c; Uwe Bergwitz 77tl, 171tr; Robert Bird 155cb; blickwinkel / McPHOTO / SBA 193br; BLM Photo 10-1b; Steve Bly 111t, 229br; Janice and Nolan Braud 97cr, 204-5t; Darryl Brooks 41tr; Ramunas Bruzas 142-3b; Ray Bulson 53b, 55clb, 173cla; Cannon Photography LLC / BrownWCannonIII 48-9t; CDM Wild 72bl; Naum Chayer 81tc, 138cla; Naum Chayer / Sculpted by Chuck Buchanan 146br; Loetscher Chlaus 155br; Tim Clark 90cl; Classic Image 57br; Rob Crandall 180-1t; David Crane 198tl; Cultura Creative (RF) / Hagephoto 76bl; Richard Cummins 116bl, 158bl; Danita Delimont / DanitaDelimont.com / Michael DeFreitas 22t, Cindy Miller Hopkins 238-9b, / Janet Muir 134bl, / Tom Norring 213cla, / Hugh Rose 193crb, / Stuart Westmorland 177br, / Art Wolfe 216-7t, / Angel Wynn 38cra; DCM / Dennis MacDonald 59bc; Design Pics Inc / Alaska Stock 109bl, / Sunny Awazuhara- Reed 70cra, 70-1b, 110crb, 242clb, / John Delapp 249cla, / Doug Demarest 56clb, 248t, / Patrick Endres 11t, 120-1b, 176bl, 214bl, 243br, 244bl, / Brian M. Guzzetti 35cl, / John Hyde 154bc, / Amber Johnson 47clb, / Michael Jones 12t, 72-3b, 82-3t, 182bl, 170t, 194t, 215tr, / Blake Kent 206tl, / Doug Lindstrand 20cr, 55cl, 121cr, Sculpted by Malcolm Alexander 57cr, / Steven Miley 30-1t, 200bl, / Lucas Payne 26-7ca, 139bl, / Don Pitcher 179br, / Gary Schultz 227, / Jeff Schultz 8clb, / Kevin Smith 27tl, 230-1b, 236t, 246tl, / Harry M. Walker 57tl, 55tr, / Alaska Stock RF / Sunny K. Awazahura- Reed 52bl, 138t, 182clb, / Carl R. Battreall 74, / Edward Bennett 77cra, / Randy Brandon 86ca, 86bc, / Milo Burcham 51tr, / John R. Delapp 20crb, 168-9b, / Mike Criss 19t, 208-9, / Matt Hage 73cla, 98bl, 102-3t, / Calvin W. Hall 51c, / John Hyde 29tr, 35tr, 140-1t, / Its About Light 224br, / Karen Jettmar 195bl, / Amber Johnson 132-3t, 206-7b, / Carl Johnson 54cl, 122bl, / Michael Jones 22cl, / Doug Lindstrand 75br, 78br, 194cra, 217tr, Inc / Yves Marcoux 10ca, 250-1, / Steven Miley 172-3b, / Clark James Mishler 13cr, 18tl, 124-5, / Null 39br, 69crb, 118t, / Don Pitcher 131cr, 152cl, / Jeff Schultz 173crb, / Robert Siciliano 169tr, 240-1t, / Kevin G Smith 30bl, 39tr, 49bl, 79c, 173c, 199b, / Joe Stock 78-9t; dmac / DCM / Sculpted by Joan Bugbee Jackson 88bl; Stephen Dorey 28-9t, 46tl, 146-7t; Richard Ellis 79cra, 230cl; Gado Images / Smith Collection 60bc; Gaertner 44bl; Kevin Galvin 156br; Renato Granieri 71crb; H. Mark Weidman Photography 31b; ML Harris 38-9b, 143tr, 143ca; Liane Harrold 13t; Heritage Image Partnership Ltd / Werner Forman Archive / Smithsonian Institution, Washington 57tl; Kirk Hewlett 154clb; History and Art Collection 58cla; Cindy Hopkins 41cl, 238clb; Dave G. Houser 152-3b; IanDagnall Computing 57cla; imac / DCM 22br; Image Professionals GmbH / TravelCollection 192b; imageBROKER / Robert Haasmann 18cb, 157cl, 164-5, / Stefan Wackerhagen 190cra; Mark A. Johnson 10clb; Paul Jones 213tl; Latitude 59 LLP 24tl; P.A. Lawrence; LLC. 191tr; Paul Andrew Lawrence 237cl; Dan Leeth 122-3t, / Created by Mark Webber 123br; Ilene MacDonald / Sculpted by Derek Freeborn 81br; Itsik Marom 45b; mauritius images GmbH / Rolf Hicker 158-9t, / Bernd Römmelt 154-5t; 221bl; Patti McConville 136tr; Mint Images Limited 245bl; MiraMira 8cla, 36-7t; Diane Modafferi 24-5ca, 53cl; David L. Moore - AK 33tr, 53tr, 162-3b; MShieldsPhotos 197tr; William Mullins 152tr; National Geographic Image Collection / Aaron Huey 169cl, / Michael S. Quinton 61cra; Nature Picture Library / Steven Kazlowski 19bl, 232-3; Niebrugge Images 26tr, 48bl, 99tr, 155cr, 228-9t; Ron Niebrugge 46-7b, 55cr, 99br, 100b, 103clb, 120t, 130bl, 160tl, 186br, 242br; Boyd Norton 218t; NPS Photo 249cb, / Planetpix / Emily Mesner 246-7b; Lucas Payne 105tl; Pictures Now 57tr; Robert Harding 36br, / Richard Cummins 163tr, / Kevin Morgans 50tl, / Michael Nolan 217cr; Pep Roig 150clb, 150-1c, 151ca, 217cb; RSBPhoto 135r; James Schwabel 17t, 25tl, 47tr, 69clb, 82br, 84-5b, 92-3, 116-7t; Richard Smith 103crb; Inga Spence 40br, 54cr; Stellamc 86-7b; stillbeyou_travel 47br; Tribune Content Agency LLC / McClatchy-Tribune / TNS / Norma Meyer 35br; Paolo Trovò / Sculpted by Jacques & Mary Regat 91br; US Air Force Photo 55crb; USFWS Photo 231tr; UtCon Collection 59clb; Greg Vaughn 91tl; Tom Walker / Sculpted by Todd and Chris 54cra; Leon Werdinger 61cr; Robert Wyatt 145br; Xavier Fores - Joana Roncero 224-5t; Zoonar GmbH / Andreas Edelmann 110bl; ZUMA Press; Inc. / Arnold Drapkin 26tl, 37br.

Alaska Craft Brew & Barley Wine Festival- (Peak 2 Peak): 43cla.

Alaska State Fair: Clark James Mishler 12clb.

Alaska State Museum (Juneau): © Lara Swimmer 2016 28tl.

The Anchorage Museum: © 2017 jodyo.photos 69bl; Jim Kohl 68tl.

AWL Images: Ken Archer 240ca; Danita Delimont Stock 178-9t; Christian Heeb 68-9t; John Warburton-Lee 97crb; Nigel Pavitt 2-3, 145tr.